500 ROCK BANDS

A QUANTUM BOOK

This edition published in 2010 by
CHARTWELL BOOKS, INC.
a division of BOOK SALES, INC.
276 Fifth Avenue Suite 206
New York, New York 10001
USA

QUMROCB

ISBN-13: 978-0-7858-2619-4
ISBN-10: 0-7858-2619-X

This book is produced by
Quantum Publishing Ltd
6 Blundell Street
London N7 9BH

Publisher: Anastasia Cavouras
Project Editor: Valeria Kogan
Production: Rohana Yusof
Design: Andrew Easton

Printed and bound in Singapore by Star Standard Industries (Pte) Ltd

500 ROCK BANDS

CHARTWELL
BOOKS, INC.

Contents

QUIET RIOT
Pearl
QUIET RIOT

Introduction

It is an incredible time to be a rock fan. With over fifty years worth of artists to choose from and with so many sub-genres and styles falling under the catch-all banner of rock, there is a seemingly endless wealth of quality music just waiting to be discovered. With so much to choose from, it's sometimes hard to know where to start. Well, right here is a good place.

This collection features a huge selection of bands and musicians whose records have made an indelible mark on the history of music. Some of the musicians here are superstars while others are lesser-known masters in their field. Hopefully reading about them here will inspire you to seek out their music and buy a record or two, or at least download a few songs.

With such a huge array of musicians to choose from, it wasn't easy deciding the criteria for inclusion in 500 Rock Bands. Was it only to be bands with the standard rock instrumentation of guitars, bass and drums? For the most part the answer is yes, although there are some notable exceptions to that rule who could not be omitted.

While the birthplace of rock 'n' roll is the United States and the British invasion of the 1960s revolutionized the sound, bands from Canada, Germany, Brazil, Japan and the Netherlands are also included. It is impossible to ignore the sounds and innovations of the international musical landscape when so many fantastic bands come from all over the world.

The sounds of early rock 'n' roll are here. We couldn't forget the pioneering steps of Buddy Holly, Eddie Cochran and Elvis Presley and we embrace the gutsy spirit of rockabilly legend Wanda Jackson. To truly do justice to this varied genre we must start at the beginning.

The '60s are well represented, too. The Beatles' revolutionary recording techniques and songwriting prowess can't be denied, nor can we ignore the different media they utilized in getting their music out into the world. Jimi Hendrix's guitar mastery was without equal, although Jeff Beck's understated style was closer to a lot of people's hearts. Then there was Pink Floyd's amazing Technicolor dream.

Glam rock, heavy metal, funk-rock, punk and the numerous other styles that sprang to life throughout the '70s and '80s shine in bands like the Runaways, David Bowie, Prince & The Revolution and Iron Maiden. Compared to the short-lived careers of many pop bands, it's incredible to think that many of these rockers are still touring and still making music.

Which brings us to the sounds of the last twenty years, decades that have seen music technology develop in leaps and bounds and the number of bands seem to double every month. Oasis is already a classic, but what about underground favorites Yo La Tengo? We think you will like them too. Then there are Gossip, the Yeah Yeah Yeahs and Interpol.

With so much choice it would be easy to just stick with old favorites, but a little look at all the other possibilities might make it interesting to take a chance with something new. Or if perhaps you just want to go back and listen to a record you haven't heard in years, this is the place. Music fuels so much of our lives and it is sometimes easy to take it for granted, so here's some inspiration to keep your music collection exciting.

Ludwig

1 The Beatles

The Liverpool quartet of John Lennon, Paul McCartney, George Harrison and Ringo Starr is the most popular rock band in the world. From their early days playing rock 'n' roll they developed as songwriters and recording artists, laying the groundwork for popular music as we know it. One of the first bands to perform its own material, Lennon and McCartney remain, almost 40 years after the band's demise, the upper-most pinnacle of songwriting. Known for bringing diverse styles including pop, ska, and British dancehall into their music, the Beatles flexed their rock muscle on songs like "Revolution", "Why Don't We Do it in the Road?" and "Taxman". (See picture opposite)

"I still like black music, disco music... 'Shame, Shame, Shame' or 'Rock Your Baby' - I'd give my eye-tooth to have written that. But I never could. I am too literal to write 'Rock Your Baby'. I wish I could. I'm too intellectual, even though I'm not really an intellectual."
- John Lennon

2 Chuck Berry

No one plays guitar like Chuck Berry. Even today, when technology enables musicians to make just about any sound imaginable, no one has matched Berry's tone. One of rock's forefathers, Berry was instrumental in turning Chess Records from a blues label to a rock 'n' roll label, when "Maybelline" topped the charts. Berry inspired legions of musicians, most notably Keith Richards, who performed with Berry in the documentary Hail! Hail! Rock 'n' Roll. Plagued with legal problems throughout his life, Berry still found time to pen classic songs like "Nadine", "Johnny B. Goode" and his only #1 hit, the salacious "My Ding-a-Ling".

3 Elvis Presley

Elvis Aaron Presley passed away in 1977 but he is still the King of Rock 'n' Roll. Taking the country and gospel music he grew up with and adding the rhythm and blues sounds that were springing up in the Southern U.S.A. during the '50s, Elvis captured the imagination of teenagers; young people who were experiencing leisure time and spending money in the post-war prosperity. Songs like "Hound Dog", "That's All Right" and "Blue Suede Shoes" highlighted Elvis's swagger and sexuality, making him an instant hit. Although he was not the first person to sing rock 'n' roll, Elvis brought it to television and the world. (See picture opposite)

> *"I ain't no saint, but I've tried never to do anything that would hurt my family or offend God...I figure all any kid needs is hope and the feeling he or she belongs. If I could do or say anything that would give some kid that feeling, I would believe I had contributed something to the world."*- Elvis

4 The Rolling Stones

Starting as a blues band, the Rolling Stones, and their fans, have called themselves The World's Greatest Rock 'n' Roll Band since the late '60s. Centered on singer Mick Jagger and guitar player Keith Richards, the band's classic line-up featured Brian Jones, Charlie Watts and Bill Wyman. Following Jones's death, Ron Wood eventually became the Stones' rhythm guitar player, forming the line-up that continued until bassist Wyman's departure in the '90s. The distorted guitar riff on "Satisfaction" is instantly recognizable to rock fans, and there are few examples of acoustic guitar sounding as aggressive as on "Street Fighting Man". (See picture below)

5 Led Zeppelin

Spawning thousands of would-be virtuosos to play "Stairway to Heaven" and "Whole Lotta Love" in guitar shops around the world, Led Zeppelin combined blues guitar (Jimmy Page) with mystical lyrical imagery (Robert Plant) and one of the heaviest rhythm sections (drummer John Bonham and bassist John-Paul Jones) in '60s rock. Often referred to as the first heavy metal band, Zeppelin released nine albums throughout the '60s and '70s. The untimely death of John Bonham cut the band's career short, though the three remaining members have all continued making music, reuniting (with Bonham's son Jason on drums) in 2007 for a charity event. (See picture below)

6 Little Richard

A whop bop-a-lu-a whop bam boo. With this one phrase, Macon, Georgia's Richard Penniman insisted his audience get up and dance. "Tutti Frutti", like his other hits, "Lucille", "Good Golly Miss Molly" and "Jenny Jenny", to name a few, centered on Richard's driving piano and breakneck vocals. His signature "Wooo!" punctuated the lyrics and provided lyrical inspiration for The Beatles in years to follow. Growing up in the American south, Richard was steeped in gospel music, but it still came as a surprise when, in 1957, he abruptly quit rock 'n' roll to become a minister. After some time spent out of the spotlight, Richard eventually returned to the stage, though today he is semi-retired.

7 Buddy Holly and the Crickets

Known for his iconic black-framed glasses, Texan Buddy Holly was a singer, a songwriter, and was one of the first rock 'n' rollers to bring the Fender Stratocaster into the spotlight. Clean cut enough to get the parents on his side, Holly's songs; "That'll Be The Day", "Rave On", "Heartbeat", and "Peggy Sue", among others, were a hit with the kids. When Holly died in a plane crash at the age of 22, he left behind one of the most significant bodies of work of the rock 'n' roll era. That his career had such an impact in only 18 months is still astonishing. (See picture opposite)

LITTLE RICHARD FACTFILE:

Born: 1935

Died: N/A

Home town: Macon, Georgia, U.S.A.

Members: Little Richard

What you should check out/why: Little Richard includes "Good Golly Miss Molly", "Ooh! My Soul", "Keep a Knockin'" and other rock 'n' roll blueprints.

Worth looking out for: Any performance footage of the legendary singer and piano player for a master class in rock 'n' roll performance.

BUDDY HOLLY FACTFILE:

Start up year: 1957

Disband year: N/A (Although Buddy Holly died in 1959)

Home town: Lubbock, Texas, U.S.A.

Members: Buddy Holly, Jerry Allison, Joe Mauldin, Sonny Curtis, Niki Sullivan

What you should check out/why: The "Chirping" Crickets contains "Oh, Boy!", "Maybe Baby", "That'll Be the Day", while the follow-up, Buddy Holly, has "Rave On" and "Peggy Sue".

Worth looking out for: Wreckless Eric's ramshackle cover of Holly's "Cryin', Waitin', Hopin'"

8 Pink Floyd

Formed in 1965, Pink Floyd's first record, The Piper at the Gates of Dawn, is a psychedelic rock masterpiece, with songs like "Astronomy Domine" and "Lucifer Sam" juxtaposing singer Syd Barrett's playful lyrics with the driving bass, keyboards and guitar lines. Barrett left the band following this album but David Gilmour, Roger Waters, Nick Mason and Rick Wright continued on, releasing numerous commercially popular and critically acclaimed albums, including The Dark Side of the Moon, one of the highest-selling rock albums of all time. In 1979, they released The Wall, a concept album which was made into a movie starring Bob Geldof.

PINK FLOYD FACTFILE:

Start up year: 1965

Disband year: 1996 (with occasional reunions)

Home town: Cambridge, England

Members: Syd Barrett, David Gilmour, Roger Waters, Nick Mason, Rick Wright

What you should check out/why: Piper at the Gates of Dawn for the brilliance of Syd Barrett's "Lucifer Sam" and "Astronomy Domine."

Worth looking out for: Dark Side of the Moon.

9 Nirvana

Arguably the most influential band of the '90s, Nirvana was at the forefront of grunge and propelled Seattle's Sub Pop records into international fame. Debut album Bleach introduced Nirvana to the world, but it was their second record, Nevermind, and the song "Smells Like Teen Spirit" that made Kurt Cobain, Kris Novoselic and Dave Grohl household names. Often alternating between soft and melodic then loud and aggressive, Nirvana brought a punk rock attitude to mainstream radio. Releasing only three albums (not including rarities collection Incesticide or MTV Unplugged) before singer Cobain's suicide in 1994, Nirvana's catalog is small but enduring. (See picture opposite)

"Punk is musical freedom. It's saying, doing and playing what you want. In Webster's terms, 'nirvana' means freedom from pain, suffering and the external world, and that's pretty close to my definition of Punk Rock."
- Kurt Cobain

10 The Who

From "My Generation" to "Substitute" and "Baba O'Reilly", few bands capture teen angst as masterfully as the Who. Driven by Keith Moon's propulsive drumming, The Who was for many years the loudest band in the world, prompting guitarist Pete Townshend's early hearing loss. In the early years, The Who's songs were amphetamine-fueled, short and choppy, but as Townshend's interest in experimental recording techniques and instruments grew, the music became more complex, resulting in albums like Quadrophenia. While Roger Daltry sings the majority of Who songs, bassist John "The Ox" Entwistle, was responsible for fan favorite, "Boris the Spider". (See picture opposite)

THE WHO FACTFILE:

Start up year: 1964

Disband year: N/A (Minus Keith Moon and John Entwhistle)

Home town: London, England

Members: Pete Townshend, Roger Daltry, John Entwhistle, Keith Moon

What you should check out/why: The Who Sings My Generation for "The Kids Are Alright"; The Who Sell Out for "Mary Ann with the Shaky Hands"; Who's Next for "Baba O'Reilly", etc.

Worth looking out for: The film that launched a thousand Mod revivalists, Quadrophenia.

"But what was interesting about what The Who did is that we took things which were happening in the pop genre and represent them to people so that they see them in a new way. I think the best example is Andy Warhol's work, the image of Marilyn Monroe or the Campbell's soup can."
- Pete Townshend

11 Queen

Few voices in rock are as striking and theatrical as that of Queen's Freddie Mercury. Bringing an operatic element to songs like "Bohemian Rhapsody" and "Killer Queen", Mercury, along with Brian May, Roger Taylor and John Deacon, brought drama to stadium rock. The driving anthem "We Will Rock You" continues to be heard in sports arenas world-wide and is the title song for a stage musical that uses Queen's songs to tell a post-apocalyptic story. While Mercury, who passed away in 1991, may be regarded as Queen's figurehead, guitarist Brian May is equally important. There is even a line of Brian May guitars for players trying to emulate his sound. (See picture opposite)

"Years ago, I thought up the name Queen...it's just a name, but it's very regal obviously, and it sounds splendid...it's a strong name, very universal and immediate. It had a lot of visual potential and was open to all sorts of interpretations. I was certainly aware of the gay connotations, but that was just one facet of it."

\- Freddie Mercury

12 The Jimi Hendrix Experience

Seattle-born guitar player and singer Jimi Hendrix was joined by drummer Mitch Mitchell and bassist Noel Redding to be 'The Experience'. While Jimi is known for his guitar pyrotechnics, the beauty of his playing is in the sensual way he made the instrument sing, not in stage trickery like holding the guitar behind his head. Framing Hendrix on classics like "Purple Haze", "Hey Joe" and "Are You Experienced" were two English musicians, Mitchell and Redding, who provided Hendrix with the insistent rhythm he required. For two years, they were one of the most exciting bands in the world and they remain among the most influential.

13 AC/DC

Lead guitar player Angus Young started wearing his school uniform on stage early in AC/DC's inception. Over thirty years later, Young still plays signature songs like "Dirty Deeds Done Dirt Cheap" and "Back in Black" while decked out in shorts, tie and jacket. Original singer Bon Scott passed away in 1980, following the release of Highway to Hell. Scott's vocal doppelganger Brian Johnson took over as the band's front man on AC/DC's seminal album, Back in Black. Back in Black made Robert "Mutt" Lange the go-to producer for rock bands and has sold over 40 million copies worldwide. (See picture opposite)

"We never thought of ourselves as a 'heavy metal band' we've always regarded ourselves as a rock band. The big difference we've always thought we had a lot more feel for rock, we always went out for songs, not riffs or heavy, heavy sounds. But every now and again it does come on like a sledge hammer."

\- Angus Young

14 Van Halen

In 1984 brothers Eddie and Alex Van Halen, along with David Lee Roth and Michael Anthony, released Jump, one of the top-selling albums of the '80s. While their best known song, "Jump", added a keyboard to the mix, Van Halen is best known for Eddie's flashy guitar diving around Alex and Michael's rhythm section, while flamboyant David Lee sings and yowls over top. In spite of 1984's staggering success, the next year Roth left to pursue a solo career and was soon replaced with Sammy Hagar. Van Halen had success with later albums 5150 and For Unlawful Carnal Knowledge, but it is the original line-up that remains the classic and best.

15 The White Stripes

The White Stripes is a duo from Detroit, Michigan comprised of former married couple Jack and Meg White. The majority of the duo's scrappy sound is comprised of guitar and drums, although on record they sometimes add piano, bass and other instruments. The band is known as much for their striking red and white visuals as they are for hits like "Fell in Love with a Girl" and "Seven Nation Army". Initially sticking to blues-based garage rock, with the occasional acoustic song thrown in, recent albums Get Behind Me Satan and Icky Thump explore more varied musical landscapes, defying expectations of what a duo can do.

16 The Kinks

Proof that two chords can change the world, the opening riff of the Kinks' "You Really Got Me" is among the most influential in rock. Technically simple, the distorted sound came from guitarist Dave Davies messing around with his amplifier. Though tame by today's standards, it was a sound unlike any heard to that point. While the Kinks went on to make many brilliant records, often based around singer Ray Davies's witty and insightful view of English culture, it is early songs like "I Need You" and "David Watts" that make the Kinks an integral part of the rock canon.

17 Sleater-Kinney

In the 1990s, Olympia, Washington was a hotbed of creativity and independent music. One band that sprung from that scene is power trio Sleater-Kinney. Comprised of singers/guitarists Carrie Brownstein and Corin Tucker, and drummer Janet Weiss, who replaced Lora MacFarlane in 1996, Sleater-Kinney released seven albums prior to calling an indefinite hiatus in 2006. Intense and melodic, Sleater-Kinney combines punk's aggression with personal lyrics that are often scathingly funny. Brownstein's intricate guitar playing is instantly recognizable to rock fans, as is Tucker's vibrato-rich voice. Sleater-Kinney's second album, Call the Doctor, included the alternative anthem, "I Wanna Be Your Joey Ramone".

18 The Ramones

Few bands of the punk era are as iconic as New York City's Ramones. Dressed in the band uniform of ripped jeans and black leather jackets, the self-named Joey, Johnny, Dee Dee and Tommy Ramone released their self-titled debut in 1976. Johnny's distinct down-stroke buzz-saw guitar style and bassist Dee Dee's "1-2-3-4" count-offs punctuate the Ramones' lightning-fast, girl group-inspired songs. In 1979, the band starred in the film Rock 'N' Roll High School, inspired by the Ramones song of the same name. While three-quarters of the original line-up is now deceased, songs like "Blitzkrieg Bop" and "I Wanna be Sedated" ensure the Ramones' music will live on.

SLEATER-KINNEY FACTFILE:

Start up year: 1994

Disband year: 2006

Home town: Olympia, Washington, U.S.A.

Members: Carrie Brownstein, Corin Tucker, Janet Weiss, Lora MacFarlane

What you should check out/why: The Woods is a brain-piercingly loud reminder that Sleater-Kinney's demise occurred too soon.

Worth looking out for: Call the Doctor

THE RAMONES FACTFILE:

Start up year: 1974

Disband year: 1996

Home town: New York, U.S.A.

Members: Joey, Johnny, Dee Dee, Marky, Tommy, Richie and CJ Ramone

What you should check out/why: The first album introduces the Ramones' trademark sound with "Beat on the Brat" and "I Wanna Be Your Boyfriend."

Worth looking out for: The Phil Spector produced End of the Century

19 Guns 'N' Roses

In the late'80s, Guns 'N' Roses sprang from L.A.'s glam metal scene with Appetite for Destruction, from which songs like "Sweet Child O' Mine" and "Paradise City" became radio staples. Controversial singer Axl Rose's high-pitched wail is instantly identifiable and perfectly suited to the accompaniment of top hat sporting lead guitar player Slash. On stage, they were perfect foils: Rose danced and worked the crowd, while Slash remained coolly detached. Line-up changes plagued the band and, following the release of 1993's The Spaghetti Incident, Slash left too. In 2008, Guns 'N' Roses, with only Axl remaining from the original band, released Chinese Democracy. (See picture opposite)

"The cool thing is that in reality you can't put a label on us. Come down to our shows and watch us. You'll see that there's every kind of fan at our shows. There s the hardcore metal heads, there's the hardcore punks, all kinds of people. There's that whole whitefaced make-up with the black hair scene and then all the really young kids that have just gotten out of junior high school."
- Slash

20 Black Sabbath

Before Ozzy Osbourne became a reality television star, he was the singer for one of the heaviest rock bands in the world. From 1970 to 1973, Black Sabbath released five classic albums: Black Sabbath, Paranoid, Master of Reality, Volume 4 and Sabbath Bloody Sabbath. Though they would continue as a band until the mid-2000s, with singer Osbourne being temporarily replaced by Ronnie James Dio and later, Ian Gillen, it's the first records that stand the test of time and establish Sabbath as the heavy metal pioneers they are. Fusing topical lyrics with bowel-churning low-end and Tony Iommi's heavy guitars, songs like "Paranoid" and "War Pigs" created Black Sabbath's signature sound.

"Everybody knows that Black Sabbath started everything and almost every single thing that people are playing today has already been done by Black Sabbath. They wrote every single good riff...ever."
- Rob Zombie

21 Metallica

In 1988, Metallica released ...And Justice For All and the band, which had already been a favorite with metal fans, got its first taste of mainstream success. Based on Dalton Trumbo's novel, Johnny Got His Gun, the song "One" became a huge hit, driven by its accompanying video that intersperses clips from the movie version of Johnny with scenes of the band playing. Three years later, the self-titled album and the single "Enter Sandman" became Metallica's most commercially successful releases to date. In 2000, Metallica sued file-sharing service Napster for violating various copyright laws. Four years later, the documentary Metallica: Some Kind of Monster, was released. (See picture opposite)

METALLICA FACTFILE:

Start up year: 1981

Disband year: N/A

Home town: Los Angeles, U.S.A.

Members: Kirk Hammett, Lars Ulrich, James Hetfield, Cliff Burton, Jason Newsted, Dave Mustaine, more

What you should check out/why: Master of Puppets remains the jewel in Metallica's crown.

Worth looking out for: Some Kind of Monster, a documentary about the making of Metallica's St. Anger.

22 David Bowie

England's shape-shifting David Bowie started out playing blues-inspired rock 'n' roll under his real name, David Jones, but found fame and notoriety as David Bowie when he embraced the theatrics of glam rock. From 1972's The Rise and Fall of Ziggy Stardust and the Spiders from Mars to 1975's Aladdin Sane Bowie transformed his stage persona, going from orange-haired spaceman accompanied by ace guitar player Mick Ronson to sophisticated blue-eyed soul singer in a few easy steps. Throughout Bowie's 40-plus year career, he's always been a musical adventurer and rarely sticks to the same sound from one album to the next.

23 Aerosmith

Nicknamed the Toxic Twins for their hard-living ways, Aerosmith's Steven Tyler and Joe Perry have endured a fickle music industry, as well as stints in rehab, to emerge as one of rock's longest-lasting bands. Early hits like "Dream On" and "Sweet Emotion" remain staples on classic rock radio, while songs that followed the band's early-'90s renaissance, "Crying", "Love In An Elevator", "Janie's Got a Gun", have arguably eclipsed the early hits in popularity. In 1986, Aerosmith confounded their fans by teaming up with Run-D.M.C. for a hip-hop take on Toys In the Attic's "Walk This Way". The result was a genre-defying hit for both groups. (See picture right)

24 Def Leppard

Sheffield, England's Def Leppard had been together about six years and had released two records when they released Pyromania and seemingly overnight became one of the biggest rock bands of the '80s. In a musical landscape dominated by synthesizers and love songs, Def Leppard made music that fused their love of '70s glam with a more muscular guitar sound produced by Mutt Lange. The result was hits like "Rock of Ages", "Photograph" and "Foolin'". Amazingly, Def Leppard followed up with Hysteria, an equally successful record that spawned one of the era's most popular hard rock songs, "Pour Some Sugar on Me".

25 Bruce Springsteen & The E Street Band

Bruce Springsteen is the embodiment of the American singer-songwriter. His lyrics are vignettes of the lives of working class heroes and their loves: cars and girls. Backing Springsteen is the E Street Band, a rock 'n' roll band that animates Springsteen's vocals and punctuates everything he says. It's hard to describe as lean a band that adds organ, guitar, and saxophone, along with second and sometimes third guitars to the standard guitar / bass / drums line-up, but these players (including Steve Van Zandt on guitar and Clarence Clemons on saxophone) play exactly what's necessary to illuminate the song. There are few bands that bring the energy of a live performance to a record but the E Street Band is one. (See picture right)

26 Joan Jett & The Blackhearts

As a teenager Joan Jett played rhythm guitar in The Runaways. Following her departure from that band, Jett formed the Blackhearts and released Bad Reputation in 1981. A mix of originals and covers, Jett establishes herself as a first class rock singer, bringing a sweet toughness to the proceedings. However, it was Bad Reputation's follow-up, I Love Rock 'N' Roll, with the song of the same name, that gave Jett her biggest hits, including a sultry version of The Shondells' "Crimson and Clover". In 2006, Jett released Sinner, featuring a fine cover of The Replacements' live and let live ode "Androgynous".

27 Smashing Pumpkins

Helmed by singer-songwriter Billy Corgan, Chicago's Smashing Pumpkins were at the forefront of '90s college rock. In some ways, songs like "Disarm" and "Cherub Rock" were too pop to be fully embraced by grunge enthusiasts. The Smashing Pumpkins became the voice of disenfranchised teenagers everywhere with the nihilist anthem "Zero" from 1995's Melon Collie and the Infinite Sadness. That same two-record collection also featured the sweet, hazy '70s pop of "1979", showing the two dominant sides of Corgan's musical palette. The band initially included bassist D'Arcy, guitar player James Iha and drummer Jimmy Chamberlain, but internal conflicts ripped the band apart. Recently Corgan and Chamberlain toured under the Smashing Pumpkins name.

JOAN JETT FACTFILE:

Born: 1960

Died: N/A

Home town: Philadelphia, U.S.A.

Members: Joan Jett

What you should check out/why: Bad Reputation for the title song and the rollicking cover of Gary Glitter's "Do You Wanna Touch Me (Oh Yeah)."

SMASHING PUMPKINS FACTFILE:

Start up year: 1988

Disband year: 2008?

Home town: Chicago, U.S.A.

Members: Billy Corgan, James Iha, D'Arcy, Jimmy Chamberlain

What you should check out/why: Siamese Dream for the dream pop of "1979".

28 The Clash

Coming out of Britain's punk scene, the Clash quickly established themselves as innovators, popularizing dub recording techniques and reggae rhythms within a rock context. Fiery and political, the Clash, Joe Strummer, Mick Jones, Paul Simonon and Topper Headon, debuted with a self-titled album that included an incendiary version of Bobby Fuller's "I Fought the Law" and the reggae hit "Police & Thieves". Growing in popularity, the Clash peaked with 1979's double-album London Calling. Mixing the pop of "Lost in the Supermarket" with anthems like "Death or Glory" and the reggae-infused "The Guns of Brixton", London Calling lays bare all of the Clash's inspirations.

29 The Yardbirds

Rarely does a band have one brilliant guitar player in their ranks, but the Yardbirds can claim Eric Clapton, Jeff Beck and Jimmy Page. Fronted by Keith Relf, the Yardbirds lost Clapton when they moved away from being a traditional blues band to embrace a harder rock sound. During Beck's reign, the band had its share of hits, including the psychedelic "Shapes of Things", "Heart Full of Soul", and a cover of Bo Diddley's "I'm A Man". Jimmy Page joined and for a short time shared lead guitar duties with Beck until Beck's departure less than a year later.

THE CLASH FACTFILE:

Start up year: 1976

Disband year: 1986

Home town: London, England

Members: Joe Strummer, Mick Jones, Topper Headon, Paul SImonon

What you should check out/why: London Calling pretty much defines the political side of England's original punk rock era.

Worth looking out for: The Future is Unwritten, the documentary about Joe Strummer.

THE YARDBIRDS FACTFILE:

Start up year: 1963

Disband year: 1968

Home town: Surrey, England

Members: Keith Relf, Jeff Beck, Jimmy Page, Eric Clapton,

What you should check out/why: Rhino Record's Greatest Hits, Volume I gives you "Shapes of Things", "I'm Not Talking" and other early hits.

Worth looking out for: Greatest Hits, Volume II.

30 Pantera

Texas powerhouse Pantera was one of the most successful and influential metal bands of the '90s. Forming in the early '80s with a lighter, more glam-inspired sound, Pantera hit the mark with the addition of vocalist Phillip Anselmo and their 1990 major label debut, Cowboys From Hell. Anselmo's powerful vocals proved to be the perfect pairing for the heavy riffs provided by guitarist Dimebag Darrell. Alongside bassist Rex Brown and drummer Vinnie Paul they went on to define the style known as groove metal, pushing their sound in heavier directions on albums like Vulgar Display of Power, Far Beyond Driven, and The Great Southern Trendkill. (See picture opposite)

"When I tried to play something and screwed up, I'd hear some other note that would come into play. Then I started trying different things to find the beauty in it."
- Dimebag Darrell

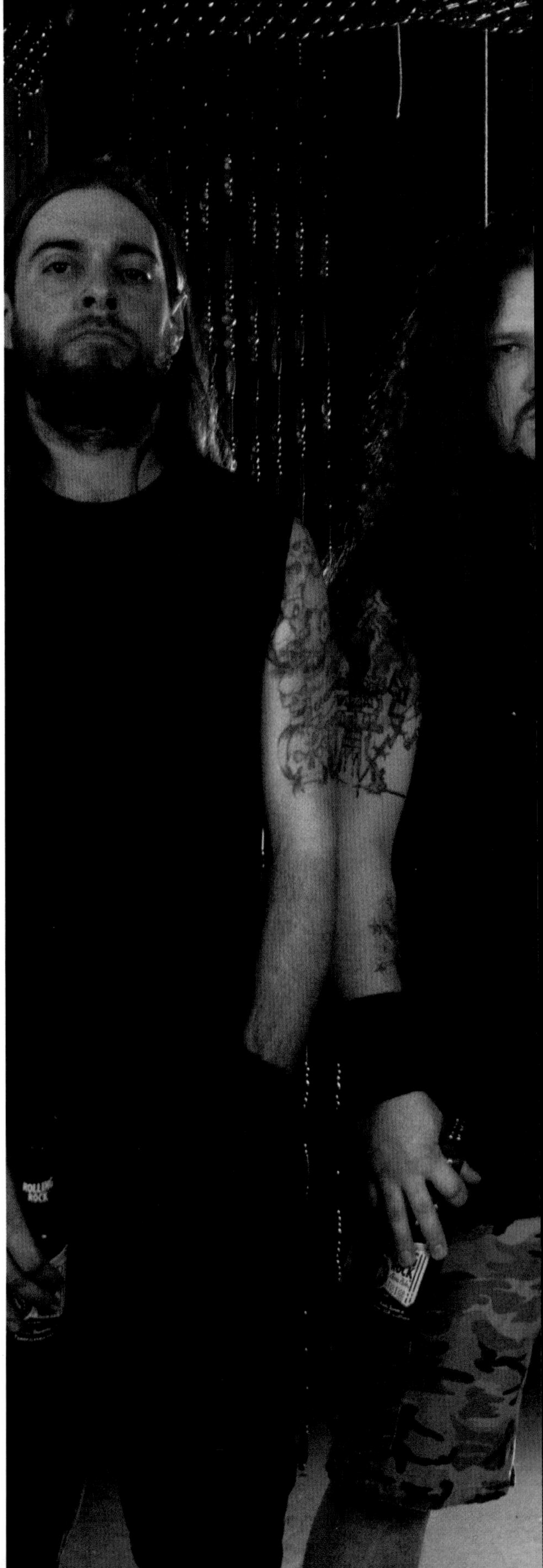

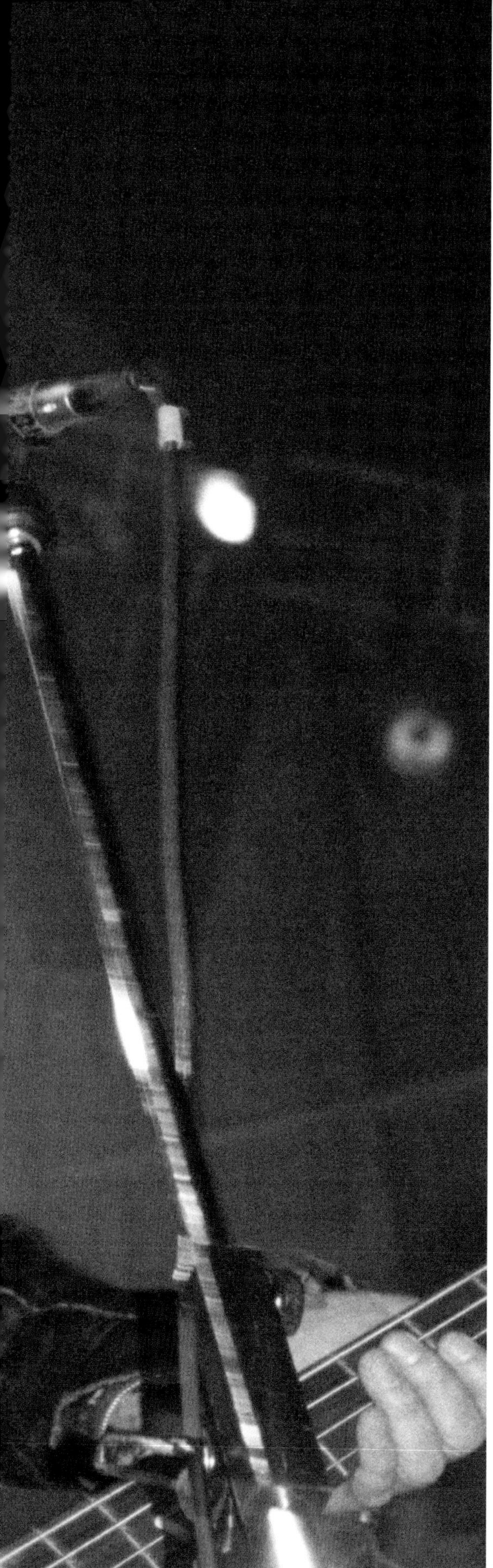

31 Guitar Wolf

Hailing from Tokyo, Japan, leather-clad, slick-haired trio Guitar Wolf is the embodiment of all things rock 'n' roll. Like their influence the Ramones, the members of Guitar Wolf employ an economical style of playing that can be summed up as loud, fast and exceptionally fun, with a guitar sound reminiscent of Link Wray. Guitar Wolf has released 14 albums since its conception in 1987 and in 2000 the band appeared in Wild Zero, the ultimate music-driven science fiction zombie movie. Named after a Guitar Wolf song, Wild Zero's premise is that rock 'n' roll, and love, truly do conquer all. (See picture opposite)

GUITAR WOLF FACTFILE:

Start up year: 1987

Disband year: N/A

Home town: Tokyo, Japan

Members: Billy, U.G., Seiji, Narita

What you should check out/why: Jet Generation includes their almost unrecognizable version of "Summertime Blues."

Worth looking out for: The movie, Wild Zero.

32 Red Hot Chili Peppers

When Red Hot Chili Peppers' fifth album, Blood Sugar Sex Magik, became a bona fide smash, it was a bit of a surprise to their long-time fans. Until songs like "Give It Away" and ballad "Under the Bridge" broke, RHCP was best known for performing naked with strategically placed socks avoiding violation of any obscenity laws. California boys Hillel Slovak (who died after 1985's The Uplift Mofo Party Plan), Anthony Kiedis, John Frusciante and Michael "Flea" Balzary started playing music during high school, blending elements of punk and funk, most notably in Flea's bass style. Fairly quiet in the early '00s, 2006's Stadium Arcadium brought them back to the airwaves. (See picture below)

33 Blondie

Although New York's Blondie scored their biggest success with the disco hit, "Heart of Glass", that song is an anomaly in Blondie's catalog, as it was more common to find drummer Clem Burke bringing the muscle. "Dreaming" from 1979's Plastic Letters exemplifies the thunderous way Burke drove Harry to greatness. Formed by Debbie Harry and guitar player Chris Stein in 1974, and centered on Harry's ethereal vocals, Blondie's use of organ (played by Jimmy Destri) makes them stand apart from the average guitar-centric punk or new wave band. Blondie was inducted into the Rock & Roll Hall of Fame in 2006.

BLONDIE FACTFILE:

Start up year: 1974

Disband year: N/A

Home town: New York, U.S.A.

Members: Debbie Harry, Chris Stein, Clem Burke, Jimmy Destri, Gary Valentine

What you should check out/why: Parallel Lines for "Picture This", "Sunday Girl" and a terrific record that straddled the line between new wave and disco.

Worth looking out for: Debbie Harry's performance in David Cronenberg's Videodrome.

34 Kiss

When Chaim Weitz's mother immigrated to the United States, it's unlikely that her hopes for her little boy would include having him dress as a demon in make-up and six-inch platform boots while spitting fire from his blood-soaked mouth and playing bass in a rock band. However, that's what happened when Chaim became Gene "The Demon" Simmons, bassist for KISS. The classic line-up, rounded out by Paul "The Lover" Stanley, Ace "Space Ace" Frehley and Peter "The Cat" Criss, was responsible for "Rock and Roll All Nite", "Love Gun" and "Detroit Rock City", songs still guaranteed to make crowds go wild. (See picture below)

35 ZZ Top

Texas trio ZZ Top has been playing its version of blues-rock since 1970, gaining popularity throughout the '70s with songs like "La Grange" and "Tush". Hitting their critical and commercial peak with 1983's synthesizer-drenched Eliminator, ZZ Top had a string of hits with "Legs", "Gimme All Your Lovin", "Sharp Dressed Man", and "TV Dinners". Fronted by bearded guitar players Billy Gibbons and Dusty Hill, with Frank Beard (ironically, the only band member with just a moustache) playing drums, ZZ Top's iconic appearance added to the band's appeal during the MTV era.

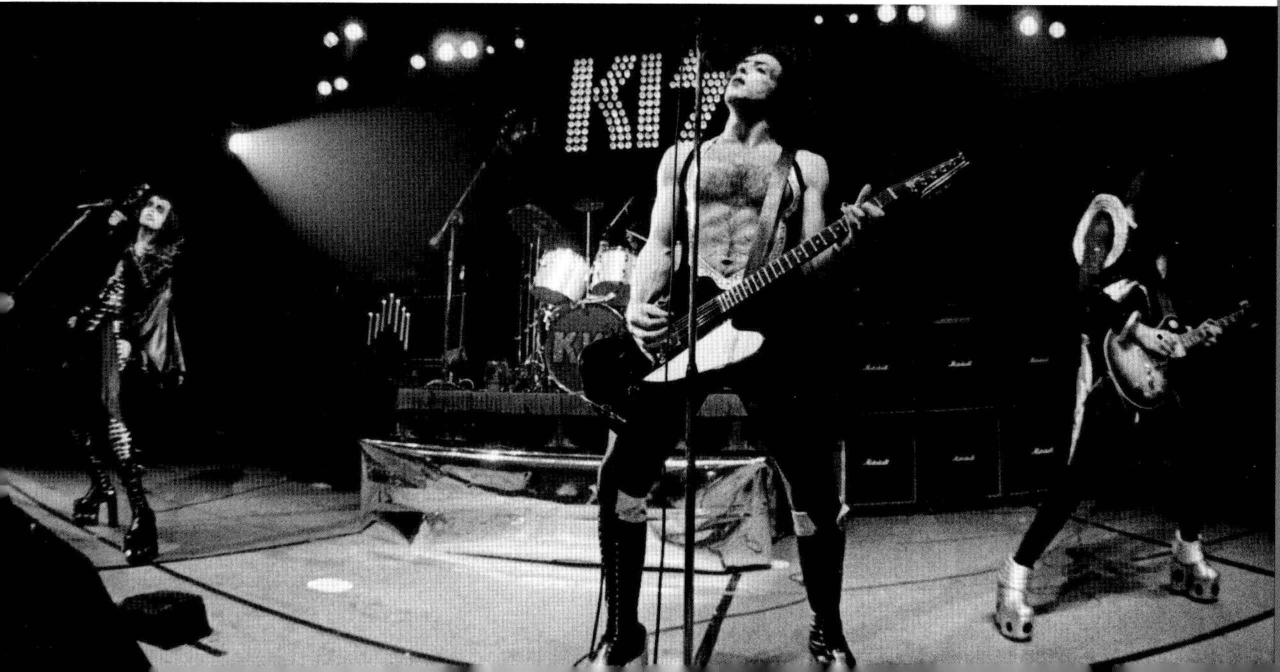

36 Dinosaur Jnr

Following the adage, "As it was, so it will be", Dinosaur Jr. started out in the '80s as the trio of guitar player J Mascis, bassist Lou Barlow and drummer Murph, broke up after seminal albums Dinosaur, You're Living All Over Me and Bug, but reunited in 2005 and released the album, Farm in 2009. Mascis continued to use the moniker and released some of the band's best albums, Green Mind and Where You Been, in the '90s. Best known for Mascis's intricate guitar playing and deadpan vocals, the beauty of Dinosaur Jr. is its ability to be simultaneously crushingly loud and perfectly melodic.

37 Heart

Sisters Ann and Nancy Wilson are the core of Heart, a Seattle-based band who spent most of the '70s and '80s at the top of the charts with rockers "Crazy on You" and "Magic Man", and ballads "Dreamboat Annie" and "These Dreams". Nancy Wilson is widely considered one of the best guitar players of all time, with a signature gallop that makes her Les Paul chime. Singer Nancy Wilson has a belting voice that gets to shine on scorching songs like "Barracuda" from the album Little Queen. With their gutsy sound and technical skill, Heart blazed a trail through '70s rock.

DINOSAUR JUNIOR FACTFILE:

Start up year: 1983

Disband year: N/A

Home town: Amherst, Massachusetts, U.S.A.

Members: J Mascis, Lou Barlow, Murph, Mike Johnson

What you should check out/why: They're all worth a listen, but try Where You Been, which may be Mascis's masterpiece.

Worth looking out for: The reunited original line-up's live shows, and new record, Farm.

HEART FACTFILE:

Start up year: 1973

Disband year: N/A

Home town: Seattle, U.S.A.

Members: Ann and Nancy Wilson, Steve Fossen, Roger and Mike Fisher, more

What you should check out/why: Little Queen for the galloping rock of "Barracuda."

38 Bob Dylan

Starting his career as a singer influenced by Woody Guthrie, Minnesota's Robert Zimmerman changed his last name to Dylan in homage to brilliant Welsh poet Dylan Thomas. Early songs like "Blowin' In the Wind" and "The Times They are A-Changin'" were acoustic guitar-based folk songs in the vein of his influences. But in 1965, he released "Like A Rolling Stone" with organ high in the mix and there was no mistaking it for a pure folk song. Folk fans felt abandoned, but this new direction took Dylan to new listeners. In the years to follow, he would incorporate many styles into his music, never resting on his laurels. (See picture opposite)

39 Audioslave

Rising from the ashes of Rage Against the Machine and Soundgarden, Audioslave is the union of singer Chris Cornell with RATM's Tim Commerford, Brad Wilk and Tom Morello. They'd been playing together for about a year before making it official, fueling anticipation amongst their fans. Audioslave released their self-titled debut in 2002, rising up the charts on the strength of first single, "Cochise", a powerful song that pleased their audience. The band released two more albums, 2005's chart-topping Out of Exile and 2006's Revelations, and played an historical show in Cuba prior to Cornell leaving the band in 2007.

40 The Doors

Fronted by the charismatic Jim Morrison, the Doors were a Californian quartet, rounded out by keyboard player Ray Manzarek, guitarist Robby Krieger and drummer John Densmore. While the verdict is still out on whether Morrison's lyrics can be considered poetry, there's little denying the Doors' sound owes a lot to the singer's voice and words. While some of their songs like "The End" and "People are Strange" explore darker themes, hits like "Love Me Two Times" and "Hello, I Love You" were bona fide pop smashes, with Manzarek's organ sound making the Doors stand out from everything else on the radio. The self-destructive Morrison died in France at the age of 27. (See picture opposite)

"I see myself as a huge fiery comet, a shooting star. Everyone stops, points up and gasps "Oh look at that!" Then, whoosh and I'm gone.. and they'll never see anything like it ever again, and they won't be able to forget me - ever."
- Jim Morrison

SONOR

41 Slade

In the '70s Birmingham, England and its surrounding area were writhing with musical talent and spawned Black Sabbath, ELO and Slade. Noddy Holder, Dave Hill, Jimmy Lea and Don Powell had been playing under different band names for about five years before becoming Slade. In 1971 they adopted the flares and make-up of the glam scene, but their music was foot-stomping party rock. Although not getting much U.S. attention until their 1983 comeback "Run Run Away", at home in the U.K. Slade had a long string of hits, including "Gudbuy T'Jane", "Coz I Luv You", "Cum on Feel the Noize" and the perennial Christmas favorite, "Merry Xmas Everybody".
(See picture opposite)

SLADE FACTFILE:

Start up year: 1966

Disband year: 1991

Home town: Wolverhampton, England

Members: Noddy Holder, Dave Hill, Jim Lea, Don Powell

What you should check out/why: There's a lot of great Slade, but Slayed has "Gudbye T'Jane" and "Mama Weer All Crazy Now", so that's a good start.

42 Radiohead

When Radiohead first came to people's attention with the song "Creep" from 1993's Pablo Honey, no one foresaw that this band would become one of the world's highest-selling and most critically beloved bands. That they followed their shoegazer/grunge debut with The Bends was a smart move on the band's part. Loaded with hits like "Fake Plastic Trees", "High and Dry" and "Just", The Bends highlighted Jonny Greenwood's guitar playing and Thom Yorke's lyrics. From there, Radiohead made experimental pop hits OK Computer and Kid A. In 2007, they released In Rainbows, for which they allowed people the Pay What You Want option to download. (See picture opposite)

43 Pearl Jam

Rising to fame during the grunge heyday of the early '90s, Seattle's Pearl Jam is a mainstream band with punk rock politics. Early hits like "Jeremy" and "Alive" sound best when performed in huge arenas, but Pearl Jam spent part of the '90s not touring while battling Ticketmaster to make the cost of concert tickets more affordable to fans. While Pearl Jam has released nine official albums since 1991's Ten, they also made an official bootleg series of every one of their recordings from their 2000 tour, making it a full-time job to be a Pearl Jam completist.

44 Nick Cave and the Bad Seeds

Nick Cave formed the Bad Seeds at the dissolution of first band The Birthday Party in 1983. Forging a sound as deeply immersed in Southern Gothic literature, in spite of Cave's Australian origins, as in any musical genre, The Bad Seeds conjure heaven, hell and all points in between on songs like "Deanna", "The Mercy Seat" and "Red Right Hand". On 1996's Murder Ballads, Cave pulled out all stops on a five-minute version of the blues classic "Stagger Lee", taking the tragic tale to new lows. While Cave went through a gentler period earlier in this decade, 2008's Dig Lazarus Dig returned him to his roots and even found him getting groovy here and there.

45 Tom Petty & The Heartbreakers

When Tom Petty & The Heartbreakers moved from Florida to California, their whole lives were riding on the hope of getting a record deal. The gamble paid off and the band recently celebrated its 30th anniversary and the release of their 14th studio album, Highway Companion. In the intervening years, the Heartbreakers' blend of Southern rock and power pop, not to mention Petty's sheer songwriting skill, found them racking up hit after hit like "Refugee", "American Girl", "Don't Come Around Here No More" and "The Waiting". While Petty's most successful work, Full Moon Fever, was released as a solo album, the Heartbreakers remain a vital touring and recording band.

46 Cream

After paying his dues as a member of the Yardbirds and John Mayall's Bluesbreakers, Eric Clapton gained international stardom as a member of Cream, along with drummer Ginger Baker and bassist Jack Bruce. In the simplest terms, Cream essentially created the rock power-trio blueprint. Relying heavily on their blues roots for inspiration, the trio was also known for lengthy jazz-like improvisational jams, scoring their biggest hits with "White Room" and "Sunshine of Your Love". In their mere two years as a band, they released three albums: Fresh Cream, double album Wheels of Fire, and Disraili Gears. A fourth album, Goodbye, was released posthumously.

"You were at school and you were pimply and no one wanted to know you. You get into a group and you've got thousands of chicks there."
– Eric Clapton

47 Motorhead

Everything Louder Than Everything Else is more than the title of Motorhead's 1999 live album; it is the foundation on which Lemmy Kilmeister has built the institution that is Motorhead. Forming Motorhead in 1975 after leaving space-rock legends Hawkwind, Lemmy did more than his fair share to help pioneer the styles that are now known as speed-metal and thrash. According to legend, there is such a toxic mix of drugs in Kilmeister's blood that a transfusion would kill him. With many personnel and record label changes and over thirty years of blasting out hits like "Ace of Spades" and "Killed By Death", Motorhead continues to blow minds with its thunderous, no-nonsense rock 'n' roll. (See picture below)

48 R.E.M

In 1981 when Mike Mills, Peter Buck, Michael Stipe and Bill Berry formed R.E.M. in Athens, Georgia, they were most notable for Buck's jangling guitar and Stipe's enigmatic vocals. Early records Chronic Town and Reckoning drew a loyal following, and by the time the video for "Can't Get There From Here" from Fables of the Reconstruction hit MTV, they were underground stars. But it was songs like "Losing My Religion" and "Everybody Hurts" from Out of Time and Automatic For the People that drove them to superstardom. While their recent albums don't get the critical adoration of their back catalog, R.E.M. continues to pack stadiums around the world.

49 Soundgarden

Seattle's Soundgarden was a potent cocktail of heavy metal, psychedelic rock, and the sound and values of the '80s underground. Though they were one of the first bands to record for grunge HQ Sub Pop, their first full length album "Ultramega OK" was released by legendary punk label SST. Soundgarden was also ahead of the pack in making the move to a major label, thus proving there was a wider audience for more adventurous rock bands. They hit their commercial peak with the albums Badmotorfinger and Superunknown, and singles "Rusty Cage", "Spoonman", "Fell On Black Days" and "Black Hole Sun".

50 Neil Young

After some time spent eking out a living in Canadian rock bands Neil Young headed to California's Laurel Canyon and together with Stephen Stills had some success with The Buffalo Springfield. After that band's dissolution, Young gathered steam as a solo artist (Harvest) and as a member of Crosby, Stills, Nash & Young. Young gathered Danny Whitten, Billy Talbot and Ralph Molina for his backing band on Everybody Knows This is Nowhere, which led to the inception of rock band Crazy Horse. To his great credit, Young has been one of the few '60s superstars who continue to make interesting and occasionally brilliant music today. (See picture opposite)

"I don't think there are too many rock bands in history that can look at the beginning and middle and ending of themselves and see what I see when I think of Soundgarden. I think from the beginning through the middle and the end it was such a perfect ride and such a perfect legacy to leave."

FDNY

51 Thin Lizzy

Formed in Dublin, Ireland in 1970, Thin Lizzy is best known for "The Boys Are Back In Town", a song that is often thought of as a fun bit of proto-metal fluff, but the upbeat tempo belies lyrics that are thoughtful, verging on introspective. This duality is the essence of Thin Lizzy: powerful instrumentation backing singer Phil Lynott's story-like lyrics on songs like "Jailbreak" and "Cowboy Song". Underappreciated by hard rock-hating critics during the band's existence, Thin Lizzy is now part of rock's pantheon. Lynott died in 1986. (See picture opposite)

THIN LIZZY FACTFILE:

Start up year: 1970

Disband year: 1983

Home town: Dublin, Ireland

Members: Phil Lynott, Brian Robertson, Scott Gorham, Brian Downey, more

What you should check out/why: Jailbreak for the rock 'n' roll storytelling triumvirate of the title track, "Cowboy Song" and "The Boys Are Back in Town."

52 The Stooges

James "Iggy" Osterberg, Dave Alexander, Ron and Scott Asheton were the original Stooges, as found on their 1969 eponymous debut and the following year's Fun House. Known for an electric stage presence, Iggy was, and remains, the ultimate front man, giving songs like "T.V. Eye" and "1970" a grittiness and sex appeal that made The Stooges stand out from the crowd. By the time they released the David Bowie-produced Raw Power, they had transformed into Iggy and the Stooges. While Raw Power is packed with some of rock's finest songs such as "Shake Appeal" and "Search and Destroy", they'd lost Alexander at this point and it wouldn't be long before Iggy Stooge became Iggy Pop.

53 Link Wray

Cited as Pete Townshend's inspiration for learning guitar, Link Wray has a sound like no one before him. Believed to be the first person to use a power chord, Wray's sound was heavier and fuzzier than his contemporaries, with first single and signature song "Rumble" sounding like nothing else on the radio. Although Wray's influence is undeniable, he's never had the commercial success of other guitar slingers because his music was often considered too wild and rebellious for labels to promote. His song "Ace of Spades" was featured in Quentin Tarantino's Pulp Fiction.

"I don't believe in organised politics, organised religion, organised music, organised anything." - Link Wray

54 The Velvet Underground

When Lou Reed, John Cale, Maureen Tucker and Doug Yule, with guest vocalist Nico, released The Velvet Underground with Nico (with Andy Warhol's iconic banana on the cover), it was greeted with a fair amount of outrage and derision. But over the years it, along with VU, Loaded and White Light, White Heat, has become a touchstone for fans and musicians, celebrated for its songwriting and its stark sound. Songs like "Heroin" and the S&M-inspired "Venus In Furs" were as far removed from the cars/girls/sunshine hits of the '60s as they could get. The band, apart for over twenty years at the time, reunited for some shows and a live album, MCMXCIII, in 1993. (See picture below)

55 The Beach Boys

Consisting of brothers Brian, Carl, and Dennis Wilson, along with cousin Mike Love and friend Al Jardine, Hawthorne, California's Beach Boys were one of the most innovative and influential bands of the '60s and '70s. Starting off singing simple surf and car songs, Brian Wilson's talents as a producer and arranger would lead them to create classics of musical depth and beauty such as Pet Sounds, Friends, Sunflower, and Surf's Up. The Beach Boys leave behind them one of the richest catalogs in American popular music, including mainstays "God Only Knows", "Surfin' U.S.A.", "Good Vibrations", and "Wouldn't It Be Nice".

56 T.Rex

Although Marc Bolan started out as a folk singer, he decided to get a little louder and more than a little sexier when he recruited percussionist Mickey Finn to form Tyrannosaurus Rex, later shortened to T-Rex. T-Rex was one of England's most popular bands during the early and mid '70s, with Bolan's signature breathy vocals and suggestive, though confounding lyrics ("You've got a hub-capped diamond star halo") juxtaposed with his loud, fuzzy guitar sounds on hits like "Telegram Sam", "Jeepster" and "Bang A Gong (Get It On)". Following the band's demise, Bolan hosted a television show. He died in 1977.

57 Slayer

Over a quarter of a century on, Slayer is still unrivaled in their metal fury. They continue to keep an ever-growing and religiously devout fan base banging their heads while never toning down their sonic assault. The twin rhythm and frenzied lead guitars of Kerry King and Jeff Hanneman produce some of the most memorable moments in the genre, while the screams of bassist/vocalist Tom Araya are instantly recognizable, and in Dave Lombardo they have one of the greatest heavy drummers in the business. No rock collection is complete without a copy of Slayer's classic 1986 album "Reign In Blood". (See picture opposite)

"We survived a Slayer crowd every night for about 50 days and thought we could do about anything after that."
- Layne Staley

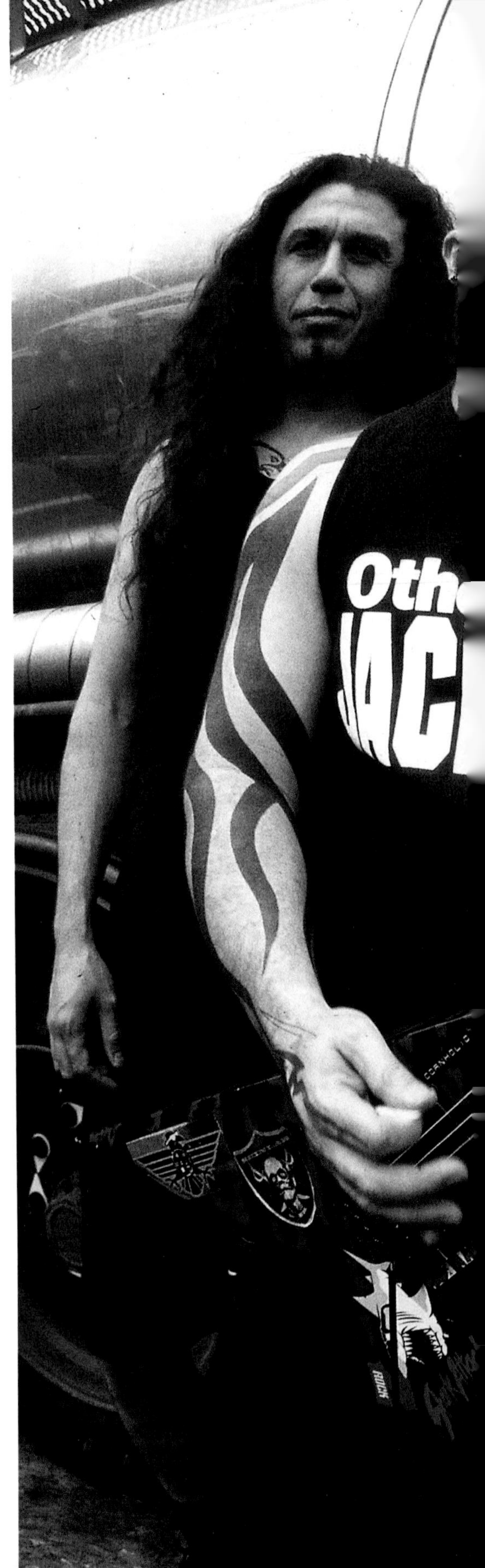

FEAR
GOD SEND DEATH
PAIN

58 MC5

From the same Detroit, Michigan scene that begat The Stooges and Ted Nugent came The Motor City 5, best known in some circles for singer Robin Tyner's profane introduction to their best-known song "Kick Out The Jams". While the MC5 didn't have a great deal of commercial success while they were together, time has found them revered as one of the greatest rock bands of all time. Nominally involved with the White Panther movement via manager John Sinclair, MC5 courted controversy. But their legacy is found in scorching songs like "Looking at You" and "I Can Only Give You Everything".

59 Creedance Clearwater Revival

Before singer/songwriter John Fogerty left to pursue a solo career in 1972, California's Creedence Clearwater Revival created a sound that was equal parts blues, rock and Cajun swamp, with a little country tossed in to keep it interesting. With its no-nonsense guitar/bass/drums instrumentation and Fogerty's workmanlike uniform of plaid shirt and jeans, C.C.R. was referred to in hindsight as the first grunge band. In the four or five years C.C.R. was together they made the classic albums Cosmo's Factory, Green River and Bayou Country and had hits with "Bad Moon Rising", "Proud Mary" and the heartbreaking "Lodi".

60 Rage Against the Machine

In the early 1990s no mainstream band was as closely associated with leftist politics as California's Rage Against the Machine. The band seems to be born into the role. Front man Zach de la Rocha is the son of Chicano political artist Beto and guitar player Tom Morello is the nephew of former Kenyan President Jomo Kenyatta. RATM deliver political sermons over an energetic blend of punk rock, hip-hop and stomping metal riffs. Their debut album was released in 1992 and earned them legions of followers with anthems like "Killing In The Name" and "Bombtrack." (See picture opposite)

61 The Cure

For the past 30 years, Robert Smith and a revolving cast of players (with bassist Simon Gallup being the only near-constant) has been creating music as The Cure. With a reputation for writing sad, some would say depressive, songs The Cure often gets stuck with the Goth label. However, while albums like Pornography, Faith and Disintegration are atmospheric and sometimes gloomy, Smith and Co. wrote a significant body of work and have had some of their biggest hits with "Let's Go to Bed" "Just Like Heaven" and "Friday, I'm in Love", which are quite removed from their sad sack reputation. Occasional threats that Smith will retire the name have gone unfounded thus far. (See picture opposite)

THE CURE FACTFILE:

Start up year: 1976

Disband year: N/A

Home town: Crawley, England

Members: Robert Smith, Simon Gallup, Lol Tolhurst, Porl Thompson, Perry Bamonte, Roger O'Donnell, Boris Williams, more

What you should check out/why: The Head on the Door for balancing pop songs and atmosphere.

Worth looking out for: Boys Don't Cry and Pornography

62 The Animals

Like many English bands of the '60s, the guys who formed the Animals bonded over a mutual love of the blues and other music coming from America. Unlike most of those bands, singer Eric Burdon possesses a voice as rough and soulful as many of the singers he admired. Coming out of Newcastle, the Animals are one of the most influential groups of the period and spent a great deal of time in the charts with songs like "House of the Rising Sun", "Don't Let Me Be Misunderstood" and "We've Gotta Get Out of This Place". Alan Price's organ arrangements are central to the Animals' distinctive sound, as they add yet another soulful level to the music.

63 The Pretenders

Few people in rock are as cool as Pretenders singer and songwriter Chrissie Hynde. Born and raised in Ohio, Hynde moved to England, the home of the music she loved, and formed the Pretenders. Emerging into the New Wave scene of the late'70s and early'80s, the Pretenders' first album, The Pretenders, spawned the hit "Brass In Pocket", but it was the sneering "Tattooed Love Boys" and "Precious" that put Hynde on the rock 'n' roll map. The Pretenders II showed a softer side with "Message of Love" and their outstanding cover of The Kinks' "I Go To Sleep". Their biggest success was 1984's Learning to Crawl with the single "Back on the Chain Gang."

64 Mötley Crüe

Mötley Crüe is a living tribute to rock 'n' roll excess, celebrating the seedier side of life on the streets of Los Angeles. Bass player and principal songwriter Nikki Sixx's vision was an amalgamation of glam rockers The Sweet, the attitude of the Sex Pistols, and the bluesy swagger of Aerosmith. Vince Neil's voice proved the perfect vehicle for Sixx's lyrics of depravity and drug abuse while the drum theatrics of Tommy Lee and the metallic guitars of Mick Mars provided the meat and backbone. Mötley Crüe became one of the most enduring and successful bands to come from the '80s glam rock movement.

65 The Buzzcocks

At the core of the Buzzcocks stand co-founders, singers and guitar players Pete Shelley and Steve Diggle. Formed in Manchester after seeing the Sex Pistols, the Buzzcocks took a shared love for '60s pop music and injected it with punk's speed and volume. While punk is generally thought of as making a political statement, the majority of Buzzcocks songs are about love ("Ever Fallen In Love?"), sex ("Orgasm Addict") and the tribulations of being a teenager ("Noise Annoys"). Although they've taken breaks throughout the years, the Buzzcocks continue to record and tour, giving young audiences a chance to see this still-vital band.

66 Nine Inch Nails

For all intents and purposes, Trent Reznor is Nine Inch Nails. An early connection to Marilyn Manson gave NIN instant underground kudos, but it was their tour with the first Lollapalooza that brought the band's electronic industrial music to a broader audience. Known for making noisy, aggressive, often grinding rock, Reznor proved his songwriting prowess when Johnny Cash covered "Hurt", turning it from a young man's lament to the words that accompanied the end of a legend's life. While Reznor recently put the band on indefinite hiatus, they went out on a high note, touring with Jane's Addiction for the album, The Slip.

67 The Replacements

New York and Los Angeles are known as the homes of American music, but the '80s saw the rise of Minnesota's music scene. Central to the scene were the Replacements, with Paul Westerberg, Chris Mars and brothers Tommy and Bob Stinson. While alcoholism eventually broke up the band, their twelve years together was long enough to amass a near-perfect body of work, including Hootenanny, Pleased to Meet Me and Tim. Primarily a rock band, the Replacements also shone during more contemplative songs like "Skyway". The album Pleased to Meet Me helped fuel the resurgence of interest in the band Big Star with the ode to singer "Alex Chilton".

68 Rush

Geddy Lee, Neil Peart and Alex Lifeson are Rush. Formed in Toronto, Canada in 1968, Rush is arguably more successful now than at any other time in their steadfast career, with their music being featured in movies like Adventureland and I Love You, Man. Technically astute and lyrically dense, with references to books like Ayn Rand's The Fountainhead abounding, Rush appeals to fans of literate, solo-laden rock. Exploring issues of alienation and existentialism, the trio's masterworks include 2112, Moving Pictures and Exit...Stage Left. Peart is among the most revered rock drummers since John Bonham. To a generation of Canadians, "Tom Sawyer" inspires as much patriotism as the national anthem.

69 Joy Division

Joy Division is a band of legendary proportions that still retains a near-cult status. Their music, sometimes dark and brooding, sometimes propulsive and radiating energy, never achieved commercial success outside of native England, but Ian Curtis, Peter Hook, Bernard Sumner and Stephen Morris were responsible for "Love Will Tear Us Apart Again" and "She's Lost Control", two of the most enduring post-rock songs. When Curtis committed suicide in 1980 it looked like the end for the band, but soon after, the surviving members re-emerged as New Order. Two films, the documentary simply called Joy Division, and the biopic Control, spawned a renewed interest in the band.

70 The Sex Pistols

One of the earliest criticisms of the Sex Pistols was that they made unlistenable noise and couldn't play their instruments, but one listen to their only official album, Never Mind the Bullocks, and it's obvious that there is plenty of punch in "God Save the Queen", "EMI" and "Holiday in the Sun". In fact, the whole thing comes across like Chuck Berry's bratty nephew. Although the Sex Pistols icons are singer Johnny Rotten and troubled bassist Sid Vicious, Vicious didn't play on Never Mind the Bullocks. Instead, the low end was provided by original member Glen Matlock, who also co-wrote most of the songs. (See picture opposite)

"I think that you have to bear in mind that music is about escape, and it's not unreasonable to think the music business would be based around escapism."
– Ian Curtis

71 The Misfits

Glenn Danzig and his band of ghouls the Misfits began their reign of terror in 1977 in Lodi, New Jersey. They quickly gained a reputation by blending ferocious punk rock with horror film-inspired lyrics. Though their musicianship was often crude, Danzig infused the songs with infectious melodies delivered in his unmistakable baritone. Bass player Jerry Only remained Danzig's only constant accomplice with frequent changes to the band's line-up. The Misfits disbanded in 1983 when Glenn began his new project Samhain, which would evolve into the more commercially successful Danzig. Jerry Only initiated a new Danzig-less Misfits in 1996. (See picture opposite)

THE MISFITS FACTFILE:

Start up year: 1977

Disband year: N/A (Jerry Only is the only remaining original member)

Home town: Lodi, New Jersey, U.S.A.

Members: Glenn Danzig, Jerry Only, Frank LiCata, "Mr. Jim" Catania, Doyle, more

What you should check out/why: Walk Among Us brings all the campy fun of '50s horror movies to music with "Vampira" and "Skulls".

72 Mudhoney

Nirvana and Pearl Jam may have had more commercial success, but Sub Pop's first signing Mudhoney is the dark horse of the grunge scene and has quietly released amazing records for twenty years. While albums from early gems like Every Good Boy Deserves Fudge and Superfuzz Bigmuff to the recent Under A Million Suns and The Lucky Ones offer fans plenty of quality listening material, it's their live shows, led by eternally youthful singer Mark Arm that turn listeners into lifelong fans. The movie Singles included an inside joke based around Mudhoney's classic song, "Touch Me I'm Sick". Like many people involved with the Sub Pop label, Arm started his career at one of Seattle's most notorious companies, Muzak.

73 Foo Fighters

After Kurt Cobain's death left drummer Dave Grohl without a band, he decided he was better suited to the front of the stage and formed the Foo Fighters. Already a home recording fanatic, Grohl had been writing songs since his teens and plays every instrument on the Foos' debut album. Throughout the band's existence Grohl has remained the only constant member. Building on the inertia of first single "This Is a Call", the Foo Fighters went platinum in the U.S. alone. Subsequent albums include hits like "Monkeywrench", "Learn to Fly" and "Lonely as You". (See picture above)

74 New York Dolls

Punks before punk even existed, David Johansen, Johnny Thunders, Sylvain Sylvain, Jerry Nolan and Arthur Kane brought sleazy glamor to a scene overrun by t-shirts and jeans. Dressed in platform heels, leather and lipstick, the New York Dolls infused their down 'n' dirty rock 'n' roll with cheeky winks to girl groups, even starting "Looking For a Kiss" by quoting the Shangri-La's "When I say I'm in love, you best believe I'm in love, L-U-V". With the dubious honor of being managed by future Sex Pistols impresario Malcolm McLaren, the hard-living Dolls only lasted a couple of albums. Sadly, Johansen and Sylvain are the only surviving members.

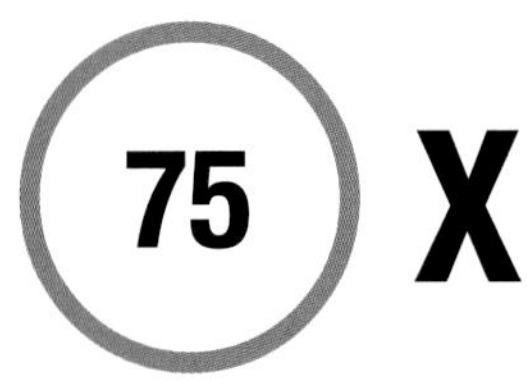

75 X

No band symbolizes L.A.'s punk scene in quite the same way X does. The classic line-up is comprised of Exene Cervenka (vocals), John Doe (bass/vocals), Billy Zoom (guitar) and DJ Bonebrake (drums). Mixing punk and rockabilly with Cervenka and Doe's powerful girl/boy vocal arrangements, X's debut, Los Angeles, made fans and critics pay attention. The 1981 follow-up Wild Gift continued the band's ascent, with the New York Times naming it Album of the Year. Although the band's members are now primarily concerned with other projects, they still reunite from time to time, giving fans old and new a chance to hear their genius.

"We thought that's the way you were supposed to be if you were in a rock 'n' roll band. Flamboyant."
- David Johansen

76 The Pixies

Charles Thompson changed his name to Black Francis and together with Kim Deal, Joey Santiago and Dave Lovering, created the Pixies, one of the most beloved bands of America's college rock scene of the '90s. Their 1989 breakthrough album Doolittle captured the minds of students everywhere with the videos for "This Monkey's Gone to Heaven" and "Debaser" becoming alternative rock hits. Deal's deadpan vocals provided the perfect counterpart to Francis' more manic style. Part of the Pixies' considerable charm lay in the use of surf guitar in a noisier, fuzzier context than listeners were used to hearing it. Personality clashes broke them up, but time healed wounds enough to allow them to reunite in 2004. (See picture below, left)

Tool

Fusing progressive art-rock with the sonic palate of thrash metal, Tool found a place for themselves on the edges of the '90s alternative rock landscape. Gaining exposure with a slot on the third Lollapalooza tour, Tool proved to be a welcome change for some with their bleak portrayals of alienation. Intricate time signatures and extended instrumental passages provided contrast to vocalist Maynard James Keenan's emotional musings of despair and everyday life. Guitarist Adam Jones is responsible for their groundbreaking videos for songs like Sober and Prison Sex as well as the elaborate artwork that makes the long wait in between albums worthwhile for fans. (See picture below, right)

78 Gossip

One of the most vibrant trios in rock today, Gossip's foundation lies in the soul, blues and gospel singing of the Southern U.S. mixed with indie-rock minimalism, and on 2005's Standing in the Way of Control and 2009's Music for Men, a disco beat. Singer Beth Ditto is a revelation and her voice is a throaty, gutsy wail. Backed by only guitar player Brace Paine and drummer Hannah Billie, Ditto is central to Gossip's sound. In the past couple of years, Ditto has become something of a celebrity in the U.K. and is as well-known for being a confident fat woman who posed nude for magazine covers as she is for Gossip's music. (See picture opposite)

"There's a lot of people in bands out there who are millionaires, and it might sound egotistical but they're no better than me. I'm not saying I'm better than them, but they're no better than I am. It has nothing to with talent, it has to do with majors, and sexism in the music industry."
- Beth Ditto

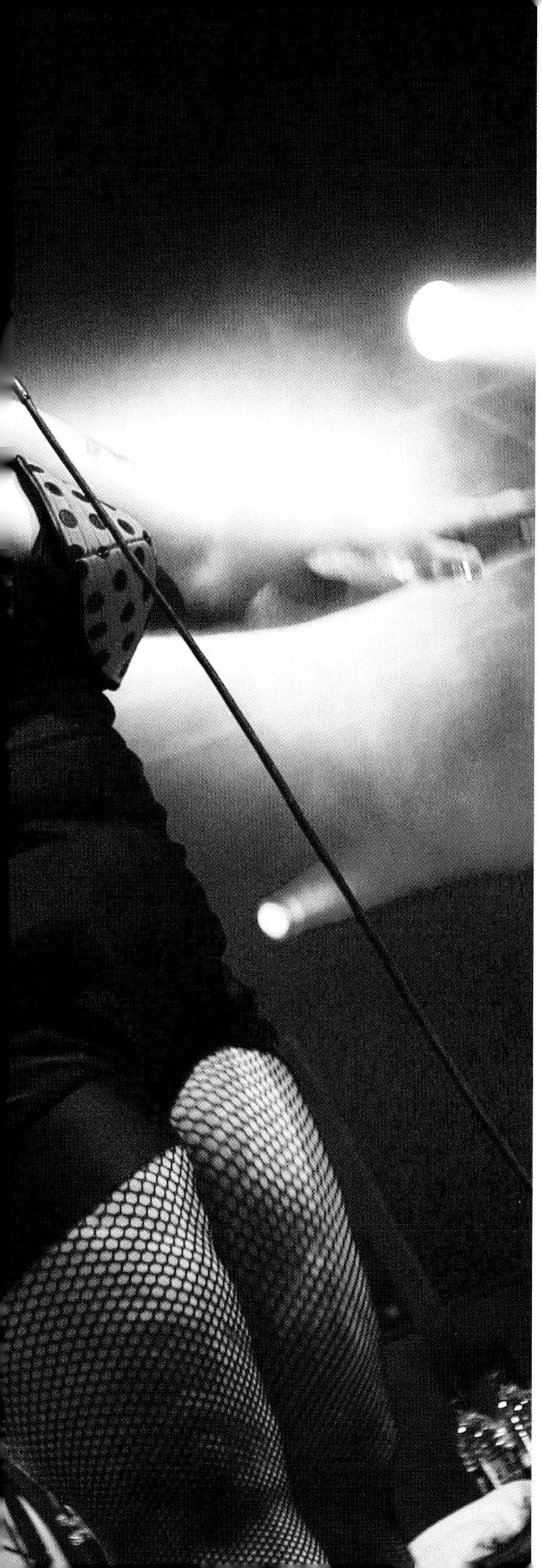

79 The Band

Starting out as the Hawks, the backing band for rock 'n' roller Ronnie Hawkins, The Band later hooked up with Bob Dylan when he, as legend says, went electric. Robbie Robertson, Levon Helm, Richard Manuel, Garth Hudson, Rick Danko made enduring music that combined traditional styles with elements of psychedelia and contemporary folk. The Band's debut, Music from Big Pink, continues to influence bands attempting to glean the formula to making an album that sounds so simple yet has so many lyrical and musical complexities. The Martin Scorcese-directed film of The Band's final concert, The Last Waltz, is essential viewing for anyone who cares about popular music.

THE BAND FACTFILE:

Start up year: 1967

Disband year: 1976

Home town: Toronto, Canada

Members: Robbie Robertson, Levon Helm, Richard Manuel, Garth Hudson, Rick Danko

What you should check out/why: Music From Big Pink was at the helm of the country-rock scene.

Worth looking out for: Martin Scorcese's documentary/concert film The Last Waltz.

80 Janis Joplin

In many ways, time hasn't been kind to Janis Joplin. The creator of classic rock albums Pearl and Cheap Thrills (with Big Brother and the Holding Company), Joplin was a sensitive woman with a passionate, gravelly voice that up-and-comers have tried to imitate ever since. However, many people think of her as a rock 'n' roll casualty with a bottle of Southern Comfort in hand. This view does a disservice to Joplin and her brand of blues-rock. Best known for "Ball and Chain" and her cover of "Summertime", her live performance of the Bee Gee's "To Love Somebody" on the Dick Cavett Show was an awe-inspiring moment in rock 'n' roll history. (See picture opposite)

JANIS JOPLIN FACTFILE:

Born: 1943

Died: 1970

Home town: Port Arthur, Texas, U.S.A.

Members: Janis Joplin

What you should check out/why: Pearl for "Mercedes Benz" and her heartbreaking version of Kris Kristofferson's "Me and Bobby McGee."

Worth looking out for: Robert Crumb's cover art on the Big Brother & the Holding Company album, Cheap Thrills.

"When I sing, I feel like when you're first in love. It's more than sex. It's that point two people can get to they call love, when you really touch someone for the first time, but it's gigantic, multiplied by the whole audience. I feel chills."
- Janis Joplin

81 Boston

Unfairly lumped in with what many consider corporate rock, Boston was an innovative band led by recording pioneer Tom Scholz. Scholz, a former product designer for Polaroid, was a home-recording enthusiast with a studio that makes gearheads drool. Boston, released in 1976, is a masterwork in hi-fidelity recording. The single "More Than a Feeling", with its slow and pretty verses and its rousing, guitar-heavy chorus, laid the groundwork for stadium rock song structure. In spite of the success of its debut, Boston has never been a prolific band, with nine years separating their second and third albums, and another eight elapsing before album four. (See picture opposite)

BOSTON FACTFILE:

Start up year: 1971

Disband year: N/A

Home town: Boston, U.S.A.

Members: Tom Scholz, Brad Delp, John "Sib" Hashian, Fran Sheehan, Barry Goudreau, more

What you should check out/why: Boston for classic rock favorites "More Than a Feeling" and "Peace of Mind."

82 Hawkwind

Forming in England in the late '60s, Hawkwind consists of core member Dave Brock and a virtually endless rotating cast of band members that has included such notable names as Motorhead's Lemmy Kilmister, and science fiction writer Michael Moorcock, as well as a brief inclusion of former Cream stickman Ginger Baker. Hawkwind's art-rock exists on a more primal plain than that of contemporaries like the more commercially successful Pink Floyd or King Crimson but they did manage brief chart success with "Silver Machine". In its various incarnations Hawkwind has released dozens of studio and live albums in its 30-plus years, leaving many melted minds behind them.

83 Fugazi

Ian Mackaye, whose list of credits already included legendary bands Minor Threat and Embrace as well as operating Washington, DC label Dischord Records, took hardcore to new places with Fugazi. Mackaye, along with Guy Picciotto, Joe Lally, and former Rites of Spring member Brendan Canty showed that a band could gain hordes of fans while still challenging them. A band that stuck to their activist roots, Fugazi maintained low costs for their CDs when major labels were gouging and kept cathartic live shows affordable to their fans. Fugazi pushed their sound in new directions while retaining their strong band identity.

84 Dick Dale

Known as the King of Surf Guitar, Dick Dale was a musical pioneer on many levels. As a performer, he had magnetism galore, drawing fans to his blend of Middle Eastern, Eastern European and rock styles. Closely associated with Fender guitars and amplifiers, he worked with the company in the '60s to develop technology that would help replicate the sounds he heard in his head. His song "Let's Go Trippin'" started a fad of surf music throughout the United States, inspiring groups like Jan & Dean and the Beach Boys. The rollicking "Pipeline" is an essential listen.

85 The Allman Brothers

Southern rock pioneers the Allman Brothers were known to make songs stretch for upwards of half an hour during their legendary performances of the early'70s. Comprised of brothers Duane and Gregg Allman and guitarist Dickey Betts, the Allman Brothers are first and foremost a live band. Songs like "Whipping Post" and "Midnight Rider" were central to the band's early sets and to the development of their career. Two weeks after the release of live album At Filmore East, band leader Duane Allman was killed in a motorcycle accident. With numerous personnel changes, the Allman Brothers remain a viable band, continuing to play its hybrid of jazz, rock, country and blues.

86 Janes Addiction

Jane's Addiction singer Perry Farrell is one of the most significant figures in '90s rock. Along with steering Jane's to success with Nothing's Shocking and Ritual de lo Habitual, Farrell is the founder of Lollapalooza, an ambitious touring music festival that brought together rock and hip-hop bands. Today it still exists as a one-day festival in Chicago, Illinois. Jane's Addiction combined art rock distortion with metal's heavy guitars to produce a sound that often sounded like waves crashing overhead. Mega-hit "Been Caught Stealing" can still be heard blaring from car stereos and university dorm rooms today.

87 The Cramps

Until singer Lux Interior's 2009 death, rockabilly and punk fans lived in hope that the Cramps would take the show on the road one more time. Slow and sludgy, the Cramps took classic rock 'n' roll to new, dark places and they did so with a sexiness today's squeaky clean pop stars couldn't even begin to dredge up. Stalking the stage in killer heels and a leather mini-skirt, guitar player Poison Ivy led The Cramps through "Goo Goo Muck" and "I Was a Teenage Werewolf". Similar to the image of Che Guevara, an iconic skull-with-a-pompadour Cramps t-shirt is worn by more people than the number who own a Cramps album.

88 Eddie Cochran

In what seems to be a familiar story for many early rock 'n' rollers, guitar player Eddie Cochran was only 22 when he died in a car crash while on tour in the U.K. with Gene Vincent. Best known for "Summertime Blues", a song that's been covered by everyone from Blue Cheer to Rush to Joan Jett, and "C'mon Everybody", Cochran had a playful style that begs to be danced to even today. His song "Twenty Flight Rock" was used in The Girl Can't Help It, one of the first films to feature rock 'n' roll.

89 Jeff Beck

After leading The Yardbirds through their commercial peak, Jeff Beck split to try his hand as a solo artist. Uncomfortable singing, he was put in front of the microphone for "High Ho Silver Lining", a song that inspires drunken sing-alongs thirty years after the fact. Joining forces with Rod Stewart and Ron Wood, Beck released Truth, a bluesy, heavy album that features an incredible cover of the Yardbirds' "Shapes of Things" and Beck's signature tune, "Beck's Bolero". Beck, known for his tasteful, non-flashy playing, rarely stays in one musical place for long, having explored jazz, blues, rockabilly and even electronic music throughout his career. (See picture opposite)

"I don't care about the rules. In fact, if I don't break the rules at least 10 times in every song then I'm not doing my job properly." - Jeff Beck

90 The Grateful Dead

Hailing from San Francisco, the Grateful Dead is best known as the premier jam band, based on lengthy live performances that found the band, led by guitar player Jerry Garcia, playing extended solos that merged songs together under shared rhythms. While the Grateful Dead are very much a part of the late '60s acid rock scene, much of their music is rooted in folk and country traditions. "Box of Rain" from American Beauty is as sweet and introspective as the best of Jackson Browne. Garcia passed away in 1995 and Bob Weir took over the reins, continuing to bring music to their many fans. Jerry would have wanted it that way. (See picture opposite)

"If we had any nerve at all, if we had any real balls as a society, or whatever you need, whatever quality you need, real character, we would make an effort to really address the wrongs in this society, righteously." - Jerry Garcia

91 Queens of the Stone Age

Queens of the Stone Age began when singer/guitarist Josh Homme and bassist Nick Oliveri's previous band, Kyuss, broke up. While Kyuss had a devout legion of followers, QOTSA was a bona fide smash. Sophomore album R (like the movie rating) wasn't as heavy as previous Homme releases, with horns and harmonies thrown into the mix, but it set up QOTSA as one to watch. The follow-up Songs for the Deaf secured QOTSA's place as one of the most significant bands of the 2000's. Oliveri was fired from or quit, depending on which story you believe, in 2004. (See picture opposite)

QOTS FACTFILE:

Start up year: 1997

Disband year: N/A

Home town: Palm Desert, California, U.S.A.

Members : Josh Homme, Nick Oliveri, Alfredo Hernandez, Dave Catching, more

What you should check out/why: Songs for the Deaf includes the crossover hits "No One Knows" and "Go With the Flow."

92 Wanda Jackson

After years of lobbying, Wanda Jackson was finally inducted into the Rock 'n' Roll Hall of Fame in 2009. That Jackson, essentially the first lady of rock 'n' roll, had to wait so long is a travesty. Songs like "Fujiyama Mama", "Let's Have a Party" and "Funnel of Love" stand with rockabilly's finest, with Jackson playing guitar and singing her guts out. As her career progressed, Jackson took on a greater country and gospel feel, with "Big Iron Skillet" being perhaps the finest warning a man has ever been given to not stay out all night drinking and carousing. Jackson, now in her 70s, still rocks like a woman less than half her age.

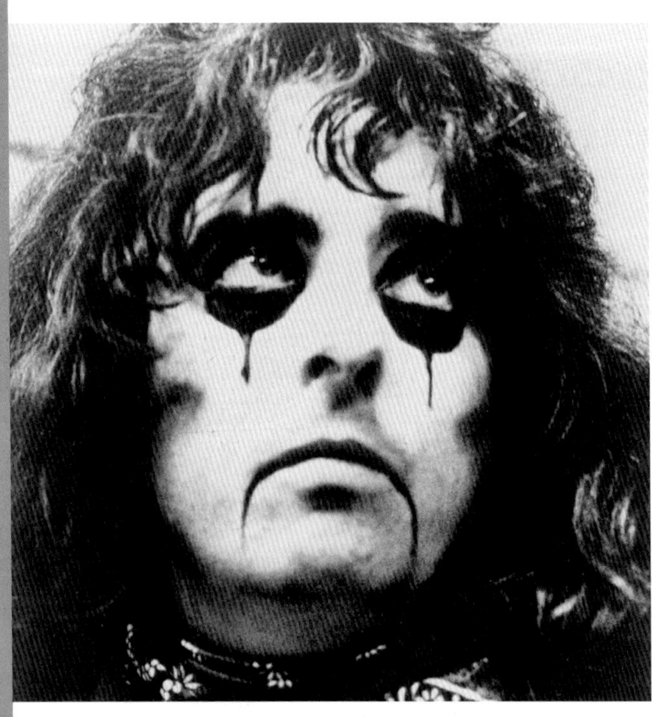

93 Alice Cooper

With today's special effects and technological trickery making almost anything seem possible, Alice Cooper's stage show's inclusion of a beheading and snake handling seems almost quaint by comparison. But when Cooper (born Vincent Furnier) introduced his theatrics to audiences in the '70s, the effect was mind-blowing. Kids rushed to hear songs of triumphant rebellion like "School's Out", "Under My Wheels" and "I'm 18", while parents feared for the souls of their offspring. While Cooper's heyday was a booze-soaked adventure, today he's sober and seems to enjoy nothing more than a nice game of golf. He still records and his live shows still impress young audiences used to modern trickery as well as his older fans. (See picture opposite)

"I appreciate an audience that reacts to the music, even if they jump on stage and try to beat us up, I think that's a fantastic reaction. I think that they're really hearing something then." - Alice Cooper

94 Cheap Trick

Rockford, Illinois' greatest export Cheap Trick took power pop to new levels. In a decade that loved live albums, Cheap Trick had a runaway success with 1979's Live at Budokan. Introducing "Surrender" with "This is the first song from our new album" was the smartest thing singer Robin Zander could have done. Not only did the crowd go wild for the song but it's one of rock's most quoted moments. Years later the Beastie Boys sampled it. Cheap Trick had hits throughout the '70s and '80s with "Dream Police", "I Want You to Want Me" and "The Flame". The original four members, Zander, Bun E. Carlos (drums), Tom Petersson and Rick Nielsen (guitar), are still touring.

95 Marilyn Manson

Ohio's Brian Warner is better known to music fans as Marilyn Manson, a singer who took the theatrics of Alice Cooper and mixed it with the electronic/industrial/metal mélange of Nine Inch Nails. With Manson and his band taking their stage names from a combination of sex symbols and serial killers, they situated themselves as creations of celebrity culture, which was a smart marketing ploy as well as a fun critique on popular culture. During the height of Manson-mania, the audience was a swarm of angst-ridden teenagers. Hits include, "The Beautiful People", "The Dope Show" and a cover of the Eurythmics' "Sweet Dreams (Are Made of This)". (See picture opposite)

96 Elvis Costello and the Attractions

Elvis Costello has been a rock icon for so long that it's hard to believe that he was once considered an anomaly on the musical landscape. Still known for his bespectacled visage, Costello's Buddy Holly glasses and ill-fitting suits made people notice him. His early albums, My Aim is True, This Year's Model and Armed Forces, made people pay attention. Armed with a razor wit and a way around a melody, Costello stormed the radio with "Allison", "Pump it Up" and "Oliver's Army". Now over three decades into his career, Costello has explored country, classical, northern soul and numerous other forms. In 2009, he released the country covers album, Secret, Profane and Sugarcane.

97 Iron Maiden

Without a doubt one of the most influential bands in the history of heavy metal, Iron Maiden has been recording classic albums and filling arenas for over 30 years. T-shirts sporting the Iron Maiden logo and their monstrous mascot "Eddie" are an iconic badge of metal loyalty. Their real breakthrough came in the form of third album, 1982's The Number of the Beast. Beast was the first to feature new vocalist Bruce Dickenson. 2009 sees the release of Flight 666, a live CD/DVD of the band in 16 different cities revisiting Maiden classics on their Somewhere Back in Time tour. (See picture above)

98 Weezer

Rivers Cuomo must have some sort of psychic powers. When he was writing and recording the band's first album, radio was filled with rage and angst. The kids were suffering, whether through anger or misery, and everyone was hearing about it. Then, as if from nowhere, came the disjointed sweetness of "Undone" and the unabashed poppiness of "Buddy Holly". The Blue Album (as it is called) said it was ok to be outside of the norm and seemed to provide reassurance to all other bands at the time. Weezer's second album, Pinkerton, was ignored upon release, but is now considered a lost treasure. The band's hits continued with "Hash Pipe" and "Island in the Sun".

99 Sonic Youth

The grandparents of what is now known as alternative rock, Sonic Youth has always walked the line between familiar rock structures and experimentalism. Thurston Moore (guitar/vocals), Kim Gordon (bass/vocals), Lee Ranaldo (guitar/vocals) and Steve Shelley (drums) were already influencing bands like Nirvana when they were signed with DGC Records at the beginning of the '90s alt-rock explosion. While the closest they have come to a radio hit is probably Dirty's "Kool Thing", it is Daydream Nation's "Teenage Riot" that remains a fan favorite. In 2009 Sonic Youth signed with indie label Matador Records and released The Eternal. (See picture opposite)

100 Patti Smith Group

Looking like a slightly more feminine Keith Richards, Patti Smith released the poetic and dissonant Horses in 1975, and audiences did not know what to think. Gut-wrenchingly emotional and raw, Smith was pretty far removed from the radio-friendly female singers of the time. Olivia Newton-John she was not. Still, she had chart success with "Because the Night", an impassioned and inspired song written for Smith by Bruce Springsteen. After a nine-year hiatus the death of her husband, MC5 guitarist Fred "Sonic" Smith, inspired Patti to get to work and she released Peace and Noise in 1997. She occasionally engages in short tours and special performances, including one that found her onstage with My Bloody Valentine's Kevin Shields.

101 Bon Jovi

Jon Bon Jovi and company's ability to grow with their audience has granted them a longevity that very few of their contemporaries have enjoyed. Letting their hair metal roots grow into those of arena rockers and seamlessly morphing into a sound that is closer to Shania Twain than it is to Mötley Crüe, Jon Bon Jovi, guitar player Richie Sambora, drummer Tico Torres, keyboardist David Bryan, and bassist Alec John Such (who parted ways with the band in 1994) have managed to keep the hits ("Livin' On a Prayer") coming throughout their career that has passed the quarter century mark, selling more than 120 million albums in process. (See picture opposite)

"Each one of you has something no one else has, or has ever had: your fingerprints, your brain, your heart. Be an individual. Be unique. Stand out. Make noise. Make someone notice. That's the power of individuals." - Jon Bon Jovi

BON JOVI FACTFILE:

Start up year: 1983

Disband year: N/A

Home town: Sayreville, New Jersey, U.S.A.

Members : Jon Bon Jovi, Richie Sambora, Tico Torres, David Bryan, Alec John Such

What you should check out/why: Slippery When Wet for the working man anthem, "Livin' On a Prayer."

102 U2

Paul "Bono" Hewson was a rebellious youth when he formed U2 with Dave "The Edge" Evans, Larry Mullen Jr. and Adam Clayton in Dublin, Ireland. Today he is middle-aged and still standing up against the world's injustices and urging others to do the same. Whether in front of thousands singing "Elevation" and "New Year's Day" or on the world's stage meeting national leaders, Bono exudes confidence, even if he seems afraid to be seen in public without sunglasses. U2's seminal album, 1987's The Joshua Tree, was produced by Daniel Lanois and Brian Eno, and produced a slew of hits, including "Where the Streets Have No Name" and "I Still Haven't Found What I'm Looking For". (See picture opposite)

103 Ministry

Ministry made their start in 1981 as purveyors of danceable synth-pop that bore little resemblance to the fierce industrial metal that was to become their signature. Front man Al Jourgensen was the only constant member in the band's 27 year history. By pairing machine-gun guitar riffs with cold drum machines and burying his vocals under a mountain of distorted effects, Jourgensen helped create a sound that bands like Nine Inch Nails would take to wider audiences. Ministry's mainstream success came in 1991 with the single "Jesus Built My Hotrod" featuring guest vocals by Butthole Surfers singer Gibby Haynes.

104 Rancid

After the demise of underground ska-punk favorites Operation Ivy, guitarist/vocalist Tim Armstrong and bassist Matt Freeman went on to form Rancid with the addition of drummer Brett Reed. For their second LP, Lets Go they brought Lars Frederiksen on board as a second guitar player. Looking to the early recordings of The Clash as inspiration, Rancid perform their roots reggae-informed street punk with a conviction and energy that easily translates from the album to the listener. By the time the band released its third album …And Out Come the Wolves Rancid had become one of the most recognizable names in American punk rock.

"Dealing with the press is a double edged knife. You know, if you believe their euphoria and you get a high, if it pushes you, then a couple of stupid rumors get you down. So the best thing is to ignore it all, because nobody can really take it for a long time." - Lars Frederiksen

105 The Runaways

Joan Jett, Lita Ford, Cherie Currie, Sandy West and Jackie Blue were the Runaways, a group of teenage rock 'n' rollers introduced by would-be Svengali, Kim Fowley in 1975 Calfornia. The young women were tough, sexy and inspired by England's glam rock outrageousness and were in many ways the ultimate rock band. Twenty years after its release, their slinky ode to teenage rebellion "Cherry Bomb" became the unofficial riot grrrl anthem. Hugely successful in Japan, the Runaways never saw commercial success in the U.S. while they were together. Jett and Ford found greater popularity as solo musicians.

106 Electric Light Orchestra

Coming from Birmingham, England's psychedelic rock band the Move, the Electric Light Orchestra started off as the vision of Jeff Lynne, Roy Wood and Bev Bevan. However, after a few performances and a little recording, Wood extracted himself to form Wizzard. With Lynne in charge, E.L.O. was an orchestral rock project that became a musical phenomenon. In the late'70s and early'80s E.L.O. had 15 songs in the Top 20, starting with "Livin' Thing" and ending with the Olivia Newton-John collaboration "Xanadu". After leaving the band, Lynne continued as a producer and was also a member of the Traveling Wilburys along with Tom Petty, Bob Dylan, Roy Orbison and George Harrison.

107 Talking Heads

The Talking Heads brought a nerdy, arty aesthetic to New York's punk scene. Art school graduates David Byrne, Chris Frantz and Tina Weymouth got together with Jerry Harrison, who had recently been a member of the Modern Lovers, to create songs that exuded paranoia ("Psycho Killer") and existential angst ("Life During Wartime") as well as a genuine sweetness ("This Must Be the Place") that is missing from most new wave music. In 1984 Jonathan Demme made Stop Making Sense, the consummate concert film that shows the art of a Talking Heads show. When they broke up Byrne went on to a solo career while the others formed the Tom-Tom Club. (See picture opposite)

108 My Morning Jacket

Based in Louisville, Kentucky, psychedelic country rockers My Morning Jacket have been making the rounds for over ten years, steadily gaining momentum with every tour, and there have been a lot of them. Not content with sticking to one sound, MMJ's music is all over the map, with singer Jim James' voice keeping things semi-consistent. Evil Urges (2008) finds the band moving furthest away from the blues-rock that grounded them in the early years, with James often using a falsetto singing voice.

109 Arcade Fire

Although Arcade Fire singer/songwriter Win Butler originally called Texas home, he met band mate and wife Regine Chassagne in Montreal, Canada, which is where the band calls home. Following a self-released EP, Arcade Fire signed with North Carolina indie label Merge Records for their full-length debut Funeral. Funeral received just about every critical accolade imaginable and consumers listened, making the Arcade Fire a rare independent success. The songs "Wake Up" and "Neighbourhood #3 (Power Out)" were ubiquitous, introducing people to the bands joyous, ramshackle sound. In 2007, Arcade Fire released Neon Bible which was not quite as beloved, but was a success nonetheless.

110 Buffalo Springfield

When Neil Young rolled into Laurel Canyon in 1966, Stephen Stills approached him about joining a band and the result was Buffalo Springfield. Releasing three albums over two years, which was far more common in the '60s than it is today, Buffalo Springfield weren't together long, but their impact was great. Collections of music celebrating the hippie era always include "For What It's Worth", Stills' meditation on the civil rights movement. But equally good were songs like "Mr. Soul", "Sit Down I Think I Love You" and "Burned", which is a classic early Young track. (See picture above)

111 Television

It's tough to have two poets in the same band. So, while the idea of having two singer/guitar players as charismatic as Tom Verlaine and Richard Hell in the same band seems like a great idea on paper, in reality it didn't last long. As a result, the classic television line-up was made up of Verlaine with Billy Ficca (drums), Richard Lloyd (guitar), and Fred Smith (bass). Following their self-released single "Little Johnny Jewel", Television signed with Elektra for their debut, Marquee Moon. For many, Marquee Moon is one of the greatest albums of all time. Verlaine is the essence of sneering cool on songs like "Venus de Milo" and "Prove It". Television reunites occasionally. (See picture opposite)

TELEVISION FACTFILE:

Start up year: 1973

Disband year: 1978 (with occasional reunions)

Home town: New York, U.S.A.

Members : Tom Verlaine, Billy Ficca, Fred Smith, Richard Lloyd, Richard Hell

What you should check out/why: Marquee Moon is among the most accessible avant-garde records to date; or else it is among the most experimental pop albums.

Worth looking out for: Tom Verlaine's live performance accompaniments to short films by Man Ray.

112 Shellac

Steve Albini made a name for himself as a producer (Nirvana, The Pixies, PJ Harvey), but he is also the brains behind Shellac, a caustic, minimalist noise-rock outfit that may not be in the mainstream, but holds throngs enraptured whenever it tours or releases a record. A tirade of singles introduced the band prior to 1994's full-length At Action Park. Shellac is known for its grating guitars, as well as the black humor of Albini's satirical lyrics. Sporadically recording albums for Chicago's Touch and Go record label, Shellac does not do anything in a traditional way and rarely tours North America.

113 Frank Zappa and The Mothers of Invention

Frank Zappa is the place where art meets rock. Composing and creating volumes of music prior to his death in 1993, Zappa is one of rock's most prolific writers. And Zappa's songs aren't simple verse-chorus-verse ditties. Influenced by classical and contemporary classical composers as well as jazz, Zappa took rock instrumentation to new levels. Zappa's sharp wit was apparent in everything he did, with songs like "Don't Eat the Yellow Snow" and "My Guitar Wants to Kill You" being obvious examples. After years of underground success, Zappa broke the charts with 1982's novelty song "Valley Girl", sung by his daughter Moon Unit.

SHELLAC FACTFILE:

Start up year: 1992

Disband year: N/A

Home town: Chicago, U.S.A.

Members : Steve Albini, Bob Weston, Todd Trainer

What you should check out/why: At Action Park is the finest in uneasy listening.

Worth looking out for: Albini's other band, Big Black

"A composer is a guy who goes around forcing his will on unsuspecting air molecules, often with the assistance of unsuspecting musicians."
- Frank Zappa

114 Shadowy Men on a Shadowy Planet

Canada's Shadowy Men on a Shadowy Planet is not a household name, but fans of surf bands and comedy love them with equal intensity. Surf fans love the interplay between guitar player Brian Connelly's riffs and Reid Diamond's melodic bass lines. They enjoy drummer Don Pyle's punchy fills and the way the three carried on the surf rock tradition without sounding like they were ripping off the past on albums like Dim the Lights, Chill the Ham. Comedy fans hold Shadowy Men dear for providing the theme ("Having an Average Weekend") and soundtrack to sketch comedy troupe The Kids in the Hall's television show.

115 Arctic Monkeys

With just two albums to their name, Sheffield's Arctic Monkeys are often cited as the saviors of English rock music. Singer Alex Turner's lyrics are so vivid that each song is like a movie, with one, "Scummy Man", having been made into a short, disturbing movie. Prior to their first album Whatever You Say I am, That's What I'm Not the Arctic Monkeys already had a significant fan-base as a result of the band's live shows and internet presence, and they are just one of the many successes that have managed to market themselves via myspace and become international stars. First single "I Bet You Look Good on the Dance Floor" is a cheeky number that set the tone for things to come.

ARCTIC MONKEYS FACTFILE:

Start up year: 2003

Disband year: N/A

Home town: Sheffield, England

Members : Alex Turner, Jamie Cook, Andy Nicholson, Nick O'Malley, Matt Helders

What you should check out/why: Whatever People Say I Am, That's What I'm Not is full of Turner's cheeky and insightful lyrics.

Worth looking out for: Alex Turner's Morricone-inspired side-project, The Last Shadow Puppets.

"I never made an effort to play an instrument or anything. I used to play the organ a bit but I was crap at that. Being in a band has got me into music more than anything else - it wasn't the other way around."
– Matt Helders

THE FACES FACTFILE:

Start up year: 1969

Disband year: 1975

Home town: London, England

Members: Rod Stewart, Ron Wood, Ronnie Lane, Kenney Jones, Ian McLagan

What you should check out/why: Ooh La La for classic Ronnie Lane songwriting on the title track and "Glad and Sorry".

THE GUESS WHO FACTFILE:

Start up year: 1963

Disband year: 1975

Home town: Winnipeg, Canada

Members: Burton Cummings, Randy Bachman, Jim Kale, Garry Peterson, more

What you should check out/why: Wheatfield Soul, along with having terrific cover art, includes "These Eyes."

116 The Faces

When Rod Stewart and Ron Wood defected from the Jeff Beck Group to join the remnants of Small Faces, the beloved mod band became the Faces, a band that made four fine albums, First Step, Long Player, A Nod's As Good as a Wink… To A Blind Horse and Ooh La La, before Stewart's solo fame overtook that of the band. While Stewart and Wood, and to a lesser extent bassist Ronnie Lane, are the names associated with The Faces, it is keyboard player Ian McLagan who brings much of the personality to the band's sound. The song "Ooh La La" was used to great effect in Wes Anderson's The Royal Tennenbaums.

117 The Guess Who

Burton Cummings and Randy Bachman, the songwriting team behind the Guess Who's massive success, come from Winnipeg, Canada, a prairie city not known for churning out rock stars. Perhaps being separate from the country's musical centers drove them harder. Whatever the reason, the Guess Who's ambition drove them to world-wide success with "These Eyes", "Undun" and "American Woman", which became a hit all over again when covered, without any sense of irony or the original's scathing meaning, by Lenny Kravitz on tk. While personality conflicts broke up the band in 1975, recent years have found Cummings and Bachman reuniting.

118 The Libertines

The beautiful mess that was the Libertines might have been one of rock's great stories. Longtime friends Pete Doherty and Carl Bernat formed the Libertines in 2001 and released two excellent albums, 2002's Up the Bracket and 2004's The Libertines, before imploding in a hailstorm of drugs and booze. By the time the Libertines toured North America for the second record, Doherty was already out of band, although the separation was supposed to be temporary. While Doherty has now become the punchline for tabloid jokes, when they were together the Libertines wrote fantastic rock songs like "Can't Stand Me Now", and it is better to remember them this way. Doherty later created the band Babyshambles. (See picture opposite)

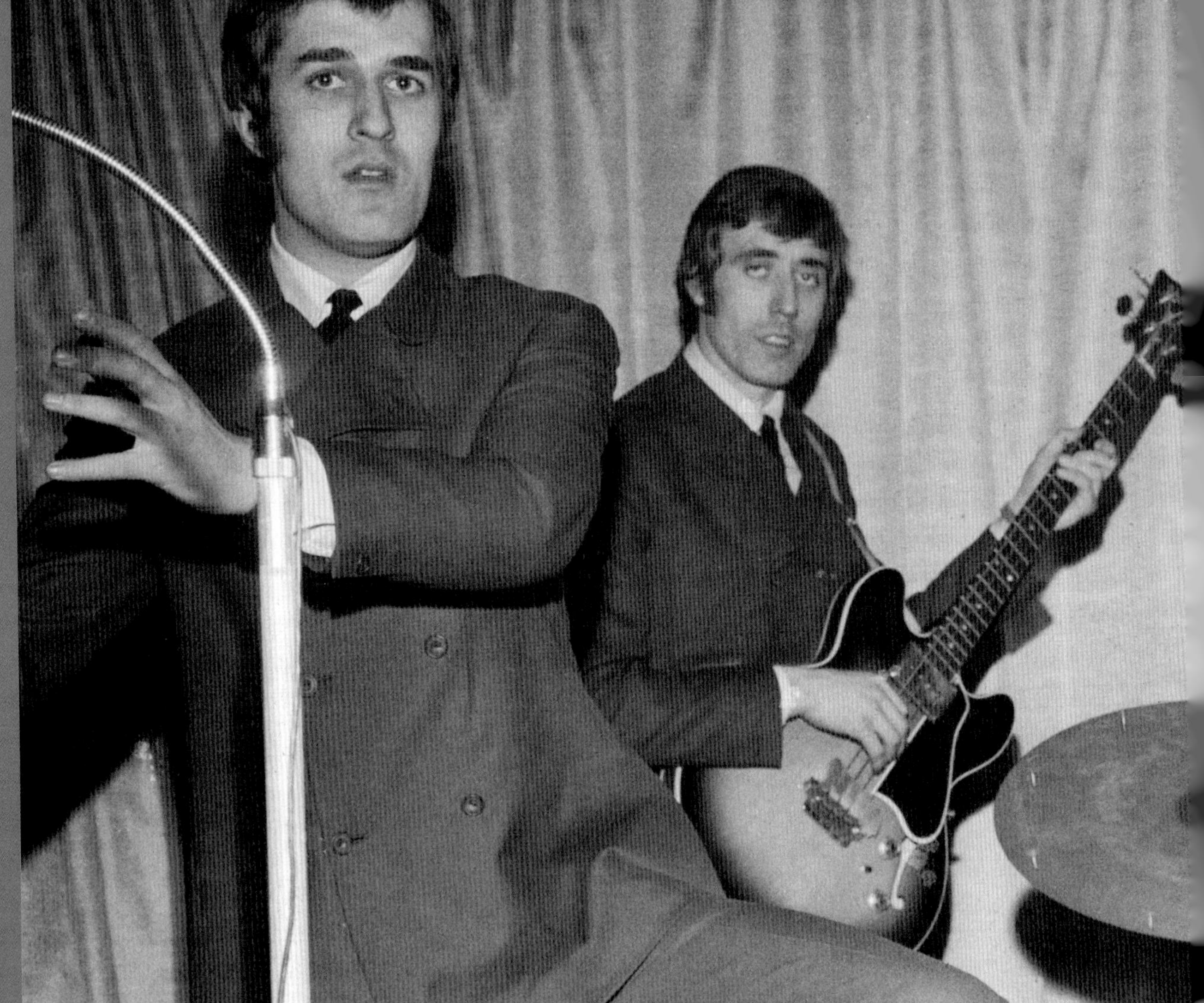

119 Sweet

When a struggling young band called Sweet signed with RCA they were introduced to powerhouse songwriters Mike Chapman and Nicky Chinn. Chinn and Chapman were the kings of writing bubblegum pop hits, and did just that for Sweet, providing them with "Little Willy", "Blockbuster", "Teenage Rampage", "Ballroom Blitz" and "The Six Teens". With their tight shiny clothes, long hair and glittery makeup, Sweet were at the top of the glam rock heap. The Chapman/Chinn songs provided them with hard rocking foot stompers with easy to learn lyrics. Although they had a hit with their own composition "Fox On the Run", Sweet's decline began when their partnership with Chinn and Chapman ended.

120 Moody Blues

The Moody Blues had their first taste of fame as part of the British Invasion with the soulful "Go Now", a song that found chart success in both the U.K. and the U.S. At that time the band included singer Denny Laine and bassist Clint Warwick. When they left the band, Justin Hayward and John Lodge were their replacements, which changed the Moody Blues from a blues and soul band to the orchestral rock band that they are best known as. The first album with the new line-up was Days of Future Passed, and featured the massive hit "Nights in White Satin". (See picture above)

121 Quiet Riot

Quiet Riot's first Top 40 success came with a cover of Slade's "Cum on Feel the Noize" that was the lead single off 1983's Metal Health. While Quiet Riot seemed to be an overnight sensation, the guys, Kevin du Brow, Rudy Sarzo, Frankie Banali and Carlos Cavazo, had been toiling away for six years. In an attempt to follow up Metal Health's success the band released another Slade cover, "Mama Weer All Crazee Now", to only marginal interest. No more hits were forthcoming. Randy Rhoads, who went on to fame with Ozzy Osbourne, was in Quiet Riot's original line-up. (See picture opposite)

QUIET RIOT FACTFILE:

Start up year: 1975

Disband year: 1988

Home town: Los Angeles, U.S.A.

Members: Kevin du Brow, Rudy Sarzo, Frankie Banali, Carlos Cavazo, Randy Rhoads, more

What you should check out/why: Metal Health for the more-rock, less-swagger version of Slade's "Cum on Feel the Noise."

122 The Eagles

Coming from the same scene that gave the world the Doobie Brothers, James Taylor and Linda Ronstadt, the Eagles embody the Laurel Canyon sound of laid-back country mixed with rock 'n' roll. Helmed by songwriters Don Henley and Glen Frey, the Eagles were popular right out of the gate, but in the four years between their formation and the release of Hotel California, they became one of the biggest bands in the world. The title song, "Life in the Fast Lane", and "New Kid in Town" were all chart hits and fans just couldn't get enough, making Hotel California one of the highest selling albums of all time. An acrimonious break-up following 1979's The Long Run led the Eagles to call their 1994 reunion tour and album Hell Freezes Over. (See picture opposite)

THE EAGLES FACTFILE:

Start up year: 1971

Disband year: N/A

Home town: Los Angeles, U.S.A.

Members: Don Henley, Glenn Frey, Timothy B. Schmidt, Randy Meisner, Joe Walsh, Bernie Leadon, Don Felder

What you should check out/why: Hotel California if you haven't already heard it a million times.

123 (International) Noise Conspiracy

Dennis Lyxzen, Inge Johansson, Lars Stromberg, and Ludwig Dahlberg came together from various Swedish punk and art-rock bands in 1998 to form the (International) Noise Conspiracy as an instrument through which to express their anti-capitalist political views. Their music owes less to other politically-aware punk bands like The Clash and the Dead Kennedys than to garage rock of the '60s, particularly the Monks. Lyxzen's vocals alternate between murmuring and wailing over a nervy, rhythm-heavy guitar rock sound. Since 2004 the band has worked with producer Rick Rubin.

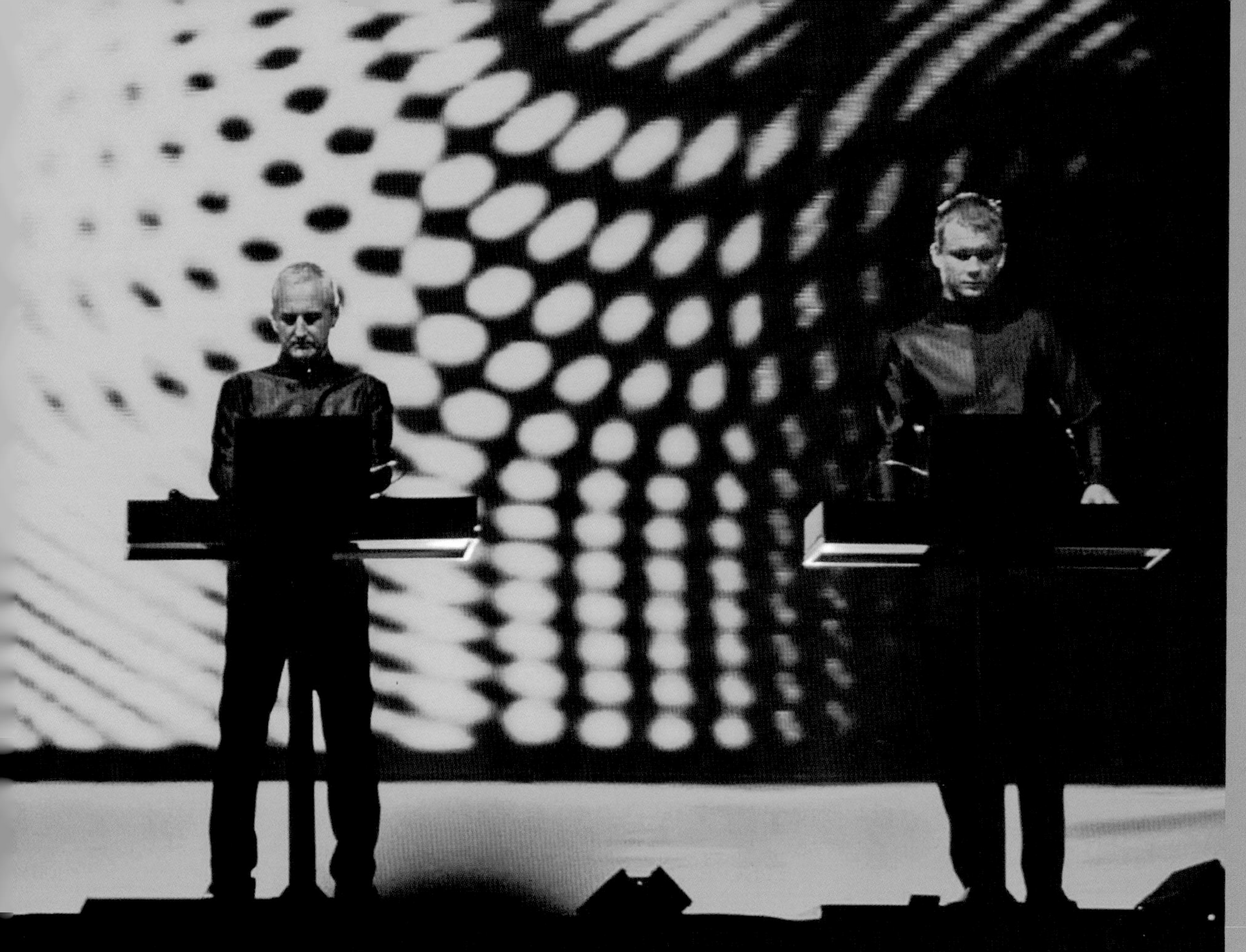

124 Kraftwork

With their matching uniforms and synthesized music, Kraftwerk became one of the first electronic bands to find worldwide popularity. Hailing from Düsseldorf, Germany, Florian Schneider, Ralf Hütter, Klaus Roeder and Wolfgang Flür are in many ways unlikely pop stars, with Kraftwerk's sound and image conjuring nothing more than that of a well-oiled machine. The band's stark sound and deadpan vocals result in minimalistic music, but their songs are not devoid of humor. Songs like "The Model", "Tour de France" and "Autobahn" remain club favorites and synth-rock standards twenty-plus years after their release. (See picture above)

125 Stone Roses

Manchester's Stone Roses were a source of frustration for fans of the dance-rock hybrid nicknamed 'baggy' by pundits. When they released The Stone Roses in 1989 it was an instant success. "Fool's Gold" and "I Want to be Adored" got people on the dance floor and singing along with Ian Brown, even when he mumbled. Poised for greatness, things soon fell apart. Label problems stalled the second album. When The Second Coming was finally released in 1994, the sound had toughened up and no longer had the shambolic charm of the debut. Band members pop up occasionally, and most successful is bassist Mani who joined Primal Scream in 1996.

126 Oasis

Band members come and go, but songwriter Noel Gallagher always had his little brother Liam to sing the songs, even if they fight about it afterwards. The notoriously funny, often at the expense of other people, and volatile Gallagher brothers made two excellent records, Definitely Maybe and (What's the Story) Morning Glory?, and have spent the last ten years trying to repeat these successes. Results are varied, though "Lyla" from 2005's Don't Believe the Truth is a rollicking single that stands with anything they've done. Popular culture will remember them as the band that did "Wonderwall" and once had a rivalry with Blur. (See picture opposite)

127 Blur

Graham Coxon, Damon Albarn, Dave Rowntree and Alex James are Blur. Labeled as shoegaze for the first record, then Britpop for albums 2 through 4, critics were left scratching their heads when Blur stopped being part of any pre-existing scene with album 5 Blur. That was the album with "Song 2", the song whose "woo-hoos" will be heard during the breaks in sports events for eternity. Prior to this, Blur wrote songs that were little glimpses into English life, not dissimilar to those of the Kinks. Coxon left the band following album number six 13 and Albarn formed cartoon-band Gorillaz, but the original foursome started playing shows again in summer 2009.

128 Shocking Blue

With a voice unlike any other woman in music, Shocking Blue's Mariska Veres led the Dutch band to the annals of rock history with "Venus", a #1 hit in the U.S. which was later covered by Bananarama, losing much of the original's sensuality in the process. Although generally relegated to One Hit Wonder status, Shocking Blue had many hits in the Netherlands like "Send Me a Postcard" and "Mighty Joe" that have been rediscovered by music fans worldwide. Sadly, Veres died of cancer in 2006, thwarting any chance of a reunion that might have given Shocking Blue the recognition they deserve. (See picture opposite)

SHOCKING BLUE FACTFILE:

Start up year: 1967

Disband year: 1974

Home town: The Netherlands

Members: Mariska Veres, Cornelius VanDer Beek, Klaasje VanDer Wal, Robby VanLeeuwen

What you should check out/why: At Home includes "Venus" (later covered by Bananarama)

Worth looking out for: Any chance to hear Mariska Veres sing.

129 Vanilla Fudge

From 1967 to 1970, Carmen Appice, Mark Stein, Tony Bogert and Vince Martell made heavy, sludgy music under the sweet name Vanilla Fudge. Although Vanilla Fudge had a number of minor hits, including a version of Cher's "Bang Bang (My Baby Shot Me Down)", which was used in the film Zodiac, they are best known for their slow, thunderous cover of the Supremes' "You Keep Me Hanging On". When Vanilla Fudge broke up, Appice and Bogert hooked up with Jeff Beck for one uneven but ambitious self-titled record. (See picture opposite)

"My cousin Joey played the drums. We used to go to his house, I liked beating on his drums. I beat the hell out of 'em, you know? Finally in 1961, I don't know, I guess I was about 15, I got serious about it. My parents bought me a little drum set and I was playing for about 6 months when I started doing gigs."
- Carmine Appice

YOUNGERS
Scotch Ales

130 The Chills

Among the many great guitar bands that came out of New Zealand in the 1980s, Martin Phillipps' Chills were one of the finest. Signed with influential indie label Flying Nun, the Chills recorded numerous singles, which were later collected as Kaleidoscope World and came out on England's Creation records in 1986. The following year, the Chills' first proper album, Brave Worlds, was released, introducing their chiming guitars to a wider audience. Although the band broke up a few times along the way, a version of the group reunited for 1996's Sunburnt and remains active, releasing records and compilations to this day. (See picture above)

THE CHILLS FACTFILE:

Start up year: 1980

Disband year: N/A

Home town: Dunedin, New Zealand

Members: Martin Phillipps, Peter Gutteridge, Faser Batts, Terry Moore, Andrew Todd, Justin Harwood, more.

What you should check out/why: 1990's Submarine Bells incorporates various pop idioms for a lovely record.

131 Genesis

There are two kinds of Genesis fans. The first swears by early Genesis, the prog-rock outfit fronted by Peter Gabriel with Phil Collins on drums, Mike Rutherford on guitar and Tony Banks on guitar. This Genesis released concept albums like The Lamb Lies Down on Broadway and encouraged Gabriel to wear elaborate makeup and costumes. The second type of fan likes everything made post-Gabriel, when Collins stepped up to the microphone. This Genesis made Genesis, which didn't do a lot for their credibility with serious music fans, but made the band a lot of money with hits like "Illegal Alien", "That's All" and "Mama". (See picture opposite)

GENESIS FACTFILE:

Start up year: 1966

Disband year: 1999 (with occasional, Peter Gabriel-free reunions)

Home town: Godalming, Surrey, England

Members: Phil Collins, Mike Rutherford, Tony Banks, Peter Gabriel

What you should check out/why: Duke straddles the line between early-Genesis art-rock and the pop band they became with songs like "Misunderstanding" and "Turn It On Again."

Worth looking out for: Selling England By the Pound

"When we were really big, and we were music gods, I couldn't leave the house and walk down to the store without people coming at me."

- Marty Balin

132 Jefferson Airplane

With her long, black hair, kohl-lined eyes and far-out attire, Jefferson Airplane's Grace Slick looked like the psychedelic '60s. But it was the way her voice connected with that of Marty Balin's that made the Jefferson Airplane stand out among a plethora of acid rock bands coming out of San Francisco. Their voices, along with guitar player Jorma Kaukonen's keening leads, are fundamental to hits like "White Rabbit" and "Somebody to Love" from Surrealistic Pillow. However, they also had a softer, folkier side, as seen on the same album's "Embryonic Journey". Eventually the band broke up, with some members becoming Hot Tuna and others going on as Jefferson Starship. (See picture opposite)

JEFFERSON AIRPLANE FACTFILE:

Start up year: 1965

Disband year: 1973

Home town: San Francisco, U.S.A.

Members: Grace Slick, Marty Balin, Jorma Kaukonen, Paul Kantner, Signe Anderson, Jack Casady, more

What you should check out/why: Surrealistic Pillow has "White Rabbit", "Somebody to Love" and the gentle folk instrumental, "Embryonic Journey".

Worth looking out for: Martin Balin's '80s hit, "Hearts."

136 Echo and the Bunnymen

Liverpool's Echo and the Bunnymen have been reduced to singer Ian McCullough and guitar player Will Sergeant. When they made classic albums like Ocean Rain and Heaven Up Here, they were a four-piece that included drummer Pete de Freitas and bassist Les Pattinson. After spending most of the '80s as an underground favorite, the inclusion of "Bring on the Dancing Horses" on the Pretty in Pink soundtrack brought their music to a wider audience. A couple of years later "Lips Like Sugar" brought them more fame. Although de Freitas passed away in 1989 and Pattinson retired from music, Echo and the Bunnymen still occasionally record and play shows. (See picture opposite)

> *"I think we just had a yearning to get back together and start playing and recording together again."*
> - Ian McCulloch

137 The Jam

Young, brash and mouthy, the Jam was part of the mod revival of the late'70s. With their smart haircuts and perfectly pressed trousers; Paul Weller, Bruce Foxton and Rick Buckler were the antithesis of punk's safety pin aesthetic. In spite of not looking the part, early Jam singles like "Eton Rifles" "In the City" and "Going Underground" painted a sharp picture of the gritty urban landscape, with Weller's guitar high in the mix. Over time, the Jam began incorporating elements of soul into its sound, with Weller eventually leaving the Jam to form the ultra urbane Style Council.

Shaftesbury

138 The Hollies

The Hollies' musical legacy is pretty interesting. Starting out making cheery pop songs like "Jennifer Eccles" and "Bus Stop", the Hollies changed with the times, taking some influence from Creedence Clearwater Revival on their huge hit, "Long, Cool Woman in a Black Dress" and a singer-songwriter vibe with, "He Ain't Heavy (He's My Brother)". Singer Graham Nash, who went on to superstardom in Crosby, Stills & Nash, was responsible for a number of the Hollies' hits, including the jangly, "King Midas in Reverse" before tensions about the group's direction drove him to leave the band and England.

139 The Move

One of the jewels in England's psychedelic crown, the Move is often overlooked in rock's history for bands with greater worldwide commercial success. The Move, featuring pre-Wizzard Roy Wood, and later Jeff Lynne, released beloved albums Message from the Country and Shazam!. Wood has always been an experimental and inventive musician who would learn an instrument if he thought a song needed it. Although Carl Wayne's soaring vocals were the official voice of the Move, his voice is similar to Wood's and Wood eventually takes over. This spirit of fun and adventure permeates songs like "Blackberry Way", "Tonight" and "I Can Hear the Grass Grow". (See picture opposite)

THE HOLLIES FACTFILE:

Start up year: 1962

Disband year: N/A (Although bearing little resemblance to the original group)

Home town: Manchester, England

Members: Graham Nash, Allan Clarke, Terry Sylvester, Eric Haydock, Tony Hicks, Bernie Calvert, more

What you should check out/why: The Long Road Home box set spans the Hollies' career, from "Bus Stop" to "The Air that I Breathe" and more.

THE MOVE FACTFILE:

Start up year: 1966

Disband year: 1972

Home town: Birmingham, England

Members: Roy Wood, Carl Wayne, Jeff Lynne, Bev Bevan, Rick Price, Trevor Burton, more

What you should check out/why: First album, The Move, includes "I Can Hear the Grass Grow", "Flowers in the Rain" and other psych-pop masterpieces.

Worth looking out for: Roy Wood's subsequent band, Wizzard.

140 The Cult

Beginning life as the Southern Death Cult with Ian Astbury and Billy Duffy as the nucleus, the Cult saw meteoric success in the '80s and '90s. In 1986, heads turned when the video for "She Sells Sanctuary", featuring a leather and lace-clad Astbury, was all over the television. Following Love was Electric, and as successful as the Cult had been before, they were suddenly one of the most popular bands on the planet with "Love Removal Machine" being played everywhere. Sonic Temple added fuel to the fire. The Cult toured summer 2009 with a song-by-song performance of their seminal album, Love. (See picture opposite)

"There will be no new album. I don't think we'll ever see a Cult album. Albums are dead. The format is dead. iTunes destroyed albums."

THE CULT FACTFILE:

Start up year: 1984

Disband year: N/A

Home town: Bradford, Yorkshire, England

Members: Ian Astbury, Billy Duffy, Jamie Stewart, Ray Mondo, Kid Chaos, more

What you should check out/why: Love has trippier hits like "She Sells Sanctuary" and "Rain", though Electric goes for the full-on rock sound of "Love Removal Machine" and "Wild Flower."

141 Steely Dan

Steely Dan is the ultimate fusion of New York cool and L.A. smooth. Over the course of their lengthy careers, Donald Fagen and Walter Becker have played host to about a million musicians to create the blend of jazz and rock that is Steely Dan. The slick production and pristine musicianship of songs like "Reelin' in the Years" make it easy to forget that Donald Fagan is virtually spitting out lyrics like, "You wouldn't know a diamond / If you held it in your hand / The things you think are precious / I can't understand". This is smooth rock's greatest band. (See picture opposite)

STEELY DAN FACTFILE:

Start up year: 1972

Disband year: N/A

Home town: Los Angeles, U.S.A.

Members: Donald Fagen, Walter Becker, Jeff Baxter, Jim Hodder, Denny Dias

What you should check out/why: Can't Buy a Thrill for "Reeling in the Years" and "Do It Again."

142 Prince and the Revolution

From the outset, Prince Rogers Nelson steeped his pop-rock melodies in funk, soul and R&B, creating a sound that is all his own. In 1984, after a couple of decent introductory records and the excellent 1999 with "When Doves Cry", he became an international superstar with Purple Rain. To say that Purple Rain is a work of genius is not hyperbole. With a slew of amazing songs, including "When Doves Cry", "Let's Go Crazy" and the title song, Prince could not go wrong. Prince has written some of pop's best songs like "Raspberry Beret" and "Sign O' the Times", but today he tends to explore jazzier musical terrain and has reverted to his original moniker after various name changes.

143 Foreigner

British ex-pat Mick Jones started found a songwriting partner in Lou Gramm, thus making Foreigner one of the biggest successes of the '70s and '80s. Early hits "Cold As Ice", "Double Vision" and "Hot Blooded" featured Gramm's soaring vocals and were rooted in the era's hard rock. Proving they were untouchable, Foreigner moved into the '80s with the album 4. While 4 included another rock smash, "Urgent", it also featured power ballad "Waiting for a Girl Like You". This song, a hit in its own right, provided the template for what would become Foreigner's biggest success, Agent Provocateur's "I Want to Know What Love Is". (See picture opposite)

PATR FACTFILE:

Start up year: 1984

Disband year: 1987

Home town: Minneapolis, U.S.A.

Members: Prince, Lisa Coleman, Wendy Melvoin, Bobby Z., Dez Dickerson, Doctor Fink, Brown Mark

What you should check out/why: Yes. Prince made good records without The Revolution, but Purple Rain has five bona fide hits, and four other songs that should have been, including "Purple Rain", "The Beautiful Ones" and "Let's Go Crazy."

Worth looking out for: Sinéad O'Conner's cover of Princes "Nothing Compares 2 U."

FOREIGNER FACTFILE:

Start up year: 1976

Disband year: Their last record was back in 1995

Home town: New York, U.S.A.

Members: Mick Jones, Lou Gramm, Ian MacDonald, Dennis Elliot, Al Greenwood, Ed Gagliardi, Rick Willis, more

What you should check out/why: 4 has the ballad, "Waiting for a Girl Like You" and "Urgent", but many people are just looking for Agent Provocateur's "I Want to Know What Love Is."

Worth looking out for: Mariah Carey's cover of "I Want to Know What Love Is."

144 The Police

Before Sting was a yoga practitioner/activist/balladeer, he was the singer and bass player for the Police, a power-pop trio completed by guitar player Andy Summers and American Stewart Copeland on drums. Coming at the end of English punk's heyday, the Police had a reggae and dub influence, especially on early singles like "Roxanne" and "Message in a Bottle". The band's good looks and Sting's raspy voice made them as popular with teenage girls as they were with serious music fans, who were thrilled by Copeland's complicated rhythms. Although the Police's fifth album, Synchronicity, was a monumental success with "King of Pain" and "Every Breath You Take", the band dissolved soon after, though they reunited in 2007.

145 The Cars

While most people equate synthesizers with a light sound, Boston's Cars were a muscular power-pop band that used synths to add another, often intense, layer of sound. While singer Ric Ocasek was the voice on the majority of the band's hits like "Let's Go", "My Best Friend's Girl" and "You Might Think", it was bass player Ben Orr who was responsible for "Drive", the ballad that pushed 1984's Heartbeat City to the top of the charts. Already a hit, "Drive" captured the public's attention again in 1985 when it was used as the theme to the televised broadcast of Live Aid. The song's melancholy lyrics wedded with images of Ethiopian poverty had a particularly haunting effect on viewers.

"I think you can get the wrong impression about me from my work and think I'm always a bit down. I'm not that way at all. I'm fun-loving." - Sting

THE CARS FACTFILE:

Start up year: 1976

Disband year:

Home town: Boston, U.S.A.

Members: Ric Ocasek, Ben Orr, Elliot Eastern, Greg Hawkes, David Robinson

What you should check out/why: The Cars for "Just What I Needed" and "My Best Friend's Girl", but Candy-O and Shake It Up are great, too.

Worth looking out for: Ric Ocasek's cameo appearance in the original movie of Hairspray.

146 Fleetwood Mac

Fleetwood Mac started off as a blues band headed by Peter Green, although the version of the band best known today is an almost entirely different group, with drummer Mick Fleetwood the sole survivor from the early days. The line-up that appeared on Fleetwood Mac's seminal pop-rock albums Rumours and Tusk is Fleetwood, John McVie, Lindsay Buckingham, Christine McVie and Stevie Nicks. The songs on Rumours reflect the emotions of Buckingham's break-up with Nicks, the veracity of which must've stirred emotions in listeners who bought Rumours by the armful, making it one of the most successful records in history.

The Kills

Alison "VV" Mosshart and Jamie "Hotel" Hince formed the Kills in 2000 after an inter-continental tape exchange collaboration proved too unwieldy. For the new project Mosshart and Hince tapped their punk roots and channeled that energy and grime into a minimal, up-tempo blues and increasingly electronics-tinged sound. Often compared with the White Stripes, the Kills share an aesthetic with the lithe rock of the Yeah Yeah Yeahs and Be Your Own Pet. Recently Mosshart has joined forces with Jack White from White Stripes, Jack Lawrence of the Raconteurs, and Dean Fertita from Queens of the Stone Age in the band Dead Weather.

THE KILLS FACTFILE:

Start up year: 2001

Disband year: N/A

Home town: London, England via Florida

Members: Allison Mosshart, Jamie Hince

What you should check out/why: Midnight Boom fleshes out The Kills' spare sound and includes the sizzling "U.R.A. Fever."

"There's a chemistry. Fleetwood Mac is a band of chemistry. It always has been. None of us are schooled; we're a bunch of primitives who have honed their art by doing it a long time and by having sensibilities that oddly mesh in a way you wouldn't expect. It just works." - Lindsay Buckingham

148 Broken Social Scene

Based around the songwriting team of Kevin Drew and Brendan Canning, Broken Social Scene is a constantly morphing band, sometimes reaching upwards of 10 people on stage. Their brand of sprawling guitar jams can be linked to '90s indie darlings Pavement and Mercury Rev, though with so many people adding to the BSS soup, influences come from all directions. Broken Social Scene's sophomore album You Forgot it in People struck a chord with rock critics who championed the collective. Fans agreed and the 2002 album remains an indie favorite seven years after its release. They released Broken Social Scene in 2005.

149 Yes

As part of England's psychedelic prog-rock scene, Yes is notable for its symphonic music and sharp harmonies formed around lead singer Jon Anderson. While Yes had been gathering steam since the late '60s, it was the addition of Rick Wakeman and his Moog synthesizer that really established the Yes sound and made Fragile a Top 10 hit, fueled by the single "Roundabout". In 1972, they released Yessounds, an ambitious, some would say excessive, triple-live collection. While the line-up bore little resemblance to that of the early days, in 1983 Yes had a resurgence via the song "Owner of a Lonely Heart", which also made them video stars. (See picture opposite)

BROKEN SOCIAL SCENE FACTFILE:

Start up year: 1999

Disband year: N/A

Home town: Toronto, Canada

Members: Kevin Drew, Brendan Canning, Andrew Whiteman, Jason Collett, Justin Peroff, Leslie Feist, Emily Haines, more

What you should check out/why: You Forgot it in People has "Cause=Time" and other songs that made it one of the most acclaimed albums of the '00s.

Worth looking out for: Occasional collaborator Gentleman Reg's album, Make Me Pretty.

YES FACTFILE:

Start up year: 1968

Disband year: N/A

Home town: Birmingham, England

Members: Jon Anderson, Rick Wakeman, Peter Banks, Bill Bruford, Steve Howe, Chris Squire, Tony Kaye, more.

What you should check out/why: Fragile for songs like "Roundabout" that laid the blueprint for prog rock to come.

150 Roxy Music

Truly a band ahead of its time, Roxy Music was unlike any other band of the early'70s, though they were the direct inspiration for numerous glam-rock and new wave bands that followed. In the beginning Roxy Music was the result of the conflicting visions of singer Bryan Ferry and keyboard player Brian Eno, who left the band after just two albums and went on to make sublime records as a solo artist. While both shared a flare for the dramatic, Eno was far more orchestral in his vision than the ironic Ferry. The first line-up had hits with "Virginia Plain" and "Do the Strand". (See picture opposite)

"Bryan used to work endlessly on lyrics and then deliver them as a live take in the studio, like a conjurer pulling rabbits out of a hat. The most thrilling of these was Love Is The Drug. It's probably been our best-selling single and the most covered." - Andy Mackay

151 Wings

When the Beatles broke up, Paul McCartney formed Wings with his wife, Linda. In the ten years Wings was together, they had a collection of Top 10 hits, often treading a fairly light lyrical path. McCartney was aware that he was not a critical darling in the way Lennon was and answered his detractors with "Silly Love Songs", which shot to the top of the charts and took the album, At the Speed of Sound with it. 1973's Band on the Run was Wings' most successful album, fueled by the title track, "Jet" and "Let Me Roll It". (See picture opposite)

"I used to think that all my Wings stuff was second-rate stuff, but I began to meet younger kids, not kids from my Beatle generation, who would say, We really love this song." - Paul Maccartney

WINGS FACTFILE:

Start up year: 1971

Disband year: 1980

Home town: England

Members : Paul and Linda McCartney, Denny Laine, Joe English, Geoff Britton, Jimmy McCulloch, Denny Seiwell

What you should check out/why: *Band on the Run* for the title song, "Jet" and "Let Me Roll It."

Worth looking out for: *Wings at the Speed of Sound*

152 Big Star

Raised to almost mythic proportions by critics over the past twenty years, Memphis-based Big Star barely caused a stir in the '70s when they were still a band. The line-up on #1Album consisted of Alex Chilton, Chris Bell, Jody Stephens and Andy Hummel. This is the band responsible for the achingly sweet, "Thirteen" and the driving "In the Street", which was later altered to become the theme to "That '70s Show". Bell participated in a minor way on follow-up Radio City, but left to record his own material. He was killed in an accident soon after. The three surviving members reunited along with members of The Posies in the 1990s

153 Sly & The Family Stone

When Sly & The Family Stone sang "I am Everyday People" this diverse group of black and white men and women were not kidding. Mixing up genders and genres, San Francisco's Family Stone were a jubilant, celebratory band that, at least in the beginning, took the '60s ideals of peace, love and equality and mixed them up in a funky rock 'n' roll stew. With titles like Stand!, Life and Dance to the Music, positivity radiated from The Family Stone. However, by 1971's There's a Riot Going On, everything from the band's music to Sly's drug use got heavier and scarier. A few years later Sly was officially a solo artist. (See picture opposite)

BIG STAR FACTFILE:

Start up year: 1971

Disband year: 1975 (reunited without the deceased Chris Bell in the '90s)

Home town: Memphis, U.S.A.

Members : Alex Chilton, Chris Bell, Jody Stephens, Andy Hummel

What you should check out/why: *#1 Record* is a near-perfect album, but they're all worthwhile.

Worth looking out for: Chris Bell's *I Am the Cosmos album.*

SLY & THE FAMILY STONE FACTFILE:

Start up year: 1967

Disband year: 1975

Home town: San Francisco, U.S.A.

Members : Sly Stone, Larry Graham, Greg Errico, Rusty Allen, Cynthia Robinson, Freddie Stewart, Rose Stone, Pat Rizzo, Andy Newmark, Jerry Martini

What you should check out/why: Stand includes "Everyday People" and "I Want to Take You Higher".

Worth looking out for: Sly & The Family Stone's performance on the Dick Cavett Show.

154 Love

Imbuing Burt Bacharach's "My Little Red Book" with so much soul that by song's end the listener wants to comfort singer Arthur Lee was a good indication that Love was capable of big things. Love's magnum opus is 1967's Forever Changes, an album that combines psychedelic rock with soul and folk. Love kicks off the album with "Alone Again Or", which finds Lee singing "You know that I could be in love with almost anyone" then dropping the kicker "And I will be alone again tonight my dear" while Spanish guitars strum the fiery background. The juxtaposition of beauty and dismissal was unusual. About a year later, Lee fired the band but retained the name. (See picture below)

155 The Pretty Things

Starting off as a wild R&B band with a fondness for Bo Diddley, history has remembered them as a psych-rock band due to the enduring popularity of 1968's rock opera, S.F. Sorrow. The embracing of this folky, trippy album makes sense and it is among the best, not to mention most listenable, concept albums of all time, and was indicative of the path the band would take into the '70's. However, the lively garage rock they made in the early years, including Get the Picture's barnburner "Midnight to Six", ranks among the best of its kind. A version of The Pretty things exists today. (See picture below)

156 Rascals

Originally known as The Young Rascals, this New York-based group based around the work of singer/songwriters Felix Cavaliere and Eddie Brigati, was given the label "blue-eyed soul", which is to say that it was a white band playing music attributed to black people. Regardless of race, songs like "Girl Like You" and "Good Lovin" are soul hits. Mindful of civil rights issues, The Rascals wrote about equality in "People Got to Be Free" and many feel that the band's outspokenness about segregation caused them to fall off the charts. Eventually the R&B sound that made them popular was eschewed for a jazzier feel. In 2008, Cavaliere collaborated with Stax guitarist Steve Cropper for Nudge it up a Notch.

157 Booker T. & The MG's

As the name implies, Hammond organ player Booker T. Jones was the central figure in Booker T. & The MG's. Prior to branching out on their own, The MG's were known as Stax records' house band, located in Memphis, Tennessee. Surrounding Booker T were stellar players Steve Cropper (guitar), Donald "Duck" Dunn (bass) and Al Jackson (drums). The MG's distinctive sound is most famously heard on "Green Onions", an instrumental that finds Cropper's fuzzy guitar running tight laps around Booker T's keyboard groove. While schedules and distance eventually ended the band, they reunited in the '90s to play with Neil Young. (See picture opposite)

THE RASCALS FACTFILE:

Start up year: 1964

Disband year: 1972

Home town: New York, U.S.A.

Members : Felix Cavaliere, Eddie Brigati, Gene Cornish, Dino Danelli

What you should check out/why: Groovin' tor summery pop hits, "A Girl Like You", "You Better Run" and "A Place in the Sun."

Worth looking out for: Felix Cavaliere's collaboration with Steve Cropper, Nudge it Up a Notch

BOOKER T. & THE MGS FACTFILE:

Start up year: 1962

Disband year: 1971 (with occasional reunions)

Home town: Memphis, U.S.A.

Members : Booker T. Jones, Steve Cropper, Donald "Duck" Dunn, Al Jackson

What you should check out/why: Green Onions showcases the band's groove; some of the best instrumentals around.

158 The Pogues

Although the years have not been kind to Pogues' singer Shane McGowan, for a time in the '80s, few songwriters could compare to him. Fronting a rag-tag mob of musicians who added traditional Irish instruments such as a tin whistle and accordion to the standard guitar/bass/drums, McGowan's gruffly beautiful vocals created a mood that was equal parts drunken brawl and first date. McGowan's poetry was central to the Pogues' first three albums, Red Roses for Me; Rum, Sodomy and The Lash, and If I Should Fall From Grace With God. The Pogues broke up in 1996, five years after McGowan left the band. (See picture above)

159 Mott the Hoople

Throughout the early '70s, Mott the Hoople, led by Ian Hunter, was one of England's finest hard rock bands. Never achieving the same popularity in the U.S. as they did at home, Mott nevertheless had a worldwide success with 1972's "All the Young Dudes" from the album of the same name. Written by David Bowie, "All the Young Dudes" is the theme for the glam era with its depiction of pretty boys and dressing up. The follow-up album, simply titled Mott, was critically acclaimed, but soon after its release, personality clashes broke up the band, causing guitar player Mick Ralphs to form Bad Company soon after.

160 Parliament Funkadelic

Parliament and Funkadelic were ostensibly two different bands under the tutelage of George Clinton, though whenever any band combines funk and rock, it's often referred to as the P-Funk sound. From 1970 to 1980 Clinton worked under the these names, adding players as he went along, including tenor sax player Maceo Parker and bassist Bootsy Collins, who had both previously played with James Brown. While the bands had R&B hits throughout the '70s, they are best known today for the riotous "Tear the Roof Off the Sucker (Give Up the Funk)". Clinton had a solo hit in the '80s with "Atomic Dog". (See picture opposite)

PARLIAMENT FUNKADELIC FACTFILE:

Start up year: 1970

Disband year: 1980

Home town: Detroit, U.S.A.

Members : George Clinton, Bernie Worrell, Eddie Hazel, Maceo Parker, Bootsy Collins, more

What you should check out/why: Mothership Connection brings the funk with songs like "Give Up the Funk (Tear the Roof off the Sucker).

"Funk is fun. And it's also a state of mind, ... But it's all the ramifications of that state of mind. Once you've done the best you can, funk it!"
- George Clinton

161 Santana

For most of guitar player Carlos Santana's career he was best known to the casual music fan for the laid back vibe of "Black Magic Woman", a song with the Latin flavor that is Santana's calling card. Long respected for his distinctive musicianship, Santana was one of the first older artists to find huge success via collaborations with young and or multi-platinum bands. In 1999 the album Supernatural sold over 10 million copies and garnered a host of Grammy nominations. Guests include Matchbox 20's Rob Thomas, who sang "Smooth", the album's first hit single, Lauryn Hill, Eric Clapton, and Dave Matthews. He made a similar album, Shaman, in 2002. (See picture opposite)

SANTANA FACTFILE:

Start up year: 1966

Disband year: N/A

Home town: San Francisco, U.S.A.

Members : Carlos Santana, Buddy Miles, Greg Errico, Pete and Coke Escovedo, Neil Schon, Michael Shrieve, Mike Carabello, more

What you should check out/why: Abraxes includes "Black Magic Woman" and Santana's version of Tito Puente's "Oye Como Va."

Worth looking out for: Santana's scorching performance in Woodstock.

162 REO Speedwagon

A band for almost ten years before scoring moderate success with 1978's You Can Tune A Piano, But You Can't Tuna Fish, Illinois' REO Speedwagon were one of the biggest pop-rock bands of the '80s. Kevin Cronin's voice was made for the airwaves and in 1980, with the release of Hi Infidelity, they struck radio gold. Scoring two gigantic hits, "Take it on the Run" and "Keep on Loving You", Hi Infidelity was sensitive yet powerful. Throughout the '80s hits kept coming with "Keep the Fire Burning" and "Can't Fight This Feeling". In 2007, they released Find Your Own Way Home.

163 Journey

The combination of Steve Perry's scratchy yet soaring voice and lone original member Neil Schon's flashy guitar proved too much for music fans to ignore during Journey's five-year peak from 1978 ("Wheel In the Sky") to 1983 ("Faithfully" and "Separate Ways"). During this period they released Escape, which practically defined '80s arena rock, with songs like "Don't Stop Believin" and "Open Arms". Lyrically, Journey tended toward the uplifting by painting pictures of triumph over the trials that try to keep average guys down. Schon's shredding and Jonathan Cain's keyboard wizardry ensured fans' fists would pump the air in victory.

164 Beachwood Sparks

A few years before Fleet Foxes made it popular again to like beautiful harmonies singing about nature and relationships, California's Beachwood Sparks released two albums, Beachwood Sparks and Once We Were Trees, and one EP, Make the Cowboy Robots Cry, that were the pinnacle psychedelic country-rock. Not unlike the best of Poco or, on songs like "The Sun Surrounds Me", Mike Nesmith's solo work, the Beachwood Sparks wrote intricate, spacious songs. A cover of Sade's "By Your Side" was released as a single. Breaking up in 2002, the Beachwood Sparks reunited for a few shows in 2008.

165 The Only Ones

Throughout the '70s and '80s Peter Perrett was the voice of the Only Ones, a band that came out of the punk scene but had shared little with the rough and tumble bands of the day. Primarily concerned with the rise and fall of modern love, the Only Ones' biggest hits were the power-pop classic "Another Girl, Another Planet" and the dreamy, hazy "The Whole of the Law", both taken from their debut album. The follow-up Even Serpents Shine does not have songs that jump out of the speakers, but is still a consistently good listen. They broke up in 1980.

166 Derek and the Dominoes

By the time Eric "Slowhand" Clapton formed the short-lived Derek and the Dominoes he had already been the guitar player for the Yardbirds, Blind Faith and Cream, which is a pretty good resume by anyone's standards. The Dominoes' lone studio album, Layla and Other Assorted Love Songs, featured an appearance by Duane Allman of the Allman Brothers. The titular hit song was later re-popularized by Clapton as an acoustic song and stripping it of all of the original's gutsiness. Layla also included a beloved rendering of Jimi Hendrix's "Little Wing". Drug use was instrumental in the band's brief lifespan. Recorded during the band's US tour, In Concert was released in 1973.

THE ONLY ONES FACTFILE:

Start up year: 1977

Disband year: 1980

Home town: London, England

Members : Peter Perrett, Alan Mair, John Perry, Mike Kellie

What you should check out/why: The rock 'n' roll romanticism of The Only Ones.

DEREK & THE DOMINOES FACTFILE:

Start up year: 1970

Disband year: 1971

Home town: New York, U.S.A.

Members : Eric Clapton, Bobby Whitlock, Carl Radle, Jim Gordon, Duane Allman

What you should check out/why: Layla and Other Assorted Love Songs for the original, riff-driven version of "Layla."

167 Traffic

In the time between his leaving The Spencer Davis Group and launching a successful solo career, singer/organ player Steve Winwood, who was 18 years old at the time, formed Traffic, a jazz-rock band that also had folk leanings in the beginning. Although it was ostensibly Winwood's band, Dave Mason (guitar/bass) provided Traffic with its first singles, "Paper Sun" and "Hole in My Shoe". By the time Traffic's first album, Mr. Fantasy hit the Top 10, Mason was out of the band, although he came back to help with Traffic, which included "Feelin' Alright", a song that later became a big hit for Joe Cocker.

168 Lynard Skynard

To all but their fans, Lynyrd Skynrd is synonymous with their lengthy, guitar solo-heavy ballad "Free Bird" and their redneck kiss-off to Neil Young's "Southern Man", "Sweet Home Alabama". But fans loved Ronnie Van Zandt's direct, story-telling lyrics and Ed King's and Allen Collins' seemingly endless country-rock guitar jams. With a few albums already under their belt, 1975's Nuthin' Fancy scored them a Top 10 album. When Van Zandt was killed in a plane crash in 1977, it looked like the end of the band; however, the surviving members started playing again in the '90s and supported Kid Rock's 2009 tour.

TRAFFIC FACTFILE:

Start up year: 1967

Disband year: 1975

Home town: Birmingham, England

Members : Steve Winwood, Dave Mason, Jim Capaldi, Chris Wood

What you should check out/why: Traffic includes Dave Mason's "Feelin' Alright", which became better known as a hit for Joe Cocker.

LYNYRD SKYNYRD FACTFILE:

Start up year: 1965

Disband year: N/A

Home town: Jacksonville, Florida, U.S.A.

Members : Ronnie Van Zant, Allen Collins, Gary Rossington, Leon Wilkeson, Billy Powell, Bob Burns, Artimus Pyle, Steve Gaines, Ed King, more

What you should check out/why: Pronounced Leh-nerd Skin-Nerd features the Southern Rock ballad "Free Bird."

169 The Soft Boys

Formed in Cambridge, England in 1976, the Soft Boys marked the debut of singer-songwriter Robyn Hitchcock as well as Morris Windsor, Matthew Seligman and Kimberley Rew, who later had a hit with "Walking on Sunshine" as part of Katrina and the Waves. The Soft Boys' debut, Underwater Moonlight showed the bands' influences (Pink Floyd, Bob Dylan) through a combination of psychedelic imagery and occasionally barbed lyrics. While album opener "I Want to Destroy You" could best be described at power-pop, that description doesn't do justice to the range of genres incorporated into the Soft Boys' sound. A short-lived reunion in 2002 resulted in a successful tour and the album, Nextdoorland.

170 Pavement

Based around the nucleus of songwriters Stephen (SM) Malkmus and Scott (Spiral Stars) Kannberg, Pavement was at the centre of the mid-'90s indie rock explosion that saw New York's Matador Records become one of the finest indie labels in the U.S. While their ramshackle debut, Slanted and Enchanted, gets cited as Pavement's seminal work, Crooked Rain, Crooked Rain, featuring "Range Life" and "Cut Your Hair", songs that poked fun at the absurdity of alternative rock, was the band's biggest success. In true indie style, fans often cite the maligned Wowee Zowee as Pavement's best work. (See picture opposite)

THE SOFT BOYS FACTFILE:

Start up year: 1976

Disband year: 1981 (with a reunion in 2002)

Home town: Cambridge, England

Members : Robyn Hitchcock, Kimberley Rew, Morris Windsor, Matthew Seligman

What you should check out/why: Underwater Moonlight is a strange, surreal delight, featuring "Queen of Eyes", "I Got the Hots" and "I Wanna Destroy You."

Worth looking out for: Robyn Hitchcock's records with The Egyptians; Kimberley Rew's solo work.

"We're probably a couple of freaks who've created their own little universe, are living in our own little world and that's the only place where we can survive."
- Steve Malkmus

171 Deep Purple

More popular in the U.S. than they were at home in England, Deep Purple made a name for themselves at the tail-end of the '60s and into the '70s with a heavy, guitar-centric sound anchored by Ritchie Blackmore's guitar. Initially sprinkling their albums and live shows with a liberal amount of covers, including Jimi Hendrix's Hey Joe" and Ike and Tina Turner's "River Deep, Mountain High", they made a lasting imprint on the musical landscape with their own "Smoke on the Water" from the Machine Head album. "Smoke on the Water" has an introduction that every beginning electric guitar player has attempted to master. (See picture opposite)

"Well, we were not a happy band. There was always an edginess to our relationship, even in the early days, but it was edginess that gave birth to a lot of creativity as well."
- Roger Glover

DEEP PURPLE FACTFILE:

Start up year: 1968

Disband year: N/A

Home town: Hertford, England

Members : Tommy Bolin, Ian Gillan, Ritchie Blackmore, Joe Satriani, Rod Evans, Nick Simper, Jon Lord, Ian Paice, David Coverdale, more

What you should check out/why: Machine Head includes "Smoke on the Water", the song that launched a million teenage boys' guitar lessons.

172 Chicago

Though Chicago's thirty-plus year career includes several stylistic touchstones, the band is perhaps best known and best loved for the tightly arranged snaking horn lines, driving rhythms, and blues guitar that characterize its jazz-rock sound. Early hits like "25 or 6 to 4" and "Does Anybody Really Know What Time It Is?" demonstrate the band's versatility, with the first number's intense and nervy juxtaposing fuzz bass and wah-wah guitar with brassy horns, and the second's relaxed stroll complimented by rich vocal harmonies and a trumpet solo. In the '80s, Chicago turned towards soft rock balladry, but retained its popular following into the present due in part to several successful singles, "best-of" packages, and a rigorous touring schedule. (See picture above)

173 Can

Among the world's most successful experimental bands, Germany's Can underwent numerous line-up changes throughout their decade-long existence, though bassist Holger Czukay and keyboardist Irmin Schmidt were always key figures and instrumental to the band's propulsive, hypnotic sound. When Can found a groove they stuck with it, sometimes for hours on end. While enthusiasts all have favorites, and the most familiar song is probably "You Doo Right" from Monster Movie, many consider the ambitious double album Tago Mago to be the band's pinnacle. Tago Mago includes vocals by Damo Suzuki, who left the band in 1973. In 1976 Can broke the British Top Ten with "I Want More".

174 Spiritualized

When trio Spacemen 3 fell apart, Jason Pierce reappeared as the brains behind Spiritualized. More pop-based than his previous band, Spiritualized still veered into hypnotic, trippy passages, especially on early records Lazer Guided Melodies and Pure Phase. Known for publicity stunts like playing on the top of Toronto's CN Tower so that they could be called The Highest Band in the World, Spiritualized does not need gimmickry to hold people's attention. 1997's Ladies and Gentleman… We are Floating in Space took things in a more orchestral direction. Although Pierce battled a life-threatening illness in 2006, Spiritualized returned with 2008's Songs in A&E.

175 The Flaming Lips

For more than ten years Oklahoma's Flaming Lips was an underground favorite. Even a guest appearance on Beverley Hills 90210 and a college radio hit with cute-yet-cosmic "She Don't Use Jelly" from 1995's Clouds Taste Metallic, did nothing to tarnish the band's cool reputation, but neither did they make the Flaming Lips a household name. All that changed in 1999 when Wayne Coyne and crew broke out with The Soft Bulletin, an album full of celebratory songs that were used in a number of commercials. The Flaming Lips became more popular when the band's live show started including people dressed in animal costumes and Coyne walking over the audience in a huge plastic bubble. (See picture opposite)

SPIRITUALIZED FACTFILE:

Start up year: 1989

Disband year: N/A

Home town: Rugby, Warwickshire, England

Members: Jason Pierce, Mark Refoy, Willie B. Carruthers, Jon Mattock, Kate Radley, Sean Cook, more

What you should check out/why: Ladies and Gentleman We Are Floating in Space features a guest appearance by New Orleans blues man, Dr. John.

THE FLAMING LIPS FACTFILE:

Start up year: 1983

Disband year: N/A

Home town: Oklahoma City, U.S.A.

Members : Wayne Coyne, Michael Ivins, Steven Drozd, Ronald Jones, Jonathan Donahue, more

What you should check out/why: Transmissions from the Satellite Heart includes "Be My Head", "Turn it On" and a ton of other psychedelic pop beauties.

Worth looking out for: The Flaming Lips' appearance on the television show, Beverley Hills, 90210

176 Gene Vincent and the Blue Caps

Gene Vincent is one of rock 'n' roll's coolest cats. Instantly recognizable for his leather outfits and slicked back curls, Vincent's voice is sweet and sultry, with an unmistakable tough guy edge. While Vincent was also a guitar player, his early songs like "Be-Bop-A-Lula" stood out thanks to the guitar playing of Cliff Gallup, who quit rock 'n' roll when he quit the Blue Caps. While his star began to wane in the U.S. following the British Invasion, Vincent remained popular in Britain, touring with Eddie Cochran on the fateful trip that took Cochran's life. Gene Vincent died from a ruptured stomach ulcer in 1971.

177 Mercury Rev

For a moment in 1990 Mercury Rev main man Jonathon Donahue was the Flaming Lips' guitar player. The union didn't last long and soon Donahue was making noisy, psychedelic rock that played fast and loose with dynamics and tempo, adding layer upon layer of sound to form the Mercury Rev sound. Never a band to make things easy, the first single from Mercury Rev's first album, Yerself is Steam, "Car Wash Hair" was a hidden track on the CD. Deserter's Songs from 1998 is widely considered Mercury Rev's best album, and it was certainly the most linear and song-based to that point.

GENE VINCENT FACTFILE:

Born: 1935

Died: 1971

Home town: Norfolk, Virginia, U.S.A.

Members : Gene Vincent, Cliff Gallup, Willie Williams, Dickie Harrell, Paul Peek,

What you should check out/why: Gene Vincent & His Blue Caps is rock 'n' roll at its purest.

Worth looking out for: Vincent's appearance in the movie, The Girl Can't Help It

MERCURY REV FACTFILE:

Start up year: late-'80s

Disband year: N/A

Home town: Buffalo, New York, U.S.A.

Members : Jonathan Donahue, Dave Fridmann, Grasshopper, Suzanne Thorpe, Jimy Chambers, David Baker, more

What you should check out/why: Yerself Is Steam is a gorgeous, hazy, topsy-turvy record; Boces takes it even further.

Worth looking out for: Hidden track "Car Wash Hair" on Yerself Is Steam.

178 XTC

Their career spanning almost two decades, XTC started out as one of the punk era's most striking bands, eschewing volume for oddball art-rock and gaining worldwide attention for "Making Plans for Nigel" from 1979's Drums and Wires. Andy Partridge, Colin Moulding and Dave Gregory stayed in the public eye with singles like "Senses Working Overtime", but 1986's acclaimed album Skylarking gave them the two huge hits "Grass" and "Dear God". In the '90s, XTC became a much mellower, smoother band and their last hit was the poppy "The Ballad of Peter Pumpkinhead", which was later covered by Crash Test Dummies.

179 The Jon Spencer Blues Explosion

After spending most of the '80s in New York City noise-rockers Pussy Galore, Jon Spencer drove the Blues Explosion throughout the '90s and '00s. The Blues Explosion strips the blues down to its rawest, most basic elements, often finding Spencer shouting one or two lines like "Bellbottoms" or "Dang" over drummer Russell Simins and second guitarist Judah Bauer's down 'n' dirty riffs. While albums like Orange and Now I Got Worry are fine examples of the Explosion's sound, it is the live shows where the band really explodes. In 1996 the Blues Explosion backed up bluesman R.L. Burnside on A Ass Pocket of Whisky.

XTC FACTFILE:

Start up year: 1976

Disband year: N/A (although they haven't released anything since 2000's Wasp Star (Apple Venus, Pt. 2))

Home town: Swindon, England

Members : Colin Moulding, Andy Partridge, Dave Gregory, Terry Chambers, Barry Andrews

What you should check out/why: English Settlement has the big jangle of "Senses Working Overtime."

Worth looking out for: Moulding, Partridge and Gregory's psych-pop side-project, The Dukes of the Stratosphear.

JOHN SPENCER FACTFILE:

Start up year: 1990

Disband year: N/A

Home town: New York, U.S.A.

Members : Jon Spencer, Judah Bauer, Russell Simins

What you should check out/why: Orange is Theremin-fueled blues trash.

Worth looking out for: Jon Spencer's other bands: Pussy Galore, Heavy Trash, Boss Hog

180 Super Furry Animals

While Cardiff, Wales may not be the first name in rock 'n' roll, that didn't stop Gruff Rhys from forming Super Furry Animals, one of the most critically beloved and, by indie standards, commercially successful bands that came up around the turn of the twenty-first century. First hit "Lord! Show Me Magic" drew listeners with its insistent guitars and Rhys's spirited vocals. Over the years, the Furries have released records in English (Rings Around the World) and their native Welsh (Mwng) to their loyal fans. In 2007 Rhys released his second solo album Candylion, which included the delightful title song. (See picture opposite)

"We're still looking for the definitive 'Furries sound,' whatever that is..." – Dafydd Ieuan

SUPER FURRY ANIMALS FACTFILE:

Start up year: 1993

Disband year: N/A

Home town: Cardiff, Wales

Members : Gruff Rhys, Huw Bunford, Dafydd Ieuan, Cian Ciárán, Guto Pryce

What you should check out/why: Mwng, a psychedelic pop dream all sung in Welsh.

Worth looking out for: Anything with the Super Furries' name on it.

ACID CASUAL

181 Teenage Fanclub

When Teenage Fanclub released the noisy, slacker rock classic A Catholic Education in 1990 the album didn't even hint that TFC would become a band known for its glorious harmonies and it barely showed that they could carry a tune. Second record Bandwagonesque still had a fair share of loud guitars, as on "Satan", but the proceedings became more melodic, and songs like "Guiding Star" and "December" foreshadowed the direction the band would take on Grand Prix and Songs From Northern Britain. While maligned at the time, their third album Thirteen more than stands the test of time. Five albums later, the Fannies have never made a bad record. (See picture opposite)

TEENAGE FANCLUB FACTFILE:

Start up year: 1989

Disband year: N/A

Home town: Glasgow, Scotland

Members : Norman Blake, Gerard Love, Raymond McGinley, Francis MacDonald, Brendan O'Hare, Paul Quinn

What you should check out/why: Grand Prix for perfect harmonies and melodies to die for.

Worth looking out for: The limited edition single of "The Ballad of John and Yoko."

182 The Sugarcubes

Before Björk became the most popular one-named celebrity since Madonna, she was the female voice (often backed by Einar Orn's oddball shouts) in the Icelandic art-rockers the Sugarcubes. When Life's Too Good was released in 1988 it came as a bit of a shock to music fans with its almost-alien sounds. The single "Birthday" included a remixed version with The Jesus and Mary Chain providing razorblade guitars and somber "Hey hey heys" contrasting with Björk's exuberant vocals. While the Sugarcubes released Here Today, Tomorrow, Next Week! and Stick Around for Joy, neither would prepare the world for the success Björk's solo career would bring.

183 The 13th Floor Elevators

In the thirty years since they broke up, Austin, Texas's 13th Floor Elevators have become revered by music fans for their psychedelic rock and folk-rock driven by singer Roky Erikson's high-pitched voice. It is a voice that seems to speak directly to whoever is listening. Second album Easter Everywhere starts with the number "Slip Inside This House" that includes over eight glorious minutes and bubbling guitar and electric jug sounds. Erikson sets a mood that is unsettling but magnetic. Drug use and supposedly anti-social behavior led to Roky being hospitalized for a number of years, which was an unfortunate series of events that changed him forever. In the past few years, Erikson has been playing shows and toured with The Black Angels in 2008.

SUGARCUBES FACTFILE:

Start up year: 1986

Disband year: 1992

Home town: Reykjavik, Iceland

Members : Björk, Einar Örn, Siggi Baldursson, Einar Mellax, Thor Eldon, Bragi Olafesson, Margret Ornolfdottir

What you should check out/why: Life's Too Good introduced the world to Björk via songs like "Motorcrash" and "Delicious Demon."

Worth looking out for: The double-grooved 12" single of "Birthday" featuring backing vocals by The Jesus and Mary Chain.

13TH FLOOR ELAVATORS FACTFILE:

Start up year: 1965

Disband year: 1968

Home town: Austin, Texas

Members : Roky Erikson, Tommy Hall, Ronnie Leatherman, Stacy Sutherland, Benny Thurman, John Ike Walton, Dan Galindo, Danny Thomas

What you should check out/why: Easter Everywhere and 13th Floor Elevators are dazzling examples of fractured psychedelic rock.

185 The Smiths

Among the most treasured groups of the '80s British pop explosion, the Smiths exposed a generation of would-be bon vivants to the wisdom of Oscar Wilde and the meaning of the term, "jumped-up pantry boy". While Andy Rourke and Mike Joyce made a formidable rhythm section, the Smiths' legacy lies in songwriting team of guitarist Johnny Marr and singer Morrissey. Considered a maudlin lyricist on "Back to the Old House", Morrissey sometimes went for humor as on "Girlfriend in a Coma". Meanwhile, Marr's guitar seemed to tell a story all its own and his sound is immediately recognizable, with the exception being on the hit "How Soon Is Now?"

186 The Electric Prunes

While the Electric Prunes have been reduced to the status of one hit wonders, at least their hit, the incendiary "I Had Too Much to Dream Last Night", is a wonder of recording techniques and an amazing song. Their debut, while primarily a prime example of psychedelic rock, also includes the surprisingly pretty ballad "Onie". In a strange twist, producer David Hassinger brought in composer David Axelrod to write and arrange the Prunes' third album, Mass in F Minor in 1968. This enormous undertaking proved too much for the garage-psych band, but it is an interesting listen nevertheless.

187 Sparks

Debuting during the transition between the psychedelic and glam rock eras, Sparks combined theatrics with an almost post-punk austerity before punk even existed. Brothers Russell (singer) and Ron Mael (keyboards) grew up in Los Angeles and knew the importance of image to a band. Russell's halo of curls and near-operatic voice contrasted sharply with Ron's slicked-back hair, trim moustache and skinny ties. In 1974, Sparks released the seminal Kimono My House and sparking the hit "This Town's Not Big Enough for Both of Us". Sparks' reputation continues to grow yearly, with the band continuing to record after almost 40 years together.

188 The Zombies

Throughout most of the 1960s, the Zombies were a singles band. Their first release, the verging on hysterical "Tell Her No" gave them a taste of success that wouldn't be matched until the band produced Odessey and Oracle in 1968. It was completely in keeping with its time, yet still manages to sound vital 40 years later. Odessey and Oracle included the smash hit "Time of the Season" along with a wealth of glorious pop songs like "This Will Be Our Year" that highlighted singer Colin Blunstone's choir boy voice. The band broke up soon after Odessey was released but Blunstone and guitar player Rod Argent currently tour and play the classics.

189 The Turtles

Howard Kaylan and Mark Volman, also known as Flo and Eddie in Frank Zappa's Mothers of Invention, were key to The Turtles sound, providing the band with the pitch-perfect harmonies that made "Happy Together" and the self-mocking "Elenore" such radio-friendly hits. The Turtles are one of the most enduring bands from '60s America, and their Greatest Hits collections truly are packed with successful songs like "She'd Rather Be With Me", "You Baby", "It Ain't Me Babe" and "You Showed Me". Although the band split up in 1970, Kaylan and Vollman continued to work together in one form or another for years afterward.

190 Sepultura

Formed in 1984 in Belo Horizonte, Brazil by brothers Max and Igor Cavalera, Sepultura would not only go on to be one of the country's largest musical exports, but they also proved to be a driving force in the 1990s metal scene. Taking early cues from underground legends like Venom, Kreator and Possessed, Sepultura incorporated punk rock as well as traditional Brazilian rhythms and instrumentation in their thrash assault. Inner tensions eventually lead to Max's departure and his taking his vocal and guitar talents to his new project Soulfly. Drummer Igor, guitarist Andreas Kisser and bassist Paulo Jr. soldiered on under the Sepultura name.

191 Belle and Sebastian

Glasgow, Scotland's Belle and Sebastian began as a college project for lead singer/ songwriter Stuart Murdoch and turned into one of the past decade's most popular independent pop-rock bands. With an almost-cult-like following springing up in the wake of their extremely limited edition debut Tigermilk, which has since been reissued, Belle and Sebastian signed with Jeepster Records in the U.K. and Matador in the U.S., giving more distribution to If You're Feeling Sinister, a highly literate and lyrical collection. While the future of the band is uncertain following the compilation Push Barman and See and the BBC Sessions, Belle and Sebastian have a strong catalog that consistently brings new fans to them. (See picture opposite)

BELLE AND SEBASTIAN FACTFILE:

Start up year: 1995

Disband year: N/A

Home town: Glasgow, Scotland

Members: Stuart Murdoch, Stevie Jackson, Chris Geddes, Sarah Martin, Richard Colburn, Isobel Campbell, Stuart David,

What you should check out/why: If You're Feeling Sinister and Tigermilk are literate, pure pop.

Worth looking out for: The "This Is Just a Modern Rock Song" EP.

192 Tommy James and the Shondells

In the '60s, songwriter Tommy James led the Shondells to the top of the charts with iconic songs like "I Think We're Alone Now", "Mirage", "Hanky Panky" and "Mony Mony", which was later a hit for Billy Idol. With easy to remember lyrics and big choruses, James was often dismissed as bubblegum by serious music fans, but there is little denying James' way with a tune. Fun touches like the tremolo-heavy vocals on "Crimson and Clover" made the Shondells stand out on the radio. Although James continued to record throughout the '70s, apart from the hit "Draggin' the Line", James never relived his earlier success.

193 Fall Out Boy

The melodic emo-pop of Fall Out Boy was born in 1991 in the Chicago suburb of Wilmette, Illinois. Naming themselves after the sidekick of Radioactive Man on television's The Simpsons, Fall Out Boy's earliest output included self-released demos, split CDs, and a mini album titled Fall Out Boy's Evening Out With Your Girlfriend. With a buzz quickly building, they broke through to the masses with their Island Records debut From Under the Cork Tree. Non-stop touring and constant radio airplay gained the band a wealth of exposure. When 2007s Infinity On High was released, it sold over 260,000 copies in its first week.

194 Plastic Ono Band

Formed in the Beatles' end days, John Lennon and Yoko Ono's Plastic Ono Band was originally meant as an outlet for the couple's experimental and artistic tendencies, with archetypal anti-war song "Give Peace A Chance" being released before Lennon's first group disbanded. The line-up of the Plastic Ono Band that included Eric Clapton, Klaus Voorman, and Alan White recorded "Cold Turkey", a song initially met with little fanfare, but one that has become a Lennon classic. While Lennon's songs still maintained a familiar pop-rock structure, Ono brought more art to the proceedings with songs like "Don't Worry Kyoko (Mummy's Only Looking for Her Hand in the Snow)".

195 Fairport Convention

Starting life as a psychedelic rock band, the addition of ethereal singer Sandy Denny and the departure of a couple of the original members turned England's Fairport Convention into one of the world's most successful folk-rock bands. While traditionalist Denny was responsible for some of the band's most popular songs like "Who Knows Where the Time Goes" and was the voice on the seminal Liege and Leaf from 1969, she left soon after due to unhappiness over Fairport's rock sound. Guitar player Richard Thompson is successful as a solo artist as well as with his ex-wife Linda Thompson.

196 Franz Ferdinand

When Alex Kapranos, Bob Hardy, Paul Thomson, and Nick McCarthy decided to form a group, legend dictates that their primary concern was making music that girls would dance to. Their wish was granted almost immediately, with single "Take Me Out" becoming one of the most played songs of 2004. Their debut record was given a load of accolades, including the prestigious Mercury Award. You Could Have it So Much Better followed a mere year later. Franz Ferdinand's third album Tonight was released in 2009 with single "No You Girls" appearing in a commercial even before the album's release.

197 New Order

Following Ian Curtis's death by hanging, Joy Division's Peter Hook, Bernard Sumner and Stephen Morris were left on the verge of a U.S. tour without a singer. Instead of breaking up, they regrouped and added Gillian Gilbert on synthesizers. The result was New Order, a band that took similar themes of isolation, loneliness and modern love and made them a little softer, sometimes even danceable. Throughout the '80s and into the '90s New Order struck gold with "Blue Monday", "Perfect Kiss", "Confusion", "True Faith" and other songs that walked the line between mumbly and atmospheric indie music and disco.

198 The Horrors

One of the most exciting bands to come out of the 21st century, the Horrors' debut Strange House was a garage rock feast, with stylish videos for "Sheena is a Parasite" featuring Samantha Morton, "She Is The New Thing" and "Count in Fives", paying homage to influences like Edward Gorey and George Franjiu's film Eyes Without a Face, not to mention Joe Meek. The screaming Farfisa provided by keyboardist Spider Webb is the heart of these early songs. In 2009, the Horrors released Primary Colours, moving away from the abject garage sound of its predecessor to explore a more spacey, post-punk sound. (See picture opposite)

199 Band of Horses

Emerging from the almost-ran '90s alt-rock band Carissa's Weird, Ben Bridwell and Mat Brooke took their music to a more roots-rock place with Band of Horses. Not unlike Sub Pop label-mates Iron & Wine, Band of Horses is known for its sensitive ballads. Everything All the Time debuted in 2006 and scored an indie hit with the piercing dirge, "The Funeral". Soon after, Brooke left the band to form Grand Archives, while Bridwell regrouped and toured the world, seeing his audience grow by leaps and bounds. In 2007, the album Cease to Begin continued to highlight Bridwell's Neil Young-like falsetto on songs like single "Is There A Ghost".

THE HORRORS FACTFILE:

Start up year: 2005

Disband year: N/A

Home town: London, England

Members: Faris Badwan, Tomethy Furse, Spider Webb, Joshua Von Grimm, Coffin Joe

What you should check out/why: Strange House features "Sheena is a Parasite" and their cover of Screaming Lord Sutch's "Jack the Ripper."

Worth looking out for: The Horrors interview with Nardwuar the Human Serviette

BAND OF HORSES FACTFILE:

Start up year: 2004

Disband year: N/A (no longer with Mat Brooke)

Home town: Seattle, U.S.A.

Members: Ben Bridwell, Mat Brooke, Creighton Barrett, Rob Hampton

What you should check out/why: Everything All the Time for the eeriness of "The Funeral"

200 Demolition Doll Rods

Like the Ramones and Guitar Wolf, the members of Detroit trio Demolition Doll Rod are siblings in rock. Actually singer/bassist Margaret Doll Rod and drummer Christine Doll Rod are sisters in real life, with guitar player Danny Doll Rod being a band mate for so long (upwards of 11 years) that he might as well be related. Playing a wonderfully sleazy brand of garage rock while wearing leather bikinis or something similar, Demolition Doll Rods were, until their demise in 2007, the ultimate in rock 'n' roll dance party fun. Songs like "Married for the Weekend", "Fast One" and "Take It Off" hint at the band's modus operandi. (See picture opposite)

"Somewhere in between the Cramps, the Donnas, Jon Spencer, and Royal Trux. this wonderfully bold Detroit trio dishes out a somewhat sparse but totally convincing brand of sexy soulful rock n' roll, often while naked."
-Skyway

201 The Birthday Party

Although Nick Cave, Roland S. Howard, Tracey Pew, Mick Harvey and Phil Calvert formed The Birthday Party in Australia, they started making waves after moving to England in 1981. Initially playing punked-up rockabilly, the Birthday Party became louder, noisier and more violent than their cute name suggests. Singer Cave was already exploring themes that still interest him and violence, religion, passion, and the underside of sex all loom large. The band's debut, Prayers on Fire, features "Nick the Stripper" and "Zoo-Music Girl". The first is slow, managing to sound simultaneously sensuous and horrifying. The second is the audio equivalent of a bludgeoning. (See picture opposite)

THE BIRTHDAY PARTY FACTFILE:

Start up year: 1977

Disband year: 1983

Home town: Melbourne, Australia

Members: Nick Cave, Roland S. Howard, Tracey Pew, Mick Harvey, Phil Calvert

What you should check out/why: Prayers on Fire for "Nick the Stripper," a slow, grinding, dirty song that demands repeated listening.

Worth looking out for: Nick Cave's books, And the Ass Saw the Angel and The Death of Bunny Munro.

HIWATT
HIWATT

202 Todd Rundgren

Getting his first taste of success with late'60s pop-rock band the Nazz, over the past four decades, Rundgren has made as much of a name for himself as a producer as he has as an extremely eclectic musician. Beloved by many for '70s ballads like "Hello, It's Me", which was used to great effect in Sofia Coppola's The Virgin Suicides, and "I Saw the Light", Rundgren has also had hits with the wacky calypso-tinged "Bang on the Drum" and the deceptively witty "We Got to Get You a Woman". Known for sticking to his artistic vision, Rundgren rarely plays his hits today.

203 Canned Heat

Best known for the songs "Going Up the Country" and "On the Road Again", Canned Heat never saw the superstardom that many other blues-based bands of the '60s saw, which is a shame because they understand the genre better than most. Harmonica player Alan Wilson and singer Bob "The Bear" Hite were the nucleus of Canned Heat, with Hite's burly presence being the focal point of the band's stage show. Prior to Wilson's death in 1970, Canned Heat backed John Lee Hooker on the blues legend's comeback, Hooker & Heat. A version of Canned Heat, minus Wilson and Hite, was playing shows in the '00s. (See picture opposite)

204 Yo La Tengo

Based in Hoboken, New Jersey, Yo La Tengo has made a living for 25 years by playing truly eclectic music. Created by guitar player Ira Kaplan and his wife drummer Georgia Hubley in 1984, Yo La Tengo added James McNew as their full-time bass player around 1990. Known as much for Kaplan's distorted guitar freak-outs like Electr-O-Pura's "Attack on Love", as for playing songs that barely rise above a whisper like Painful's "Nowhere Near", Yo La Tengo has also made diversions into jazz that include a cover of Sun Ra's "Rocket #9. Singles like "Tom Courtenay" and "Sugarcube" raised the band's profile, making Yo La Tengo one of the most beloved independent bands around.

205 Poco

Originally named Pogo after Walt Kelly's famous comic strip, Poco is one of the most critically acclaimed country-rock bands that sprang from late'60s Los Angeles. While never reaching the commercial heights of colleagues like the Eagles, Poco's sound stands up well 40 years later. A problem that plagued Poco was maintaining a line-up from one record to the next, but that didn't deter them from making two of the best albums of the genre, Pickin' Up the Pieces (1969) and Poco (1970), with Rusty Young's astonishing steel guitar giving the band a genuine country feel that was missing from many others of the time.

206 PJ Harvey

Originally claiming that P.J. Harvey was a band, singer/guitar player Polly Jean Harvey has had a longer career using the PJ Harvey name without original sidemen Steve Vaughan and Rob Ellis. Bursting onto the scene with 1991's Dry and the incendiary singles "Sheela-Na-Gig" and "Dress", Harvey's songs were powerful and impassioned with a sound she elaborated on for the equally riveting Rid of Me. Since then her songwriting has become more nuanced, treading similar lyrical and musical territory to Nick Cave and the Bad Seeds. Her Stories From the City, Stories From the Sea in 2000 was widely praised for its maturity.

207 The Donnas

Having been in bands together since they were pubescent, Maya Ford, Torry Castellano, Brett Anderson and Allison Robertson started calling the group The Donnas and calling themselves Donna Ford, Donna Castellano, Donna Anderson and Donna Robertson in 1995 at the encouragement of former manager Darin Raffaelli. The Donnas' first albums are punk-pop classics, though the band was not as confident then as they are today. While there's no denying The Donnas' musical prowess, and as much as guitarist Robertson shreds with the best of them, lyrics about boys like "40 Boys in 40 Nights", junk food and partying that were all fun when The Donnas were teenagers don't sound as fresh as they used to.

208 The Vaselines

Frances McKee and Eugene Kelly, who went on to underground success in Eugenius throughout the '90s, started The Vaselines in Glasgow, Scotland in 1986. Sweet, yet sassy, the Vaselines's sound is unpolished, but has an advanced sense of melody. Lyrically, they dabbled in cute double-entendres like "Rory Rides Me Raw", which they said is about a bicycle, but also tended toward heartfelt and tender as on "Jesus Doesn't Want Me For a Sunbeam". Covered and championed by Kurt Cobain, the Vaselines became more popular after they had already been broken up for a couple of years. They reunited in 2009, playing shows world-wide.

209 Black Mountain

With a seemingly endless amount of songs running around his head, Vancouver, Canada's Stephen McBean, who does double-duty with Pink Mountaintops, formed Black Mountain in 2004, signing with renowned independent label Jagjaguwar that same year. Their eponymous first record includes the single "Druganaut" as well as the tellingly titled "No Hits". Musically, Black Mountain treads stoner-rock territory, with heavy grooves and layered guitars, rising above the chaff through the stellar vocals of McBean and keyboard player Amber Webber of Lightning Dust. Black Mountain released In the Future in 2008, delving deeper into prog-rock than they had on the first record.

210 Velvet Cush

Perhaps the most unjustly neglected band of the '90s, Velvet Crush is power pop perfection. Although working as a duo for much of their existence, drummer Ric Menck and guitar/bass player Paul Chastain were joined by Jeffrey Underhill on guitar for the band's most successful period. After releasing swirly delight, In the Presence of Greatness to press accolades, they followed up with Teenage Symphonies to God, an album of heavenly harmonies and perfect pop-rock, including a stunning cover of Gene Clark's "Why Not Your Baby". 1999's Free Expression is a lost gem, with the trumpet line of "Melody #1" paying homage to another underrated band, Material Issue.

211 Flying Burrito Brothers

Often considered a dilettante for having more money than the musicians he hung around with, Gram Parsons nevertheless loved country music, knew how to play it and, with the Flying Burrito Brothers, set about pioneering the genre of country-rock. The original Burritos released two near-perfect albums, though various members continued using the name for much longer. The group's first album, Gilded Palace of Sin, is almost straight-up country and though it sold less than 50,000 copies when it was first released, fans like The Rolling Stones helped to build the band's legend for years to come. Parsons died in 1973. (See picture opposite)

BURRITO BROTHERS FACTFILE:

Start up year: 1969

Disband year: Gram Parsons left the band in 1970; other versions of the band continue to pop up

Home town: Los Angeles, U.S.A.

Members: Gram Parsons, Chris Hillman, Sneaky Pete Kleinow, Gene Parsons, Chris Etheridge, Bernie Leadon, more

What you should check out/why: Gilded Palace of Sin is among the finest, most soulful, country-rock (with the emphasis on country) records ever made.

Worth looking out for: Gram Parsons' solo records, Grievous Angel and GP.

212 My Bloody Valentine

Until they reunited for a series of shows in 2008, My Bloody Valentine was among rock's most enigmatic bands. With fans still waiting for a successor to 1991's Loveless, songwriter Kevin Shields remained almost totally reclusive and only occasionally popping up to produce or remix another band's music or to tell the press that he was working on new MBV material. Over a series of singles and the albums Isn't Anything and Loveless, My Bloody Valentine became one of the most treasured of the bands labeled 'shoegaze'. MBV's wall of sound is breathtakingly beautiful, even if the guitars are fed through layers of distortion. (See picture below)

213 Ride

Although Oxford, England's Ride only released four full-length records over its eight-year run, they supplemented those with numerous EPs and singles that helped chart the band's change from the huge guitar waves of Nowhere to the '60s pastiche of Tarantula, which is essentially a solo record for songwriter Andy Bell as a result of his conflict with Ride's other songwriter Mark Gardner. While Ride could never be described as passionate, at its best the band could conjure some glorious pop-rock such as "Twisterella". Ride often sounds like the aural equivalent of waves crashing over the listener's head, particularly so on "In a Different Place" and "Vapour Trail".

214 Neutral Milk Hotel

Athens, Georgia's Neutral Milk Hotel was at the core of America's indie pop explosion in the mid '90s. While their 1996 debut, On Avery Island, received some great reviews and was praised by fans of folk-and-pop-informed rock, it is Neutral Milk Hotel's second album, In the Aeroplane Over the Sea, that has become canonized in the past decade. Over 11 songs, singer-songwriter Jeff Mangum offers vivid glimpses into his thoughts, without ever giving too much away. Glorious single "Holland, 1945" refers to the life of Anne Frank without being obvious. Best heard in its entirety from beginning to end, In the Aeroplane… is a prime argument against the random culture of the iPod generation.

NEUTRAL MILK HOTEL FACTFILE:

Start up year: 1989

Disband year: 1998

Home town: Ruston, Louisiana via Athens, Georgia, U.S.A.

Members: Jeff Mangum, Julian Koster, Scott Spillane, Jeremy Barnes

What you should check out/why: In the Aeroplane Over the Sea is the masterpiece, but On Avery Island has "Song Against Sex."

Worth looking out for: Scott Spillane's other band, The Gerbils.

RIDE FACTFILE:

Start up year: 1988

Disband year: 1996

Home town: Oxford, England

Members: Andy Bell, Mark Gardener, Loz Colbert, Steve Queralt

What you should check out/why: Songs like "In A Different Place" and "Vapour Trail" make Nowhere a hazy, dream-like delight.

Worth looking out for: The "Leave Them All Behind" EP.

215 Red Kross

Brothers Steve and Jeff McDonald started Redd Kross, which was initially spelled Red Cross, when they were respectively in junior high and high school. Although there was a period of inactivity during the 2000's, punctuated by a side project called Ze Malibu Kids featuring both brothers, Redd Kross has existed since 1978. Growing up in Hawthorne, California, the McDonalds started out playing punk rock with titles like "Linda Blair", but eventually their love for the music of the '60s and '70s overtook them and they started playing ultra-catchy songs with big hooks and guitar solos. Redd Kross had its biggest success with 1993's Phaseshifter and the single "Jimmy's Fantasy".

216 The Creation

History has vindicated The Creation. This North London band sprang up in the late'60s with a brace of singles that should have been chart toppers, but never managed to make much of an impression with the kids of the day. However, with various Mod revivals, the emergence of Brit-pop, and some decent CD collections, The Creation found a new generation of fans rabid to hear the psychedelic "How Does It Feel to Feel?" and the jagged guitar of "Making Time". Guitar player Eddie Phillips was among the most innovative of the day, implementing distortion and preceding Jimmy Page in playing his guitar with a bow.

217 The Seeds

Sky Saxon, who passed away in 2009 on the verge of a North American tour, was the voice of one of the '60s rawest, sexiest and heaviest garage bands, the Seeds. First single "Pushin' Too Hard" is prototypical punk, galloping along at break-neck speed with a fuzzy guitar solo accenting Saxon's menacing vocals. Follow-up single "Can't Seem to Make You Mine" finds the Seeds at their slinkiest, with Saxon imploring his lost love to "come back" over Jan Savage's punctuating guitar twang. Toward the end of the decade, the Seeds veered toward a more psychedelic sound, but it never found an audience outside of a few hardcore devotees.

218 Devo

Based on the concept that society is de-evolving, Devo, headed by Jerry Casale and Mark Mothersbaugh, released their first album Q: Are We Not Men? A: We Are Devo in 1982. Using synthesizers to create a cold, processed sound, the Brian Eno produced debut introduced listeners to the band's jerky theme song "Jocko Homo", but it was 1980's Freedom of Choice that provided middle America with a glimpse of the flower-pot-hat-wearing Devo via the video for "Whip It", a song that looks at issues of domination in daily life. Together into the 1990's, Devo recorded the single "Watch Us Work It" in 2007.

219 Bauhaus

Considering the fact that chart toppers in 1979 included the Village People's "Y.M.C.A.", it is both fitting and surprising that Daniel Ash, David J, Peter Murphy and Kevin Haskins, a.k.a. Bauhaus, released the creepy epic "Bela Lugosi's Dead" the same year. Although it didn't make a dent in the charts, it nevertheless made Goths everywhere almost crack a smile. Bauhaus's first album In the Flat Field made the British charts and secured their popularity with the title song and "Stigmata Martyr". Bauhaus broke up in 1983, but reunited in 1998 and recorded Go Away White a decade later.

220 The Breeders

Initially meant as a side-project for the Pixies' Kim Deal and Throwing Muses' Tanya Donnelly, the Breeders only kept Donnelly for one album (1990s Pod) and one E.P. (1992's Safari) before heading off to form Belly. Left to her own devices, Deal recruited sister Kelley and set about writing Last Splash, an album that would spawn one of the era's biggest songs, "Cannonball". That song has a bass line so hooky that it has become a common sample in hip hop and still gets people on the dance floor. After years of breaking up and making up the Breeders released their fourth album, Mountain Battles, in 2008.

221 Hole

Hole only released three albums between 1991 and 2002, but nevertheless left an indelible mark on modern rock that has weathered the increasingly bizarre, incoherent public persona of front-woman Courtney Love. Love and guitarist Eric Erlandson formed the band in 1989 and released the noisy Pretty on the Inside in 1991. Their legacy would rest on 1994's Live Through This however, which welded the frayed, aggressive sound of their previous record with more conventional pop structures, allowing Love's vocals to alternate between mumbled drawl and throaty scream. Hole followed Live Through This with 1998's Celebrity Skin, trading noise and aggression for a slick modern rock sound. Despite continued success, Hole broke up in 2002, though rumors of a reunion remain evergreen. (See picture opposite)

HOLE FACTFILE:

Start up year: 1989

Disband year: 2002

Home town: Los Angeles, U.S.A.

Members: Courtney Love, Eric Erlandson, Patty Schemel, Kristen Pfaff, Melissa Auf der Mar, more

What you should check out/why: Live Through This is the record Love has never lived up to and songs like "Doll Parts" and "Miss World" still sound as vulnerable and angry as they did in 1994.

Worth looking out for: A young Courtney Love in Alex Cox's Straight to Hell.

222 Dave Clark Five

Bucking the trend in naming a band after the singer, drummer Dave Clark was the bandleader who led his Five to the top of the charts time and again. “Over and Over”, “Do You Love Me” and “Bits and Pieces” all worked in the DC5’s favor, making them teen idols on both sides of the Atlantic. With singer Mike Smith’s soulful voice and Clark’s heavy, almost tribal drumming, creating the backbone of the band’s sound, they made a simple pop song like “Glad All Over” into something unique. Unfortunately a failed attempt at engaging the psychedelic generation caused the Dave Clark Five’s break-up in 1970.

223 The Ventures

Tacoma, Washington’s Ventures are the most successful instrumental combo of all time, having sold over 100 million records worldwide. Scoring major hits in the ‘60s with “Walk Don’t Run” and “Hawaii Five-O”, they went on to inspire an endless list of teenagers to pick up the guitar. Grouping their melodic effect-laden guitar twang in loosely themed albums based around concepts like ‘colors’ and ‘space’, almost 40 albums saw the charts. After the band’s popularity began to wane in the U.S., they found legions of new fans abroad, especially in Japan, for whom they recorded exclusive albums and filled concert halls.

224 Del Shannon

As popular in Britain as he was at home in the U.S., Michigan native Del Shannon’s falsetto singing voice on hits like “Runaway”, “Hats Off to Larry” and “Little Town Flirt” made him an enduring figure from the early‘60s. When keyboard player Max Crook added his homemade invention the Musitron to create a piercing, high-pitched sound as the foreground instrument on “Runaway”, Shannon created a lonely sound of desperation even within the confines of a three-minute rock ‘n’ roll song. Shannon continued making records into the ‘80s and Tom Petty produced Drop Down and Get Me. Shannon committed suicide in 1990.

225 Afghan Whigs

Perhaps too idiosyncratic to have shared the success of early '90s contemporaries like Nirvana and Pearl Jam, the Afghan Whigs nonetheless gathered a significant popular and critical following through a dense grunge sound spliced with soul-derived rhythm and dynamic vocals. When Greg Dulli, Rick McCollum, John Curley and Steve Earle formed the band in 1986 they looked to post-punk stalwarts The Replacements and Hüsker Dü, but by the time they released their major label debut, Gentlemen, the Whigs had begun to temper the aggression with a more melodic yearning, appropriate to Dulli's dark, anguished lyrics. The Afghan Whigs officially split in 2001, but reunited briefly in 2006.

226 Spaceman 3

Sticking to their motto "Taking drugs to make music to take drugs to", Spacemen 3 and their minimalist drone helped influence an entire generation of reverb-obsessed shoegazers. Meeting in Art College in Rugby, Warwickshire, Jason Pierce (a.k.a., J. Spaceman) and Peter Kember (a.k.a., Sonic Boom), who were both born on November 19, 1965, were the core members in a band with a revolving door of supporting players. Taking their cue from bands like The Velvet Underground and the 13th Floor Elevators, the men from space incorporated long, single chord meditations, blues-influenced dirges, and feedback-drenched lullabies about themes as diverse as Jesus Christ and recreational drugs.

227 Screaming Trees

Emerging from Tacoma, Washington in the early-'90s, Screaming Trees were automatically part of the grunge scene, if judged by location alone. Early records on taste-making indie labels Sub Pop and SST gave Mark Lanegan and crew indie credibility and enough of a buzz so that they became the first band on the scene to sign with a major label like Epic Records. Although the majority of Screaming Trees' music is more rock 'n' roll than the sludge-rock that is closer to grunge, the band's biggest hit "Nearly Lost You" from the soundtrack to the movie Singles fits the Seattle sound pretty well. They disbanded in 2000.

228 The Verve

Making gentle waves in the early '90s with their lustrous, swirling debut, A Storm in Heaven, Wigan, England's version of the Verve gained much of their American audience while playing the second stage of the Lollapalooza festival. Following the release of their second album A Northern Soul singer Richard Ashcroft broke up the band, only to have them reunite a year or two later with Urban Hymns, an album that delivered the band more popularity—and more legal headaches—than they ever imagined. The moody single "Bittersweet Symphony" was a worldwide success, but the band was disappointed by their losing all rights to the song due to the inclusion of an unauthorized sample of the Rolling Stones' "The Last Time".

229 Coldplay

Coldplay emerged from the tail-end of Brit-pop in 2000 to become one of the most successful bands of the 21st century. "Yellow", the breakout single from their debut album Parachutes exemplifies the light-touch pop that has earned the band such popularity for their melodic hooks, broad production, emotive lyrics, and most notably singer Chris Martin's soaring falsetto. Martin, along with Jon Buckland, Will Champion and Guy Berryman found continued success with follow-up albums that tweaked their signature sound with electronics, denser soundscapes, and darker lyrics, but never moving too far from mainstream pop. Coldplay has also been active politically and philanthropically by donating 10% of their profits to charity.

230 The Damned

As part of Stiff Records' roster of ramshackle, verging on comical, punk artists, the Damned were poster boys for the label's aesthetic. Early singles "Smash It Up" and "New Rose" had a tough sound that was ideal for pogo dancing and shouting along, but had lyrics that seemed to be making fun of the scene that embraced them. This is especially true of "Smash It Up". Following Captain Sensible's departure, Dave Vanian took the band down more gothy roads on songs like "Grimly Fiendish" which once again seemed to be more of a jibe at a genre than an anthem for the movement. (See picture opposite)

"Somewhere in the world Alan McGee is having a heart attack. He said we'd never make it."
- Chris Martin

SAVAGE

231 Husker Du

Trio Husker Du was central to the Minneapolis music scene that spawned the Replacements and Prince. Throughout the '80s, Bob Mould, Grant Hart and Greg Norton forged a sound that mixed pop with a tougher punk sound as on "New Day Rising". Early in the band's career they released a punchy cover of the theme from the Mary Tyler Moore Show. Steadily growing their audience with albums like Candy Apple Gray and Warehouse Songs and Stories, Husker Du made a lasting impression on a generation of young punks. Hart's composition "Could You Be the One?" got some alternative radio play and is arguably the band's catchiest song. (See picture opposite)

HUSKER DU FACTFILE:

Start up year: 1979

Disband year: 1987

Home town: Minneapolis, Minnesota, U.S.A.

Members: Bob Mould, Grant Hart, Greg Norton

What you should check out/why: New Day Rising is punchy, sweet and includes the sublime, "The Girl Who Lives on Heaven Hill", while Warehouse: Songs and Stories includes their biggest hit, "Could You Be the One."

Worth looking out for: The use of "Don't Want to Know if You Are Lonely" in the movie Adventureland.

232 The Hold Steady

The Hold Steady formed in Brooklyn in 2003, and early on displayed an affinity for precise biting lyrics and a broad rock sound that proudly wears the influence of Bruce Springsteen and Hüsker Dü. Band members Craig Finn, Galen Polivka, Tad Kubler, and Judd Counsell released their debut album Almost Killed Me in 2004 and earned instant critical acclaim. Accolades followed subsequent albums Separation Sunday and Boys and Girls in America, and the band added drummer Bobby Drake and multi-instrumentalist Franz Nicolay to its line-up. Though Finn's lyrics are often caustic and dark, his talk-sing vocal delivery and the grand character of the backing guitars and keyboard are decidedly upbeat.

233 Psychedelic Furs

In 1981 singer Richard Butler along with bass playing brother Tim and guitar player John Ashton released their second record Talk Talk Talk, a record that established them as a vital part of the artier side of new wave. Featuring "Pretty in Pink" in a rawer, more engaging form than the re-recorded version that appeared in the John Hughes movie of the same name, Talk Talk Talk was literate pop-rock made unique by Richard Butler's raspy voice. But it was 1984's Mirror Moves that propelled them to their greatest success via singles "Heaven" and "The Ghost in You".

234 Wilco

Jeff Tweedy formed Wilco in 1994 after previous band Uncle Tupelo imploded. Two 1996 releases, A.M. and Being There picked up where Uncle Tupelo left off with alternative country-rock favorites "Passenger Side" and "Outta Sight (Outta Mind)" coming from that era. While becoming a popular touring band, Wilco hit its most fertile period creatively at the end of the 20th century with Summerteeth and Yankee Hotel Foxtrot, records that saw founder Jeff Tweedy find his creative equal in multi-instrumentalist Jay Bennett. Following Bennett's departure and eventual death Wilco released A Ghost is Born, Sky Blue Sky and Wilco (The Album) to mixed reviews.

235 Paul Revere and The Raiders

With a name like Paul Revere Dick it was only natural that stardom would find the keyboard player and his young Raiders. Dressed in Revolutionary War garb and blessed with the powerful and charismatic vocals of front man Mark Lindsay, Paul Revere and The Raiders shared the charts with British invasion heavyweights such as the Beatles, the Stones and the Animals. Making their way into the homes of Americans as the house band on Dick Clark's Where the Action Is, they had exposure that most of their contemporaries could only dream of attaining. This provided a forum for hits like "Kicks" and "Hungry".

236 Van Morrison

With a reputation as one of music's most curmudgeonly characters, Van Morrison stands among the most influential songwriters in music, as well as an excellent example of never sticking to the script of what people expect him to be. Starting out as the singer of blues-inspired rock 'n' rollers Them, Belfast, Ireland's Morrison's solo career includes two jazz-inspired gems, the dreamy Astral Weeks and the poppier Moondance, and the soulful His Band and Street Choir. Continuing to tour and record, Morrison's best known song is "Brown-Eyed Girl", a bittersweet depiction of a lost love that has become a misinterpreted karaoke favorite due to its catchy chorus.

237 The Feelies

If the original Modern Lovers had recorded a follow-up to their debut album it might have sounded something like The Feelies' Crazy Rhythms. All nervous energy and herky-jerky rhythms, Crazy Rhythms and its single "Fa-Ce-La" didn't sell well when it was released in 1980 but in subsequent years it has influenced everyone from Yo La Tengo to R.E.M. While the band's recording history is sporadic at best, with founding member Bill Million leaving town without so much as a goodbye at one point, The Feelies briefly reunited for some live dates in 2008.

238 The Stray Cats

Single-handedly reviving a mainstream interest in rockabilly music, the Stray Cats were a unique voice in the synth-pop and hard rock that dominated early'80s radio. The bare-bones trio of drummer Slim Jim Phantom, stand-up bassist Lee Rocker and singer/guitar slinger Brian Setzer managed to sound modern even while remaining true to the roots of rock 'n' roll. Songs like "Stray Cat Strut" and "Sexy and 17" are as rooted in the '50s as the band members' pompadours and tattoos. Although Stray Cats and Built for Speed maintained them throughout the '80s the Stray Cats broke up in 1984. Numerous reunions have followed.

239 The Distillers

Previously married to Tim Armstrong, Distillers singer/guitar player Brody Dalle gave the Rancid front man a run for his money in the raspy vocals department. Releasing their first two albums The Distillers and Sing Sing Death House on Epitaph Records, the band was doing well in punk rock circles before the song "Seneca Falls" was used in a video game and became the band's unofficial anthem. Band members were constantly shifting before third album and major label debut Coral Fang was released in 2003. Dalle, who disbanded The Distillers in 2006, has a new band, Spinnerette. (See picture opposite)

240 Girlschool

Rarely given their due, England's Girlschool, formed by bassist Enid Williams and guitar player Kim McAuliffe, is one of the era's best hard rock bands regardless of gender. Endorsed by Mötörhead, Girlschool had a U.K. hit with their debut, Demolition and its single "Emergency", but the record was not released in the U.S. where they never attained the success they had at home. They also recorded the St. Valentine's Day Massacre E.P. with Mötörhead and had a hit with a cover of Johnny Kidd & The Pirates' "Please Don't Touch". Continuing to record throughout the '80s and '90s, Girlschool continues to play shows when the mood strikes.

241 The Raconteurs

Although the White Stripes are one of the busiest bands of the 2000s Jack White doesn't seem to be able to sit still, forming not one but two side-projects, the other being Dead Weather with Kills singer Alison Mosshart. The Raconteurs finds White getting hooking up with long-time Detroit pals Jack Lawrence and Patrick Keeler, both of the Greenhornes, and Brendan Benson to make some music that is less restricting than his day job. Their 2006 debut Broken Boy Soldiers kicked off with single "Steady As She Goes", a scorcher of a song that highlights White's yelping vocals. The Raconteurs released their second record Consolers of the Lonely in 2008. (See picture opposite)

RACONTEURS FACTFILE:

Start up year: 2005

Disband year: N/A

Home town: Detroit, Michigan, U.S.A.

Members: Jack White, Brendan Benson, Jack Lawrence, Patrick Keeler

What you should check out/why: Broken Boy Soldiers for "Steady As She Goes", for which there's also an incredibly fun video.

Worth looking out for: Brendan Benson's solo records, especially Lapalco.

242 Faust

The experimental art-rock group Faust formed in Wumme, Germany in 1971. Though critical acclaim and being one of the first acts to sign with Richard Branson's Virgin Records did not translate into high record sales, Faust's journeys into ambient, industrial and psychedelic rock proved to have a lasting effect in popular music. Their influence can be heard in the multi-platinum recordings of Radiohead and in the work of Super Furry Animals and Stereolab. Faust have re-formed and toured in various incarnations since their initial break-up in 1975. They now exist simultaneously as two separate representations of the same legacy. (See picture below)

243 The Shadows

Starting out as Cliff Richard & The Shadows, this iconic British group dominated the charts in the '50s and '60s with songs like "Living Doll" and "Summer Holiday". While Richard, who would later pursue a solo career, was the face of the band, guitar player Hank Marvin and bassist Jet Harris were slowly becoming the most influential musicians in early British rock 'n' roll. In 1960, the Shadows had a string of instrumental hits, including "Apache" and "Kon Tiki". Although the Shadows broke up in 1968 they have reformed on numerous occasions. Legend has it that Marvin was the first person in Britain to own a Fender Stratocaster.

A good-looking guy, Lemonheads' stalwart Evan Dando was saddled with the 'alterna-hunk' crown in the early '90s and in spite of building a reputation with rough-around-the edges albums Lick and Creator, he was taken less seriously, even as masterwork It's A Shame About Ray became a hit. An introspective and bittersweet collection of ballads and rockers, Ray contained many songs that were written by Australians Nic Dalton (Godstar) and Tom Morgan (Smudge), but Dando made them his own. Dando's subsequent career has been scattershot, with occasional flashes of genius to remind listeners of what he can produce. He released a covers album, Varshons, in 2009.

THE SHADOWS FACTFILE:

Start up year: 1960

Disband year: 1990

Home town: Chesthunt, Hertfordshire, England

Members: Hank Marvin, Terry Smart, Norman Mitham, Ian Samwell, Ken Pavey, Tony Meehan, more

What you should check out/why: The Shadows was the band's first post-Cliff Richard album and lets Hank Marvin's guitar work shine on songs like "Sleepwalk."

THE LEMONHEADS FACTFILE:

Start up year: 1986

Disband year: N/A

Home town: Boston, U.S.A.

Members: Evan Dando, John P. Strohm, David Ryan, Murph, Nic Dalton, Jesse Peretz, Ben Deily, more

What you should check out/why: It's A Shame About Ray includes altern-pop sweetness like "My Drug Buddy" and "Allison's Starting to Happen".

Worth looking out for: Former bass play Nic Dalton's band, Godstar.

245 Gang of Four

Informing their sometimes-groovy post-punk with political theory, Gang of Four, made up of Dave Allen, Hugo Burnham, Andrew Gill and Jon King, are widely considered to be one of the most important bands of the late'70s and early'80s. Debut album Entertainment spawned an underground hit with the off-kilter "At Home He's a Tourist". By the time they released 1982's Solid Gold they had become funky enough to have a club hit with "I Love a Man in a Uniform" which still maintained the band's sense of humor as well as some disgust. After a couple of partial reunions all four original members toured in 2005.

246 Wire

In the tradition of bands who met in art school, Wire used this background to create something different from the simple rock 'n' roll that sprang up around them in the form of punk. Formed in 1976, Wire's first single "12XU" was indicative of the energy of debut record Pink Flag. Out of print for years following its release, Pink Flag was highly sought-after and it remains a critical milestone. Equally important is 1989's Chairs Missing, a cleaner more sophisticated affair highlighted by "The 15th", a song that's as minimalist as it is memorable. Although the band has ebbed and waned as a working outfit, they released Object 47 in 2008.

247 Phish

In its '80s incarnation Phish was Trey Anastasio (guitar/vocals), Jon Fishman (drums), Jeff Holdsworth (guitar) and Mike Gordon (drums), though this line up would change and be augmented over the years. Finding a built-in fan base in the Deadhead community, Phish's jazzy jams and extended solos were custom-made to help fans get over Jerry Garcia's death. Although Phish had existed for years at this point it wasn't until their fifth album Hoist that they gained mainstream attention. Their making of a video for the song "Down With Disease" certainly paid off. Although Phish had continual success throughout their career, in 2004 they announced it was all over.

248 The Jesus Lizard

Fronted by energetic, aggressive and confrontational singer David Yow, Chicago's The Jesus Lizard is legendary for its live shows that often found Yow stripped down and immersed in the audience. Although albums Goat, Head and Liar all found an audience, it was a split-single with Nirvana, "Puss" on the Jesus Lizard side and "Oh the Guilt" on Nirvana's, which made the general public aware of them. From 1989 to 1996, The Jesus Lizard was signed with influential indie label Touch & Go but in 1996 they jumped ship to Capitol for two records before breaking up.

249 The Offspring

Frequently lumped in with punk-revivalists like Green Day and Rancid, the Offspring share less in common with those bands than with Metallica and Nirvana, perhaps their most direct point of reference. Dexter Holland, Kevin "Noodles" Wasserman, Greg Kriesel and Ron Welty formed the band in 1984 but 1994's Smash brought the band's chugging guitars and quiet verse/loud chorus song structure to mainstream radio. Singles "Self Esteem" and "Come Out and Play" helped the Offspring achieve unprecedented success for an independent act. The Offspring later signed with Columbia and hit again with Americana's "Pretty Fly (For A White Guy)" and "Why Don't You Get a Job", which showcased the band's sense of humor.

250 NOFX

Though certainly part of the punk revival of the early '90s, NOFX had been playing and recording in various incarnations for a decade before mainstream attention turned to the high-energy, attitude-heavy sounds coming from California. Unlike many of their genre brethren however, "Fat" Mike Burkett, Eric Melvin, Erik Sandin and Aaron "El Hefe" Abeyta have long resisted the pull of major labels and MTV exposure, earning a wide audience through steady touring and recording. Breakneck drumming, sneering vocals, and sarcastic lyrical jabs at American politics and the recording industry characterize most NOFX recordings, borrowing equally from hardcore and ska-influenced punk.

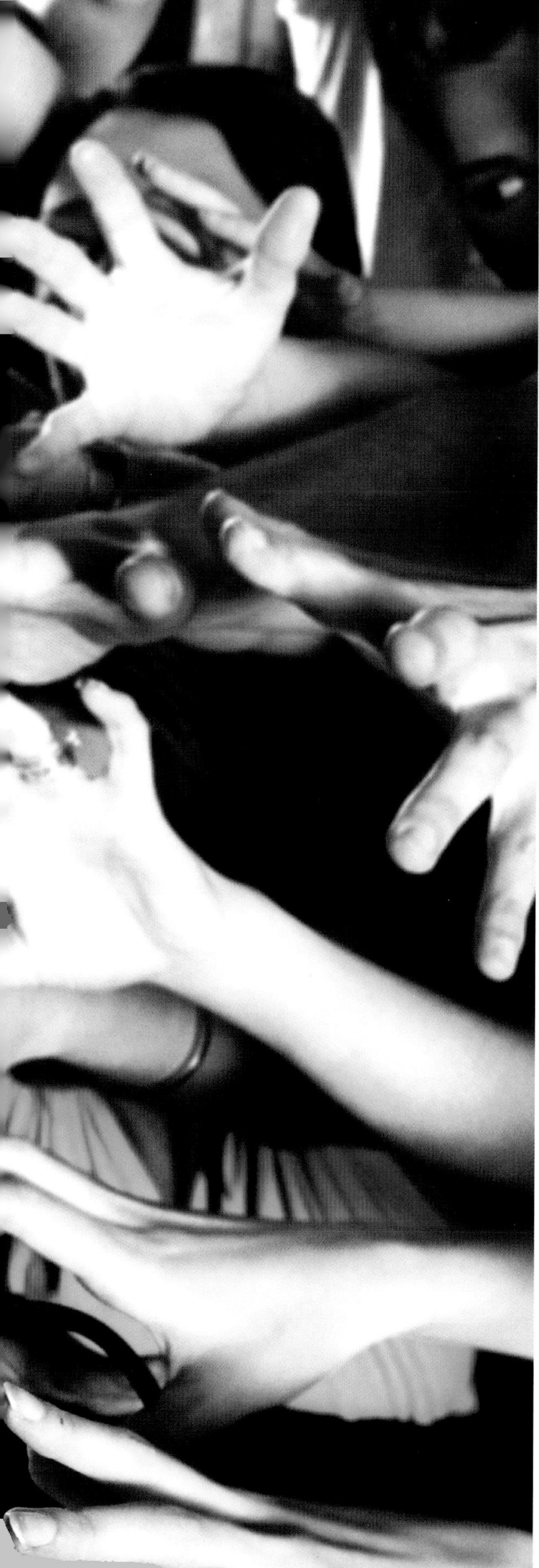

251 The Sonics

More popular now than they were as youths, the garage-rocker Sonics made a lasting impression with "The Witch", "Psycho", "Strychnine" (which was later covered by the Cramps) and "Boss Hoss", all of which featured Andy Parypa's dirty guitar sound. But what really made the Tacoma, Washington band stand apart from other bands of the day was singer Gerrie Roslie's voice, which was always soulful, but was also capable of letting out blood-curdling screams. Although they broke up in the early '70s, the Sonics reunited in 2008 and put on a live show that's more rock 'n' roll than bands half their age. (See picture opposite)

"Although their chief period of success was coincident with the release of Gibson's first fuzzbox, The Sonics' fuzzy sound was their own creation." - Sonics fanpage

THE SONICS FACTFILE:

Start up year: 1960

Disband year: 1968 (They are currently reunited)

Home town: Tacoma, Washington, U.S.A.

Members: Gerrie Roslie, Andy and Larry Parypa, Rob Lind, Bob Bennett,

What you should check out/why: Debut Here are the Sonics is packed with hits like "The Witch," "Strychnine" and "Psycho."

Worth looking out for: The Sonics reunion shows prove how gracefully the band has aged.

252 Supergrass

While Oasis and Blur were busy trying to be the quintessential English band of the '90s, Oxford's Supergrass in many ways topped them both. Snotty, brash and teenage, Supergrass's debut I Should Coco is still remarkable for its energy and spirit. A trio consisting of Gaz Coombes (voice/guitar), Danny Goffey (drums) and Mickey Quinn (bass), Supergrass had their first hit with "Caught By the Fuzz", a cheeky ode to youthful bad behavior. Supergrass surprised people with the sober second album In it for the Money, although it shows the group's songwriting growth. Over the years, Supergrass continued having hits including "Pumping On Your Stereo", "Moving" and "Grace".

252 Bad Religion

Formed in 1980 by Greg Graffin, Jay Bentley, Brett Gurewitz and Jay Ziskrout, Bad Religion remains an influential Southern California punk band, not to mention one the most enduring, now pushing the 30-year mark. With fourteen albums to their credit, it was the mid'90s one-two punch of Recipe for Hate and Stranger Than Fiction that really grabbed fans. Known for their interesting lyrics and tight harmonies, Bad Religion is not your average punk band. Gurewitz's devotion to punk rock can also be seen in Epitaph Records, the label he created in 1981.

253 Green Day

From 1989 to 1993 Billie Joe Armstrong, Tré Cool and Mike Dirnt were the jewels in the crown for San Francisco pop-punk label Lookout! Records. But it took a jump to Reprise and the release of 1994's Dookie to turn Green Day from a successful punk band to the mega-stars they are today. Lead single "Longview" was ubiquitous, with Armstrong's nasal voice opening "Sometimes I give myself the creeps". When a band seemingly comes out of nowhere to become the biggest thing in the world, success is often fleeting. Not so for Green Day, who regained their hold on the charts with American Idiot (2004) and again in 2009 with 21st Century Breakdown.

255 Os Mutantes

People outside of the genre's culture of origin often make great music. To whit, Brazil's Os Mutantes took British and American psychedelia and infused it with traditional sounds and melodies and made some forward-thinking rock that is unfettered by dated production techniques. Os Mutantes began as Arnaldo Baptista, Sergio Dias Baptista and Rita Lee. Relatively unknown during the '60s and '70s, in time word of the band spread to music fans worldwide and the fuzzy guitar tones of "A Minha Menina" made it a cult favorite. Taking an entirely different tone all together, the oft-covered "Baby" is a sweetly sexy number that highlights singer Lee's inviting voice.

256 Wolf Parade

Although Montreal quartet Wolf Parade's two main songwriters, keyboard player Spencer Krug and guitar player Dan Boeckner, also have bands of their own (Krug's is Sunset Rubdown, Boeckner's is Handsome Furs) and have two very distinct sounds, Wolf Parade has a cohesive sound that developed over debut Apologies to the Queen Mary and 2007's At Mount Zoomer. Initially inspired and produced by Modest Mouse's Isaac Brock, Wolf Parade took matters into their own hands for Mount Zoomer, with songs like "Call it a Ritual" maintaining their status as critical darlings, not to mention a hit with indie rock fans.

257 Guided By Voices

Dayton, Ohio's Guided by Voices' only constant is singer Robert Pollard, who is arguably the hardest working living man in showbiz. Although popular, Guided By Voices never reached stadium status, but that never stopped Pollard from working high kicks and microphone twirls like an indie rock Roger Daltrey. With a career as a school teacher already behind him by the time GBV made a significant splash with the albums Bee Thousand and Alien Lanes, Pollard's abstract yet vivid lyrics belie his facility with words. Although Pollard rarely stuck with the same band from one album to the next, he retired the name in 2004.

258 Sloan

Part of Halifax, Canada's early'90s music explosion, Sloan is one of the sole survivors of the scene that included Jale, Thrush Hermit and Hardship Post. Plagued by label issues, Sloan resurrected their own label Murderrecords in 2006 for Never Hear the End of It, which was released on Yep Roc outside of Canada. Becoming Canadian hit-makers with first single "Underwhelmed", it was "Coax Me" from beloved second album Twice Removed that secured their reputation. Continuing their success with songs like "The Good in Everyone", "The Lines You Amend" and "Money City Maniacs", Sloan's latest is Parallel Play.

259 The Go-Go's

The first all-female band as opposed to singing group to top the Billboard charts, the Go-Go's started in L.A.'s punk scene, but soon became international pop stars. Although their frothy image suggested they were a label creation, the Go-Go's were their own women, masterminding a string of hits including "We Got the Beat", "Vacation" and "Our Lips Are Sealed", which was co-written by the Specials' Terry Hall and Go-Go's guitar player Jane Wiedlin. Fronted by singer Belinda Carlisle, the Go-Go's also featured Wiedlin, keyboard player Charlotte Caffey, who was the songwriter behind many of the band's hits, drummer Gina Schock and bassist Kathy Valentine. They released God Bless the Go-Go's in 2001.

260 The Minutemen

Comprised of singer/guitar player D. Boon, bassist Mike Watt and drummer George Hurley, the Minutemen played a jazz-infused punk and fiercely stuck the Do It Yourself credo. Renowned for their independent spirit, the Minutemen are featured in a documentary called We Jam Econo that shows the band's penchant for touring and recording on the cheap. Constant touring engaged a devout following that gobbled up records like Double Nickel on the Dime. Watt and Boon were school friends and learned their instruments together, later spending years touring America. When Boon was killed in a car accident in 1985, it seemed like Watt would never play music again. To this day, everything Watt does is dedicated to his friend and bandmate.

261 The Shins

James Mercer, Jesse Sandoval, Marty Crandall, and Neal Langford formed the Shins from the remnants of their previous band Flake in 1999. A few regionally popular singles led Sub Pop to sign the band and release Oh, Inverted World in 2001, which is a showcase for singer and lead songwriter Mercer's high calling vocals and playful lyrics and the band's polished pop sound which would become shorthand for indie rock in the early 21st century. The band received a bump in notoriety thanks to a name-check in the 2004 film Garden State and released follow-up albums Chutes Too Narrow and Wincing the Night Away to an ever-broadening audience. (See picture opposite)

"I can sympathize with how seeing that jock in high school that you hated wearing your favorite band's shirt, I can see how that would tick you off." -James Mercer

THE SHINS FACTFILE:

Start up year: 1997

Disband year: N/A

Home town: Albuquerque, New Mexico, U.S.A.

Members: James Mercer, Neal Langford, Jesse Sandoval, Marty Crandall, Dave Hernandez

What you should check out/why: Chutes Too Narrow for "Fighting in a Sack" and "Pink Bullets".

262 TV on the Radio

Though often categorized as indie rock or even post-rock, TV On the Radio has long defied genre conventions by employing loops, samples, Tunde Adebimpe's expressive vocals, doo-wop harmonies, and hip-hop beats all mixed together. Adebimpe formed the band with David Andrew Sitek in 2002, and was joined later by Kyp Malone. Following a few critically successful EPs and a self-released debut the band broke through with 2004's Desperate Youth, Blood Thirsty Babes, which won that year's Shortlist Music Prize. Since then TV On the Radio has released two more albums, Return to Cookie Mountain and Dear Science, and collaborated with David Bowie and members of Blonde Redhead and Yeah Yeah Yeahs.

263 The Meat Puppets

The Meat Puppets emerged from hardcore punk in 1984 after releasing an EP and a self-titled full-length on SST records with a sound equal parts rock, country, bluegrass and psychedelia and forming part of the foundation for the grunge sound. Brothers Curt and Cris Kirkwood joined drummer Derrick Bostrom in 1980 and released nine albums including the classic Meat Puppets II before splitting in 1996. The Meat Puppets earned a brief mainstream spotlight when Kurt Cobain invited them to perform on the Nirvana's "MTV Unplugged" special, and a single from their eighth album Too High to Die, "Backwater", became a minor radio hit. Curt Kirkwood reformed the band without Bostrom or his brother in 1999 and reunited with Cris in 2006.

264 The Raspberries

Coming out of the unlikely city of Cleveland, Ohio, the Raspberries were the quintessential power-pop band. Led by singer Eric Carmen, who would go on to significant solo success with songs like "All By Myself", the Raspberries shared a similar aesthetic to England's Badfinger, alternating a chunky pop-rock sound with soft and pretty numbers. A string of hits including "Go All the Way", "I Wanna Be With You" and "Come Around and See Me" inspired '90s bands like Jellyfish and Redd Kross. The Raspberries third album, Side 3, tried to entice listeners with die-cut packaging that looks like a carton of raspberries, but the album does not hold up to its predecessors.

265 Refused

Prior to forming (International) Noise Conspiracy, singer Dennis Lyxzén was a member of Swedish anarcho-punk band Refused, one of the most intensely exciting punk groups of the '90s. Over a seven-year period Refused released five albums, culminating in The Shape of Punk to Come. Released in 1998 The Shape… included the closest thing Refused had to a hit with "New Noise", a song that combined screaming vocals and harsh guitars with jazzy bass lines and melodic passages in a way that makes the listener feel invigorated and not overwhelmed as one might think.

266 Yeah Yeah Yeahs

Part of the New York garage rock revivalists of the early 2000's, the Yeah Yeah Yeahs have one of the most unique sounds in the genre, freely mixing energetic art punk with electronics and, most notably, singer Karen O's Chrissie Hynde-like vocal strut. Each of the Yeah Yeah Yeahs' three full-length albums, Fever to Tell, Show Your Bones, and It's Blitz, have earned significant popular and critical acclaim, with early single "Maps" remaining one of the most haunting songs of the modern age. Guitar player Nick Zinner moonlights as a photographer.

267 Violent Femmes

Gord Gano, Brian Ritchie and Victor DeLorenzo comprised Wisconsin's Violent Femmes. Together for almost 30 years, the Violent Femmes had their most significant commercial and critical success with their first album, Violent Femmes. With a stripped down sound featuring acoustic guitar and limited drums backing Gano's neurotic whine, songs like "Add It Up" and "Blister in the Sun" became a hit with university students and other fans of twitchy rock 'n' roll. Although they had minor success with covers of T-Rex's "Children of the Revolution" and a radical reworking of Culture Club's "Do You Really Want to Hurt Me", the Femmes never achieved the perfection with which they began their careers.

268 L7

Named after a slang term for a square or uncool person, Los Angeles' L7, made up of Suzi Gardner, Donita Sparks, Jennifer Finch and Dee Plakas, got together in the '80s, though they had their greatest commercial success in the '90s. While second album Smell the Magic got some college radio play in the U.S., it was 1992's Bricks are Heavy that really hit the mark. At the time when radio was embracing the 'grunge' sound even though few of the bands involved really sounded alike, L7 struck gold with "Pretend We're Dead" and "Wargasm", a couple of sludgy, fuzz-soaked hits that remain two of the toughest songs by women to hit the charts.

269 Superchunk

Without Superchunk independent music in the U.S. would be nowhere. While the Chapel Hill, North Carolina band has never attained significant commercial success, they're beloved by music critics and other bands, inspiring a new generation to form bands. Singer Mac McCaughan and bass player Laura Ballance also head Merge Records whose catalog includes Arcade Fire, Magnetic Fields, the Rosebuds and others. Although McCaughan's high-pitched vocals and heartfelt lyrics seem to be the impetus for emo bands everywhere, Superchunk's own music is less maudlin and more rocking than what it inspired. Classic songs include "Driveway to Driveway" and "Seed Toss".

270 No Doubt

No Doubt had been playing sunny buoyant ska-punk for almost ten years before their 1995 album Tragic Kingdom and particularly the singles "Just A Girl" and "Don't Speak" brought them to mainstream attention. Gwen Stefani started the band with her brother Eric and John Spence, whose suicide rocked the lineup. By the release of Tragic Kingdom Eric Stefani had left and Tony Kanal, Adrian Young, and Tom Dumount joined. No Doubt's follow-up album, 2000's Return to Saturn, showcased a sound that dropped some of their more overt ska inclinations in favor of hip-hop and new wave. This direction continued in 2002's Rock Steady and in Stefani's solo recordings. (See picture opposite)

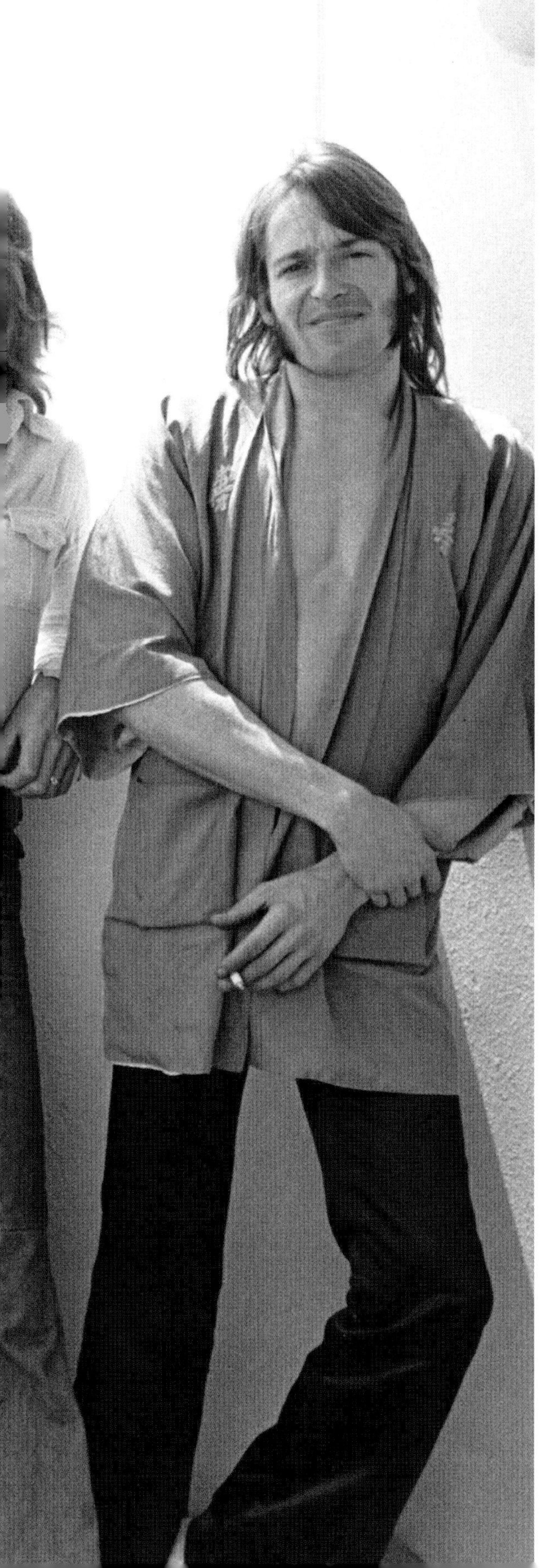

271 Bad Company

An early '70s supergroup composed of former members of King Crimson, Mott the Hoople and Free, perennial classic rockers Bad Company are known for their longevity and a bunch of hits, including "Feel Like Making Love," "Rock 'N' Roll Fantasy," and "Can't Get Enough", the latter of which showcases their hard-edged blues-rock style. Founding members Paul Rodgers, Mick Ralphs and Simon Kirke remain with the band today, though Rodgers left the band in 1982 and didn't rejoin until 1998. Original bassist Boz Burrell died in 2006 and was replaced by Lynn Sorensen in the band's current touring lineup. (See picture opposite)

BAD COMPANY FACTFILE:

Start up year: 1973

Disband year: N/A

Home town: England

Members: Paul Rodgers, Mick Ralphs, Simon Kirke, Boz Burrell, Lynn Sorensen, Robert Hart, more

What you should check out/why: The debut features the blues-rocker, "Can't Get Enough."

272 Steppenwolf

Native American John Kay was the leather pants wearing singer of '60s rock outfit Steppenwolf. Best known for their anthem of rebellion "Born to Be Wild" which was used in the film Easy Rider, Steppenwolf also had a hit with "Magic Carpet Ride". "Born to Be Wild" has suffered the fate of being over-played, especially in movies that use it pretty much any time a character dons a pair of sunglasses or gets on a motorcycle. Nonetheless, "Magic Carpet Ride" stands tall as a hard-rocking fist-pumping song despite the stigma of showing up in too many bad comedies and commercials.

273 Ian Dury and the Blockheads

More a storyteller than a singer, Ian Dury has a distinct voice that is instantly recognizable in songs like "Sex & Drugs & Rock & Roll", "Hit Me with Your Rhythm Stick" and "My Old Man". Ian was backed by the Blockheads, a band that was a little bit funk, a little bit rock 'n' roll. In many ways, Dury, who passed away in 2000, sang about archetypal fish 'n' chips England while embracing the multiculturalism of the present. Among his best songs is "Reasons to Be Cheerful (Part 3)", a list song that cites Buddy Holly, goats, singing along with Smokey Robinson and yellow socks as just a few of those reasons.

274 Napalm Death

Known as the godfathers of grindcore, Napalm Death is an institution that has served as a finishing school of sorts for some of the most notable bands in extreme music. With a lineage that has included members of Carcass, Cathedral, Godflesh, Scorn, Unseen Terror and more, Napalm Death is a self-contained musical movement. Inspired by acts like Discharge, The Ex and Crass, Napalm Death takes their punk politics and love for fast and raw music to its limits with undecipherable growling vocals, buzzing de-tuned guitars, and lighting fast blast-beat drums. Though they have undergone numerous personnel changes the power of the music and the intelligence behind their message, remains unchanged. (See picture opposite)

motörhead

275 Acid Mothers Temple

Less a band than a collective of like-minded musicians who collaborate on various projects, the many incarnations of Japan's Acid Mothers Temple have been exploring psychedelic rock, free jazz, noise-drenched soundscapes, and other experimental forms since 1995. The collective's flagship group Acid Mothers Temple & the Melting Paraiso U.F.O. is composed of leader/guitarist Kawabata Makoto, drummer Shimura Koji, bassist Tsuyama Atsushi and guitarist Higashi Hiroshi, but Kawabata and Tsuyama participate in most of the other ensembles as well. The Melting Paraiso U.F.O. and Cosmic Inferno offshoots are the most prolific, often releasing several recordings in a single year.

276 Swervedriver

London's Swervedriver brought a harder rock edge to the short-lived shoegaze movement, eschewing the dreamy ambience favored by My Bloody Valentine and Slowdive for Sonic Youth-inspired noise. Only Adam Frankline and Jimmy Hastridge stayed with the band through all its incarnations from the drive of early EPs Son of Mustang Ford and Sandblasted and full-length debut Raise to the more relaxed Mezcal Head, which was their most successful album. Swervedriver released one more album with Creation Records, Ejector Seat Reservation, and then moved to Geffen for their final album 99th Dream. After a decade of inactivity Swervedriver reunited in 2008 at the Coachella Music and Arts Festival.

277 The Strokes

When The Strokes' The Modern Age started making the rounds in 1998 it was difficult not to be charmed by singer Julian Casablanca's laconic vocals and the band's rough-and-tumble garage rock sound. When their album Is This It? came out, songs from the E.P. had been re-recorded with all the edge removed, but the album, from start to finish, remained a fine rock 'n' roll record, with "Last Nite" and "Barely Legal" being stand-outs. The momentum was lost due to a lag between the first and second albums, although they did continue to receive good reviews.

278 The Box Tops

Singer/guitarist Alex Chilton, lead guitarist Gary Talley, and bassist Bill Cunningham comprised the core of Memphis blue-eyed soul group The Box Tops through its four-year career and spawning hits like "Cry like a Baby" and "The Letter". The latter topped the Billboard charts when they were all still teenagers. Much of that success is due to Chilton's preternaturally soulful vocals and the band's easy pop sound. Despite early success, the band chaffed at the micromanagement of their songwriters and producers and dissolved in 1970. Everyone went on to further careers, including Chilton in next band Big Star, and various line-ups of the group reunited off and on from 1989 through the present.

279 The Amboy Dukes

Before he became better known for advocating bow hunting than for being a musician, Detroit, Michigan's Ted Nugent (a.k.a., The Motor City Madman) brought his guitar-playing wizardry to the Amboy Dukes. Moving to Chicago with his family in 1964, Nugent started the Amboy Dukes a couple of years later and saw numerous members walk through the door throughout the band's duration. Best known for the psychedelic hit "Journey to the Centre of Your Mind", today Nugent claims the song is about self-knowledge and has nothing to do with hallucinogens. In 1976, after a series of disappointments, Nugent went solo, becoming one of the busiest live artists of the '70s and '80s.

280 Anthrax

Of the early speed-metal pioneers, only Metallica and Megadeth enjoyed more commercial success that New York's Anthrax. Forgoing the Satanic imagery and doom and gloom trappings of their contemporaries, they delivered their tales of comic villains with a healthy dose of humor. Always open-minded, Anthrax was one of the first metal bands to experiment with hip-hop and collaborated with Public Enemy on a reworking of their classic "Bring The Noise". Anthrax also looked outside of the comfort zone of heavy metal for their inspired cover of Joe Jackson's "Got The Time".

BUTT
BLAC
FLAG
POLICE
STORY
MAKE
ME COME
FAGGOT!

281 Black Flag

One of the most influential American bands of the '70s and '80s, if not all of modern rock, Black Flag helped define hardcore punk and provided a home, SST Records, for likeminded bands with an independent streak and DIY attitude. Guitarist Greg Ginn started Black Flag in 1977 with singer Keith Morris, bassist Chuck Dukowski and drummer Brian Migdol, though the lineup would fluctuate over the years. 1980's Damaged, Black Flag's first full-length record, features the band's signature heavy-bass, call and response vocals, and wry social commentary. Notable alumnus Henry Rollins took over vocal chores in 1981 and brought a serious, activist sensibility and spoken-word approach to subsequent recordings. (See picture opposite)

BLACK FLAG FACTFILE:

Start up year: 1977

Disband year: 1986

Home town: Los Angeles, U.S.A.

Members: Greg Ginn, Henry Rollins, Keith Morris, Chuck Dukowski, Brian Migdol, Chavo Pederast, Robo, Dez Cadena, more

What you should check out/why: Damaged includes Black Flag classics like "Rise Above" and "TV Party"; it's a touchstone of Californian hardcore.

Worth looking out for: The advertisements Henry Rollins did for The Gap in the '90s.

282 Archers of Loaf

While singer Eric Bachmann has made a post-Archers of Loaf career out of solid stripped-down singer/songwriter material, he led the Archers through some noisy and unusual indie rock throughout the '90s. Debut album Icky Mettle gained them instant fame, albeit on a small scale, with the song "Web in Front" making it onto a generation's mix tapes and dance-party play lists. Punk enough to be enjoyed by hardcore fans, but melodic and accessible enough to be embraced by the same people that like early R.E.M., Yo La Tengo and Pavement, Archers of Loaf remain one of the strongest bands of that era. (See picture opposite)

283 Bad Brains

Bad Brains were anomalies in the Washington, D.C. punk scene of the '70s and '80s. In the first place, they were African-American. Secondly, they had jazz and reggae tendencies. Thirdly, and to the band's detriment, following most of the band's conversion to Rastafarianism in the '80s, they were known more for making homophobic statements than for the music they made, although some members have since distanced themselves from those remarks. Despite the controversy surrounding the band, Bad Brains, Rock For Light and I Against I all stand as excellent examples of reggae-tinged punk, with debut single, "Pay to Cum" being one of the best and fastest songs of the time.

ARCHERS OF LOAF FACTFILE:

Start up year: 1991

Disband year: 1998

Home town: Chapel Hill, U.S.A.

Members: Eric Bachmann, Mark Price, Matt Gentling, Eric Johnson

What you should check out/why: Icky Mettle for the glorious "Web in Front".

Worth looking out for: Bachmann's solo records as Crooked Fingers.

BAD BRAINS FACTFILE:

Start up year: 1979

Disband year: 1995

Home town: Washington, D.C., U.S.A.

Members: H.R., Dr. Know, Darryl Jenifer, Earl Hudson, more

What you should check out/why: The self-titled debut is fast, furious and occasional reggae-infused.

284 Faith No More

San Francisco's Faith No More successfully fused the unlikely combination of heavy metal, hardcore punk, funk, and hip-hop to produce one of the signature hard rock sounds of the '80s. Chuck Mosley, Jim Martin, Billy Gould, Roddy Bottum, and Mike Bordin, the first stable lineup, recorded We Care A Lot in 1985 to moderate success. The title track demonstrates the heavy groove and social consciousness that came to define Faith No More, this success was continued with the release of the band's third album The Real Thing and its breakthrough single "Epic." Faith No More recorded until their 1998 break-up, but recently reunited for a European tour. (See picture opposite)

285 The Hives

Sweden's The Hives are known not only for their music, which is a brash, driving rock sound similar to fellow garage rock revivalists the Strokes, but also their flamboyant live performances, which incorporate exaggeratedly boastful chatter, matching black and white outfits, and inventive stage names. The singles "Hate to Say I Told You So" and "Main Offender" from their 2000 breakthrough album Veni Vidi Vicious brought the band an international audience, though they had recorded and performed together since 1995. Subsequent full-length albums Tyrannosaurus Hives and The Black and White Album demonstrate expanded instrumentation while maintaining a focus on energy and tongue-in-cheek humor.

286 Polvo

Polvo were more tuneful than their '90s noise-rock contemporaries like Slint and Chavez, but nonetheless shared an affinity for cryptic lyrics, shifting time signatures, and density, effectively leading the musical movement known as math-rock. Ash Bowie, Dave Brylawski, Steve Popson, and Eddie Watkins formed the band as students at the University of North Carolina, and released two albums each on Merge and Touch and Go Records. The latter two demonstrate a growing interest in non-Western tunings and instruments. Polvo broke up in 1997 but reformed and resigned with Merge in 2009.

287 Suicidal Tendencies

Venice, California natives Suicidal Tendencies began as a hardcore band with a devoted following of local skaters. A self-titled album contained the underground hit "Institutionalized", a song that received regular airplay on MTV and was featured in cult film Repo Man, solidified the band's reputation. Suicidal Tendencies started to take a more metal direction on future releases. Along with D.R.I. and Corrosion of Conformity, Suicidal Tendencies are credited with being the fathers of crossover metal which is a fusion of hardcore punk and heavy metal. As the only constant member, vocalist Mike Muir keeps the Suicidal Tendencies name alive.

POLVO FACTFILE:

Start up year: 1990

Disband year: 1997 (Reunited in 2009)

Home town: Chapel Hill, North Carolina, U.S.A.

Members: Ash Bowie, Dave Brylawski, Steve Popson, Eddie Watkins

What you should check out/why: Today's Active Lifestyles for the unbelievable layers of songs like "Time Isn't on My Side" and "Tilebreaker."

Worth looking out for: Reunion shows.

SUICIDAL TENDENCIES FACTFILE:

Start up year: 1982

Disband year: 1994

Home town: Venice, California, U.S.A.

Members: Mike Muir, Grant Estes, Louiche Mayorga, Amery Smith, more

What you should check out/why: The self-titled debut for the archetypal skate punk song, "Institutionalized."

288 Voivod

Voivod was one of the most interesting bands to emerge from the thrash movement of the 1980s. They incorporated progressive rock influences and developed lyrical themes based around science fiction and technology. After releasing the classic albums War and Pain and Dimension Hatröss, their commercial peak came in the form of major label debut Nothingface, which contained an inspired cover of Pink Floyd's "Astronomy Domine". In 2005 guitarist Denis "Piggy" d'Amour lost a battle with colon cancer but left behind a surplus of guitar parts with the hope that Voivod would continue. The band released Katorz in 2006, utilizing the riffs and some help from former Metallica bassist Jason Newstead. (See picture opposite)

289 Them

With a number of skiffle, R&B and blues bands already under his belt, a young Van Morrison joined the band that became Them in the mid'60s. Always iconoclastic, Morrison shied away from becoming a pop star, even as the band had hits with the blues song "Baby Please Don't Go" and the snarling hiccup of "Here Comes the Night". B-side "Gloria" also garnered Them some success and has been covered by a number of artists including Patti Smith. Them only lasted a couple of years, breaking up after a tour of America that took a heavy toll on the band.

VOIVOD FACTFILE:

Start up year: 1984

Disband year: N/A

Home town: Jonquière, Quebec, Canada

Members: Denis "Piggy" d'Amour, Denis "Snake" Belanger, Michel "Away" Langevin, Jean-Yves "Blacky" Theriault, Jason Newsted

What you should check out/why: Nothingface includes a cover of Pink Floyd's "Astronomy Domine" and other songs that explore metal's progressive side.

THEM FACTFILE:

Start up year: 1963

Disband year: 1971 (Van Morrison left in 1966)

Home town: Belfast, Northern Ireland

Members: Van Morrison, Pete Bardens, Alan Henderson, Jim Parker, John Starks, more

What you should check out/why: Them has "Gloria" and "Mystic Eyes", but the compilation, The Story of Them Featuring Van Morrison also includes "Because the Night" and "Baby Please Don't Go."

290

Queensryche

Though they sometimes get lumped in with the pop hair-metal that dominated the '80s hard rock scene, Queensryche's roots were artier and firmly planted in progressive rock. Albums like The Warning and Rage for Order helped to put the band on the map but it was their 1988 concept album Operation: Mindcrime, featuring orchestral arrangements from renowned composer Michael Kamen, which cemented their status as a hard rock contenders. Follow-up Empire was the band's commercial peak thanks to the runaway success of their Pink Floyd-style ballad "Silent Lucidity". In 2009 Queensryche released Operation: Mindcrime II, a follow-up to their breakthrough classic. (See picture opposite)

QUEENSRYCHE FACTFILE:

Start up year: 1981

Disband year: N/A

Home town: Bellevue, Washington, U.S.A.

Members: Scott Rockenfield, Chris DeGarmo, Eddie Jackson, Geoff Tate, Michael Wilton

What you should check out/why: Empire features "Silent Lucidity", Queensryche's most popular song.

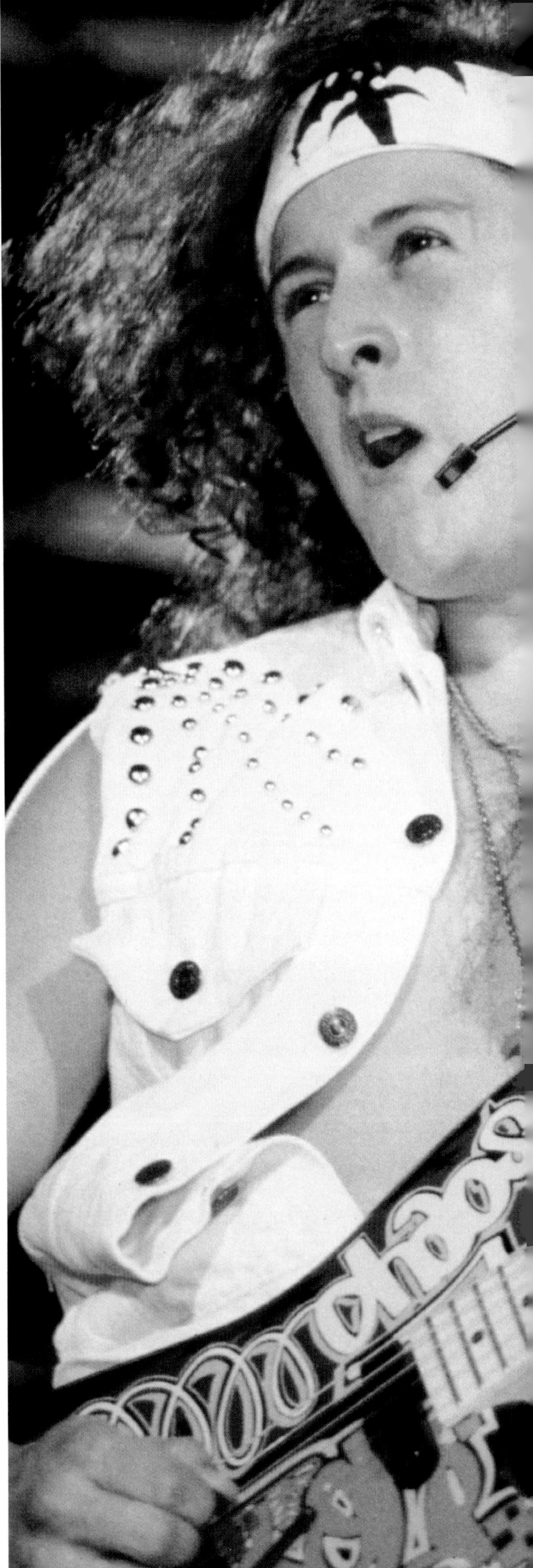

291 Dokken

The history of rock 'n' roll is rich with singer/guitar player teams like Mick Jagger and Keith Richards or David Lee Roth and Eddie Van Halen. Similarly, the driving force behind '80s rockers Dokken was vocalist and namesake Don Dokken and shred-god George Lynch. Though their roots date back to the late '70s it was not until 1983 that debut album Break The Chains was released. MTV took a shine to the photogenic Dokken and featured their videos in regular rotation. Visibility increased when they provided the title track for the third installment of the Nightmare On Elm Street series, Dream Warriors . (See pictue opposite)

DOKKEN FACTFILE:

Start up year: 1978

Disband year: N/A

Home town: Los Angeles, U.S.A.

Members: Don Dokken, George Lynch, Mick Brown, Jeff Pilson, more

What you should check out/why: Tooth and Nail includes "Just Got Lucky", which has a place in the hearts of many metal fans.

292 Johnny Burnette

Best known for his recording of Richard Sherman's "You're Sixteen", Johnny Burnette enjoyed some success as a rockabilly guitarist and singer with the Rock 'N' Roll Trio before turning to romantic pop as a solo artist. Burnette formed the Trio in Memphis, Tennessee in 1956 with older brother Dorsey on bass and Paul Burlison on electric guitar. Despite their blistering blues approach, evident on recordings of "Tear It Up" and "The Train Kept A Rollin'", and their proximity to the Sun Records scene, the Rock 'N' Roll Trio never charted, though they are revered today. Johnny spent six years as a solo artist, recording for various labels and starting his own before he drowned in a fishing accident at age 30.

293 The Hellacopters

Sweden's Hellacopters disbanded in 2008 following a 14-year career that kept fans busy with the sheer volume of singles and albums the band released. Despite having made albums with the esteemed indie labels Man's Ruin and Sub Pop, the Hellacopters released their masterpiece By the Grace of God on Universal, causing some long-time fans to abandon them for selling out. However, song-for-song, this album is packed with real rock 'n' roll, showcasing singer Nicke Andersson's songwriting prowess on songs like "Carry Me Home" and "All New Low". Andersson has also spent time as the drummer for death metal band Entombed. (See picture opposite)

JOHNNY BURNETTE FACTFILE:

Born: 1934

Died: 1964

Home town: Memphis, U.S.A.

Members: Johnny Burnette

What you should check out/why: Train Kept A-Rollin' – Memphis to Hollywood: The Complete Recordings 1955-1964 compilation to hear rockabilly at its rawest, and the booklet is an added bonus.

Worth looking out for: His recordings with the Rock 'n' Roll Trio.

THE HELLACOPTERS FACTFILE:

Start up year: 1994

Disband year: 2008

Home town: Stockholm, Sweden

Members: Nicke Andersson, Robert Dahlqvist, Kenny Håkansson, Robert Eriksson, Anders Lindström

What you should check out/why: By the Grace of God is pure rock 'n' roll pleasure, especially "It's Good But It Just Ain't Right" and the title song.

294 Porcupine Tree

It is easy to focus on Porcupine Tree's indebtedness to psychedelic and progressive rock, and to Pink Floyd in particular, but to do so ignores the influence of krautrock, Brian Eno, and Mastodon on the band's ever-evolving sound. Though "Porcupine Tree" was initially just a joke between friends about a fictional '70s progressive rock band, Steve Wilson's mock recordings gained a following and he began recording in earnest, eventually adding Richard Barbieri, Colin Edwin and Gavin Harrison for a full-band lineup. Layered, melodic, and heavy on atmosphere, Porcupine Tree albums often develop a concept or theme, ranging from paranoia and social disorders to the Bret Easton Ellis novel, Lunar Park.

295 Judas Priest

In the early '80s Judas Priest was at the forefront of heavy metal. The band's macho biker image framed the band's powerful music, making Priest the band to beat on albums like British Steel and Screaming For Vengeance. Backed by K.K. Downing and Ian Hill with a series of drummers, singer Rob Halford's alternately gruff and soaring vocals brought a level of rarely heard drama to songs like "You've Got Another Thing Coming" and "Living After Midnight". When interest in heavy metal hit a lull during the late'90s Priest went on hiatus. In 2009 Judas Priest went on tour performing British Steel in its entirety.

296 Scorpions

Around since 1969, the Scorpions have the distinction of being the most popular rock band to come out of Germany. Led by singer/guitar player Rudolf Schenker, and still going today, the Scorpions are best known for the 1984 gargantuan hit "Rock You Like A Hurricane" from the album Love at First Sting, although its predecessor "No One Like You" from 1982's Blackout did not do too badly either. On the cusp of a fickle music scene rendering hard rock unfashionable for a time, the Scorpions managed to squeeze in one more hit with 1990's power ballad "Winds of Change".

297 Opeth

Sweden's Mikael Åkerfeldt is for all intents and purposes Opeth. Various bandmates have come and gone but for close to 20 years Åkerfeldt has been incorporating folk, blues and other genres into the death metal that forms the basis of Opeth. While his musical variations alone are enough to set Opeth apart from its death metal brethren, that Åkerfeldt also sometimes sings clean, as opposed to the growling technique that inhabits the genre, is testament to his faith in the open-mindedness of the audience. Opeth's first release outside of Sweden was My Arms, Your Hearse, giving the band a solid international following.

298 White Zombie

Rob Zombie had a career in art, most notably as set designer on Pee-Wee's Playhouse, prior to forming White Zombie. This highly attuned sense of design and style helped form White Zombie's image. With its insistent chugging riff, "Thunder Kiss '65", from the album La Sexorcisto: Devil Music Vol. 1, became an unlikely dance floor hit. They followed that up with the same album's "Black Sunshine" and maintained momentum with "More Human Than a Human" from Astro-Creep: 2000. Rob Zombie went on to success as a solo artist and as a horror filmmaker (The Devil's Rejects).

299 Widespread Panic

Like fellow jam bands Phish and Gov't Mule, Widespread Panic has gathered a dedicated following through rigorous touring, a network of bootleg tape distributors, and a string of ten studio albums over its twenty-plus year career. John Bell, Michael Houser, Dave Schools, Todd Nance, and Domingo S. Ortiz first performed as Widespread Panic at a charity concert in Athens, Georgia in 1986, solidifying not only the initial line-up of the band but beginning of a trend of charity and fundraising performances that continues to the present. Guitarist Houser died in 2002, but the band continues to develop its blues-rock sound with new guitarist Jimmy Herring.

300 Primus

Though Primus front-man Les Claypool describes his band as "psychedelic polka" the band's iconic bass-heavy approach is more like funk stripped of the rhythm. Heavily influenced by Frank Zappa, Claypool formed Primus in the mid'80s with guitarist Todd Huth and drummer Jay Lane, both of whom left by 1989 and were replaced by Larry LaLonde and Tim Alexander. Known for their technical skill and offbeat humor, Primus's popularity grew with their first studio album Frizzle Fry and peaked with their fifth album Tales From the Punch Bowl, gaining some mainstream success with Sailing the Seas of Cheese. Primus went on hiatus in 2001 but reformed two years later. (See picture opposite)

"Well, it's better than digging a ditch is one of the good things about it. I would've never thought that you would have to do it 24 hours a day." - Larry "Ler" LaLonde

GUMP
Another
ANDY GU

solda

301 Gov't Mule

Guitarist Warren Haynes and bassist Allen Woody formed Gov't Mule in 1994 as an outlet for their small combo blues-jam ambitions when their other band, the reformed Allman Brothers, was not touring or recording. The side-project became a full-time band with the addition of drummer Matt Abts and the release of their eponymous debut album in 1995. Gov't Mule performances and recordings regularly feature guest musicians, and following Woody's death in 2000 bassists of all stripes filled in on several recording sessions and concerts to pay tribute. In 2003 bassist Andy Hess and keyboardist Danny Louis joined the band, which continues to tour and record. (See picture opposite)

GOV'T MULE FACTFILE:

Start up year: 1994

Disband year: N/A

Home town: U.S.A.

Members: Warren Haynes, Allen Woody, Matt Abts, Andy Hess

What you should check out/why: Live at Roseland Ballroom is the band at its live best.

TyCo
TROPHIES FOR LO
MISSIS
NIGH
THE MUSIC CLUB IN

302 Accept

While break-out German music of the '70s tended to be experimental in nature (Kraftwerk, Can), in the '80s things took a definite turn for the metal, and Soligen's own Accept was at the top of the heap. Singer Udo Dirkschneider had a wail that could wake the dead and used it on their biggest international hit "Balls to the Wall", taken from the album of the same name. Interestingly, although the band's sound and appearance is exceptionally macho, most of the lyrics on this and a number of future albums were co-written by the band's manager, a woman named Gaby Hauke.

303 Black Rebel Motorcycle Club

Peter Hayes, formerly of the Brian Jonestown Massacre, formed Black Rebel Motorcycle Club with Robert Turner and Nick Jago in 1998. Taking influence from the Jesus and Mary Chain and Hayes' previous band, B.R.M.C. offered hazy, noise-drenched variant rock on their self-titled debut album and its follow-up, Take Them On, On Your Own. 2005's Howl marked a change from the previous albums, emphasizing blues and Americana, though with a distinctly dark tone. Jago left the band shortly before the sessions that produced Howl and was replaced by Leah Shapiro of the Raveonettes. B.R.M.C. returned to a grittier sound with their fourth full-length album Baby 81 in 2007. (See picture opposite)

ACCEPT FACTFILE:

Start up year: 1978

Disband year: N/A (Without Udo Dirkschneider)

Home town: Soligen, Germany

Members: Udo Dirkschneider, Wolf Hoffman, Frank Friedrich, Peter Baltes, Jorg Fischer, Stefan Kaufmann, more

What you should check out/why: Balls to the Wall includes the infamous title track and eye-catching cover art.

BMRC FACTFILE:

Start up year: 1998

Disband year: N/A

Home town: San Francisco, U.S.A.

Members: Peter Hayes, Robert Turner, Nick Jago,

What you should check out/why: Take Them On, On Your Own is a confident second album that gets off to a great start with "Stop."

304 Marillion

From 1979 to the present day Marillion has carried the torch for progressive rock and has a worldwide legion of fans to show for it. Taking their name from the J.R.R. Tolkien short story collection The Marillion, one-named singer Fish and the band released three albums before finding mainstream success with the song "Kayleigh" from 1983's Misplaced Childhood. Although Fish left the band shortly after that, Marillion continues to sell millions of records worldwide, with 2007's Somewhere Else cracking the U.K. Top Thirty and being their first album to do so in a decade.

305 The Equals

Best known for the single "Baby Come Back" and for launching future Electric Avenuer Eddy Grant's career, the Equals made lively, energetic music that mixed rock, pop and soul with a bit of reggae thrown in. A still teenage Grant formed the Equals with twin brothers Lincoln and Dervin Gordon, Pat Lloyd and John Hall. Some of them were white and some were black, prompting the band's name. Although songs like "Hold Me Closer" and "Christine" tread a similar funk-pop territory to "Baby Come Back", they failed to stir much consumer interest at the time, making the Equals another band that has been left for time to vindicate.

MARILLION FACTFILE:

Start up year: 1979

Disband year: N/A

Home town: Aylesbury, England

Members: Steve Rothery, Brian Jelliman, Doug Irvine, Mick Pointer, Fish, more

What you should check out/why: "Kayleigh" from Misplaced Childhood was this long-standing band's lone chart hit.

THE EQUALS FACTFILE:

Start up year: 1965

Disband year: Eddy Grant left the band in 1971

Home town: London, England

Members: Lincoln and Dervin Gordon, Pat Lloyd, John Hall, Eddy Grant

What you should check out/why: Black Skin Blue Eyed Boys: The Anthology compiles 50 songs spanning The Equals' career, including the brilliant "Police on My Back".

Worth looking out for: Eddy Grant's solo work.

306 Anvil

Toronto, Canada's speed-metal pioneers Anvil never got the attention afforded to British bands that were part of the New Wave of British Heavy Metal scene, though over the course of making three albums, Hard 'n' Heavy, Metal on Metal and Forged in Fire, in the early'80s, Anvil were contenders, with audiences drawn to singer Steve "Lips" Kudlow's on-stage antics and the band's powerful musicianship. In a story now immortalized in the documentary Anvil! The Story of Anvil, poor management and band timing served to stop the band's progress in its tracks. Ever persistent, the band is currently working on a new album.

307 Eagles of Death Metal

Josh Homme and Jesse Hughes began recording as the Eagles of Death Metal in 1998, at the same time Homme was kick-starting Queens of the Stone Age, as a means of exploring a classic rock sound that owes less to either of their obvious namesakes Eagles and death metal, and more to the Rolling Stones and Guns N' Roses. Their debut album Peace, Love, Death Metal featured the single "I Only Want You" which demonstrates the gruff rock and swagger that has become the band's trademark. High-profile tours, collaborations and two subsequent recordings have further raised the band's profile.

"You shouldn't just be a band, ... If you've got the time and you've got the space you've got to make something of it. We might balls the whole thing up but you've got to try!" - Josh Homme

308 Dragonforce

English power metal band Dragonforce is as inspired by genre-brethren Manowar and Stratovarious as by the video games of their youths, the sounds and effects of which frequently accentuate the band's rapid guitar onslaught, propulsive drumming and hyperbolic lyrics that describe epic quests and the value of camaraderie in the face of adversity. ZP Theatrt, Steve Scott, Sam Totman, Herman Li, Didier Almouzni, and Steve Williams formed the band in London in 1999 and released their first studio album Valley of the Damned. Dragonforce won a Grammy for Best Metal Performance for their 2008 album Ultra Beatdown.

309 Minor Threat

Minor Threat's deceptively brief career, which included only one album and a handful of EPs and singles from 1980 to 1983, belies their influence on hardcore punk. Ian MacKaye, Jeff Nelson, Brian Baker, and Lyle Preslar comprised the initial line-up but were joined by Steve Hansgen before the recording of their only LP Out of Step. Characterized by a blistered guitar sound and breakneck tempos that condensed an entire song's worth of musical and lyrical ideas into only a few minutes or even seconds, Minor Threat's first two EPs gained a dedicated following and inspired the straight-edge movement, an affiliation MacKaye has since downplayed. Confusion about the band's direction led to its break up in 1983.

DRAGONFORCE FACTFILE:

Start up year: 1999

Disband year: N/A

Home town: London, England

Members: Steve Scott, ZP Theart, Sam Totman, Herman Li, Didier Almouzni, Steve Williams, Vadim Pruzhanov, Adrian Lambert, more

What you should check out/why: Ultra Beatdown for the sheer virtuosity of "Inside the Winter Storm."

MINOR THREAT FACTFILE:

Start up year: 1980

Disband year: 1983

Home town: Washington, D.C., U.S.A.

Members: Ian MacKaye, Jeff Nelson, Brian Baker, Lyle Preslar, Steve Hansgen

What you should check out/why: Out of Step is their only album.

Worth looking out for: The "Minor Threat" EP includes the song that defined the movement: "Straight Edge."

310 Cradle of Filth

Suffolk, England's black metal band Cradle of Filth creates a division within the scene's fans. Some adore singer Dani Filth's over-the-top theatrics and high-pitched vocals while others deride their heavily produced sound as being too commercial and denounce Cradle of Filth as pretenders. Whichever side of the fence you are on, there's no denying that Cradle of Filth have people talking. Formed in 1991, Filth's 1997 Dusk and Her Embrace pushed them into the mainstream and made the band's T-shirts a necessity for young metal fans. Cradle of Filth released Devil's Thunder in 2008. (See picture opposite)

"You tend to get rather bored with people or bands not making an effort to look less than ordinary, so we just try and be a little flamboyant, it's just the way we like; we're into this kinda thing."
- Dani Filth

CRADLE OF FILTH FACTFILE:

Start up year: 1991

Disband year: N/A

Home town: Suffolk, England

Members: Dani Filth, Paul Ryan, Benjamin Ryan, John Richard, Darren, Paul Allender, more

What you should check out/why: Dusk and Her Embrace is theatrical, somewhat cartoonish black metal that gets witty with songs like "Malice Through the Looking Glass."

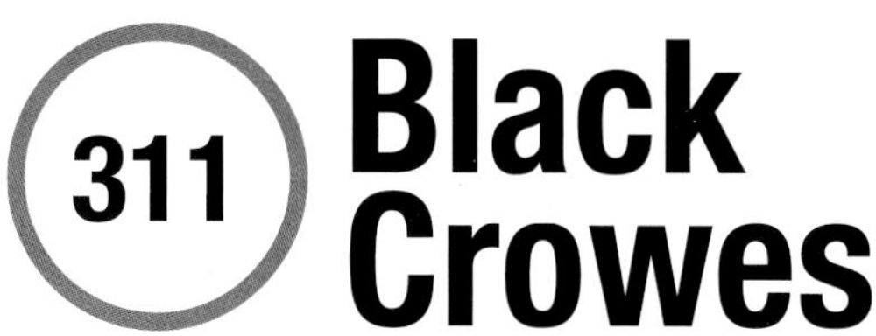

311 Black Crowes

Based on singer Chris Robinson's soul-inflected voice and his brother Rich's guitar playing, the Black Crowes made a name for themselves with 1990's Shake Your Moneymaker. That album included a hit cover of Otis Redding's "Hard to Handle", as well as "Twice as Hard", turning them into stars immediately. Follow-up album Amorica had more attention paid to its controversial cover-art than to the album's music. On 2001's Lions the Crowes channeled "Rocks Off" era Rolling Stones for "Lickin". The Black Crowes continue to tour and released Warpaint Live in 2009. (See picture opposite)

"But now we're the Black Crowes and I don't think we owe anything to anyone. We made it all on our own. I really used to hate it when we got compared to other bands all the time, but now I think it's quite all right." -Steve Gorman

BLACK CROWES FACTFILE:

Start up year:

Disband year: N/A

Home town: Athens, Georgia, U.S.A.

Members: Chris and Rich Robinson, Johnny Colt, Steve Gorman, Jeff Cease, more

What you should check out/why: Shake Your Money Maker is a fine '60s throwback, with "She Talks to Angels" keeping the ladies happy.

Worth looking out for: "Lickin'" on Lions.

312 In Flames

Together for almost 20 years, Sweden's In Flames takes the black metal genre to a more melodic place than most, which was singer Jesper Strömblad's intention when he formed the band. In the early years, In Flames was essentially a solo project for Strömblad, with him picking up band members as they were needed. But the band has remained unified since 1997, with Björn Gelotte, Anders Fridén, Peter Iwers and Daniel Svensson completing the line-up. Following a flurry of activity in the '00s, In Flames' most recent release was 2008's Sense of Purpose.

313 Liars

Liars defy all attempts at categorization, refusing a niche or trademark sound in favor of continued experimentation. Cal Arts students Angus Andrew and Aaron Hemphill joined Pat Noecker and Rob Albertson in 2001 and released Liars' first album They Threw Us All in a Trench and Stuck a Monument On Top. The straight-ahead dance/punk sound of that record all but disappeared when Julian Gross replaced Noecker and Albertson. Their follow-up album They Were Wrong, So We Drowned replaced the full-band assault with a minimal, nervy, metallic sound likened to Public Image Ltd. and Suicide. Subsequent releases demonstrate continued interest in non-linear structures, often recombining musical styles within a single song.

314 Dropkick Murphys

Many bands come to be identified with a region or city, but the Dropkick Murphys take their affiliation with south Boston to the extreme. Formed in 1994 by Mike McColgan, Rick Barton, Ken Casey, and Matt Kelly, the band members tapped their Irish roots and fused heavy, guitar-driven punk and shout-along choruses with traditional Celtic instruments, eventually growing to a seven-piece band with full-time mandolin and bag pipe players Tim Brennan and Scruffy Wallace. "I'm Shipping Up to Boston" from their 2005 album Warrior's Code, which exemplifies the band's Celtic punk sound, gained national attention when it was featured in the 2006 film The Departed.

315 Comets on Fire

Aggressive, extended noise jams and gut-churning low-end characterize most of Comets On Fire's four albums, beginning with their 2001 self-titled debut. And though Ethan Miller, Ben Flashman, Ben Chasny, Utrillo Kushner and Noel von Harmonson use feedback and distortion generously, even including von Harmonson's Echoplex as a full-time instrument, their songs are rarely unstructured or amorphous. Comets On Fire found a wider audience with 2004's Blue Cathedral on Sub Pop, and opening dates for Sonic Youth, Dinosaur Jr. and other discordant bands.

316 Jimmy Eat World

Jimmy Eat World grew from its roots as a mid '90s Arizona punk band to one of the standard-bearers of the new emo style of the late '90s, along with the Promise Ring and the Get Up Kids. Jim Adkins, Tom Linton, Rick Burch, and Zach Lind perfected the clear guitar sound, tight harmonies, and introspective and at times anguished lyrics that defined the genre on their break-through album, 1999's Clarity. Following label strife and extensive touring, Jimmy Eat World released their self-titled fourth album in 2001. Singles "Bleed American" and "The Middle" exemplify the shift to a straight-forward power pop less beholden to emo conventions.

317 Babes in Toyland

Discordant, powerful, and dark, Babes In Toyland occupied the more aggressive niche of grunge. Kat Bjelland, Lori Barbero, and Michelle Leon comprised the core line-up until Leon left and was replaced by Maureen Herrman. Spanking Machine, their 1990 debut album, showcases Bjelland's alternately coy and abrasive vocals and Barbero's heavy, thumping drums. Lee Renaldo of Sonic Youth produced their first major label release Fontanelle in 1992. It was followed three years later by the band's final album Nemesisters. Bjelland and Barbero reunited with new bassist Jesse Farmer for a one-off performance in 2001.

"Usually, old ladies tell me to find Jesus. Look, I'm just trying to find some chai and a good vegan muffin." - Davey Havok

318 Roy Orbison

A singular voice in rock 'n' roll, Roy Orbison was truly unique. The only contemporary singer to come close to Roy's vocal prowess is Chris Isaak, and he rarely approximates Orbison's lyrical weight. Best known for "Pretty Woman", the lightest song on his hits list, Orbison had success with "Only the Lonely", "Running Scared" and "In Dreams", each one an exercise in drama and heartbreak. With a purity of tone seldom heard in rock 'n' roll, Orbison's tragic personal life seemed to come through on each note he sang. After years out of the spotlight Orbison had late '80s hits with "You Got It" and as part of the Traveling Wilburys with "Handle With Care".

319 AFI

Sometimes persistence pays off. Twelve years after Davey Havok formed AFI, aka A Fire Inside, they found mainstream success with 2003's Sing the Sorrow. Produced by Butch Vig (Nirvana, Shania Twain) and Jerry Finn (Green Day), Sing the Sorrow was released on major label Dreamworks. This was the most pop-oriented effort the gothy punk band had made to date, with the single "Girls Not Grey" being positively upbeat. They continued experimenting with more diverse musicality, including a more up front electronic sound in 2006 on Decemberunderground, an album that debuted at #1 in the U.S.

320 Alkaline Trio

Heart-on-sleeve lyrics, earnest vocals, and a propulsive sound align Alkaline Trio with other late '90s pop-punk bands, like Saves the Day and the Movielife, who take young male angst and soured relationships as their subject. The initial line-up of Matt Skiba, Glenn Porter, and Dan Andriano formed in Illinois in 1996 and released their debut full-length Goddamnit in 1998. They signed with soon-to-be emo stronghold Vagrant Records and found greater mainstream success with From Here to Infirmary. Alkaline Trio continues to tour and record, and all members are active in side-projects in the Chicago punk scene. (See picture opposite)

321 Alice In Chains

Alice In Chains was one of the most popular bands to come from the Seattle grunge scene of the '90s that also gave birth to Nirvana, Soundgarden and Pearl Jam. Alternating between sludgy, metallic guitar riffs and introspective acoustic songs, Alice In Chains enjoyed success with both the alternative and metal crowds. Sophomore album Dirt and the appearance of the song "Would" on the soundtrack to the grunge-centric Cameron Crowe flick Singles helped propel the band to mega-stardom but drug dependency and a lack of touring eventually caused a divide in the band. Tragically, singer Layne Staley died of an overdose in 2002. (See picture opposite)

"There's no huge, deep message in any of the songs. We recorded a few months of being human."

ALICE IN CHAINS FACTFILE:

Start up year: 1987

Disband year: N/A

Home town: Seattle, U.S.A.

Members: Layne Staley, Jerry Cantrell, Mike Starr, Sean Kinney, Mike Inez

What you should check out/why: Dirt is a bleak, confessional album that fans love.

Worth looking out for: Alice in Chains on tour without singer Staley.

322 My Chemical Romance

My Chemical Romance vocalist Gerard Way says he made the decision to form a band while watching the September 11, 2001 attacks on New York City. It should come as no surprise that the seed planted at such an unfortunate time would grow into a band lyrically obsessed with tragedy. Mixing slick, aggressive emo-punk, with gothic imagery, the band struck a chord with their second album Three Cheers For Sweet Revenge. Their next studio full length was The Black Parade, an ambitious concept album that plays out like a mall-punk answer to Pink Floyd's The Wall. (See picture opposite)

323 New Bomb Turks

Jim Weber, Eric Davidson, Sam Brown, and Bill Randt formed garage punk outfit New Bomb Turks in Columbus, Ohio in 1993, but aside from speed had little in common with the contemporary punk revival simultaneously taking place in California. Their debut album Destroy-Oh-Boy! features the short, loud, bracing blasts of noise and low humor that would come to characterize their sound over six albums, several EPs and singles and three outtakes collections. The New Bomb Turks continue to perform, but have not released any recordings since 2003.

324 The Killers

Perhaps the most successful of the synth-laden dance pop bands that surfaced in the fist half of the 2000s, the Killers have enjoyed a high profile since the release of their debut album Hot Fuss, in 2003. Singles "Mr. Brightside" and "All these Things That I've Done" demonstrate Brandon Flowers, Dave Keuning, Mark Stoermer, and Ronnie Vannucci Jr.'s affinity for new wave rhythms and instrumentation, merged with a modern rock sensibility. On subsequent albums the Killers have collaborated with Lou Reed, Neil Tenant of the Pet Shop Boys and producer Alan Moulder from Depeche Mode.

325 Against Me!

Against Me! missed the punk revival by a few years, so it fits that Tom Gabel's somewhat heavier approach to the volume, aggression and political awareness that defines most contemporary punk recalls those bands only faintly, favoring instead the folk- punk niche. Gabel began performing and recording along with various lineups as Against Me! in 1997 but released their first widely distributed album Reinventing Axl Rose on No Idea Records in 2001. In 2006 the band stirred minor controversy in punk circles when it signed with Sire Records and began to pursue a more straight-ahead modern rock sound with New Wave.

326 Mission of Burma

Boston's Mission of Burma built an enduring legacy on a few singles, one EP and one full-length album, all of which grew from local acclaim to influence a bevy of college and indie bands, and helped define post-punk. Guitarist Roger Miller, bassist Clint Conley, and drummer Peter Prescott began playing together in 1979 and were joined by sound-manipulator Martin Swope in 1981. Both their 1981 EP Signals, Calls, and Marches and the following year's full-length Vs. showcase the band's nervy but ferocious guitar sound and ominous and literate lyrics. Miller's worsening tinnitus led the band to break up in 1983, but they reformed in 2002 with Bob Weston replacing Swope at the soundboard.

327 Dream Theater

Originally formed under the name Majesty in 1985 by Berklee College of Music attendees John Myung, John Petrucci, and Mike Portnoy, Dream Theater has immense technical skill. After a few personnel changes they found a vocalist in Canadian James LaBrie and their most recent keyboard player is Jordan Rudess. Known for virtuosic performances and captivating live shows, Dream Theater has also been known to pay tribute to their musical heroes by covering albums like Metallica's Master of Puppets and Iron Maiden's Number of the Beast in their entirety. 2009 saw the release of their aggressive and musically challenging Black Clouds & Silver Linings.

328 Good Charlotte

Twin brothers Joel and Benji Madden, Billy Martin, Paul Thomas and Aaron Escolopio formed Good Charlotte in Maryland in 1996, and garnered success in the Washington, D.C. area with the single "Little Things" from their self-titled debut album. The angst and sarcasm in the song's lyrics and simple repetitive guitar lines mark the band's modern punk sound, though Good Charlotte's approach to the genre is less energetic than that of the bands like NOFX and Green Day that they claim as influences. "Lifestyles of the Rich and the Famous" from 2002's The Young and the Hopeless earned significant radio and MTV airtime.

329 North Mississippi All-Stars

Brothers Cody and Luther Dickinson are the sons of famed producer Jim Dickinson (Big Star, The Replacements) which may account for some of their musical ability, or at least their interest. Raised in Mississippi, and hence the band name, Cody and Luther had a punk band before opting to make bluesier, rootsier music under the North Mississippi All-Stars moniker. Spending their early years as a touring band, they released their debut Shake Hands with Shorty in 2000. In 2009 they delivered a two-disc live collection called Do It Like We Used To.

330 Taking Back Sunday

Formed in 1999 in Amityville, New York, Taking Back Sunday has taken their pop-infused emo-punk to the big leagues. Their punky yet melodic two guitar arrangements proved to be the winning backdrop for the emotional wail of singer Adam Lazzara. Taking Back Sunday helped further spread their name with successful tours with the likes of At The Drive In and Jimmy Eat World. Although there have been line up changes over the years, Taking Back Sunday's popularity seems to rise continuously. 2009's New Again is their first album to feature contributions from new guitarist, Matt Fazzi.

331 Blue Oyster Cult

Best known for the somewhat psychedelic cowbell-heavy suicide pact that is "Don't Fear the Reaper", Blue Oyster Cult formed in 1969 and although it has undergone numerous changes to the line-up, has never officially broken up. Although BOC has the underpinning of a hard rock band, with squealing guitars, thunderous bass and mystic lyrics, they also have a way with melody, making them accessible to more casual listeners. Interestingly, punk poet Patti Smith, who was romantically linked with keyboard/guitar player Allen Lanier, co-wrote a number of songs with the band, as did science-fiction writer Michael Moorcock, who was previously connected with the band Hawkwind. (See picture opposite)

BLUE OYSTER CULT FACTFILE:

Start up year: 1969

Disband year: N/A

Home town: Long Island, New York, U.S.A.

Members: Andy WInters, Donald Roeser, Allen Lanier, John Wiesenthal, Albert Bouchcard, more

What you should check out/why: Agents of Fortune includes "Don't Fear the Reaper", but any of BOC's early records are worth a listen.

TYPE O NEGATIVE FACTFILE:

Start up year: 1989

Disband year: N/A

Home town: Brooklyn, New York, U.S.A.

Members: Peter Steele, Sal Abruscato, Josh Silver, Kenny Hickey, Johnny Kelly

What you should check out/why: Bloody Kisses has songs like "Christian Woman" and "Set Me on Fire."

Worth looking out for: Their cover of "Angry Inch" from Hedwig and the Angry Inch.

KYUSS FACTFILE:

Start up year: 1989

Disband year: 1997

Home town: Palm Desert, California, U.S.A.

Members: Josh Homme, Nick Oliveri, Brant Bjork, John Garcia, more

What you should check out/why: Blues for the Red Sun is stoner rock bliss.

332 Type O Negative

After spending the better part of the'80s in the punk and thrash bands Fallout and Carnivore, Peter Steele created the gothic rock band Type O Negative. With heavily atmospheric songs that sound like funeral processions married to the power of heavy metal, Type O found a home with Roadrunner Records and recorded their debut album Slow, Deep, and Hard. Their next release would be a fake live album charmingly titled The Origin of the Feces. Momentum began to build with the release of the second studio album Bloody Kisses. It showed Steele's growth as a songwriter and the Beatles-based melodies helped to elevate his often tongue-in-cheek tales of vampire lust.

333 Kyuss

Though largely unheard of when they were together, the legend of Kyuss grows stronger with every passing year. Forming in Palm Desert, California in 1989, they honed their skills as a live band at outdoor parties where power had to be supplied by gas generators. With their detuned guitars played through bass amps, the name Kyuss has become synonymous with the term "stoner metal". After Kyuss called it a day in 1997, a plethora of new bands would rise from Kyuss' ashes. Among these bands are Queens of the Stone Age, Mondo Generator, Che, and Brant Bjork & The Bros.

334 Spinal Tap

Although Spinal Tap is a fictional band created by comedians Christopher Guest, Michael McKean and Harry Shearer, they are similar to the Monkees in that they took a concept and made it a reality by releasing albums, like Break Like the Wind, and playing concerts. As legend has it, Spinal Tap began as a pop band, playing British Invasion-style songs like "Give Me Some Money" before becoming heavy metal giants with songs like "Sex Farm" and "Big Bottoms". Guitar player Nigel Tufnel, played by Christopher Guest, is best known for being able to turn his amplifier volume up to eleven, while all other bands can only go to ten. (See picture opposite)

335 Avail

Richmond, Virginia's Avail plays melodic punk rock that is rich in the traditions of their Washington, DC neighbors. Avail is known for their dynamic live shows, as documented on their Live at the Bottom of the Hill in San Francisco album. Forming in 1987, the band has released their aggressive, sing-along hardcore on premier punk labels like Lookout, Fat Wreck Chords and Jade Tree. Albums like Satiate, Dixie and Front Porch Stories helped to grow their loyal fan base. Though no official break up has been announced the band is said to be on "permanent standby".

336 Jethro Tull

To many, singer and flute player Ian Anderson is the face of England's Jethro Tull. Considering the internal grievances within the band, this perception isn't far off. With a handful of albums already to their credit in 1971, Jethro Tull released Aqualung, arguably the most commercially successful concept albums to combine folk, jazz and rock with lyrics about the relationship between God and man and religion in general. Tull followed this massive success with another huge success, Thick as a Brick. By this time Anderson was the band's only remaining original member; he remains so today.

337 The Dead Kennedys

Although a legal battle over the band name between singer Jello Biafra and the three other band members, Klaus Fluoride, East Bay Ray, and D.H. Pellegro, may have marred the Dead Kennedys' legend, throughout the '80s the San Francisco band was at the vanguard of West Coast hardcore punk with albums like Bedtime for Democracy. Biafra used his high-pitched, vibrato-laden warble to lash out against injustices and stupidity, often finding the band censored for its lyrics and imagery. As part of the senate hearings concerning the Parents Music Resource Centre, Biafra attempted to convince Middle America that their children didn't need to be protected from words.

338 Stone Temple Pilots

Though they were despised by rock critics and branded grunge imitators by many, the Stone Temple Pilots managed to be one of the most successful bands of the '90s. Releasing their debut album Core, in '92, STP had massive hits with songs like "Plush", "Sex Type Thing" and "Wicked Garden", and earned a Grammy, putting their name at the top many year-end polls. The quartet of Scott Weiland, brothers Robert and Dean DeLeo, and Eric Kretz toured and recorded tirelessly until singer Weiland's drug and legal troubles became problematic. After an extended hiatus a new album and 2009 tour are in the works.

339 Everclear

Growing up was no picnic for songwriter/singer/guitarist Art Alexakis. He was abandoned by his father, his brother died of a heroin overdose, his girlfriend committed suicide and he had his own battle with drug addiction. He managed to clean himself up and channel many of those feelings and experiences into the songs of Everclear. Forming the band in Portland, Oregon, Alexakis spent his time writing songs and tirelessly promoting Everclear. Inspired by the Replacements, Pixies, and X, their records were first released on indie labels like Tim/Kerr and Fire Records, but came to worldwide recognition via their Capitol Records debut Sparkle and Fade.

340 The Jesus and Mary Chain

Jim and William Reid wrote songs using the structures of some of the sunniest music like surf songs and '60s girl groups, and fed them through fuzz and distortion. The result was the underbelly of '60s pop as performed by two disenfranchised Scottish brothers. Psychocandy introduced the JAMC, although the recorded material was far tamer than the band's early live shows, which often lasted for less than 20 minutes and frequently ended in punches thrown. Over the years the band mellowed and had a number of alternative rock hits, including "Automatic", "April Skies" and "Sometimes Always", a duet with Mazzy's Star's Hope Sandoval.

341 Melvins

Started in the mid '80s in Aberdeen, Washington, the punk-metal sludge that oozed from King Buzzo and Co.'s amplifiers was a major influence on some of the most successful bands of the '90s. Both Nirvana and Soundgarden, albeit in an easier to swallow fashion, would drink from the cup of the Melvins. Like a deranged Black Sabbath or Black Flag at the wrong speed, they feel no need for conventional song craft. Over twenty years later the Melvins are still standing, having turned the band into a two drummer juggernaut by incorporating drum and bass duo Big Business. (See picture opposite)

"We went into that knowing that we were never going to sell a major record 'cause we didn't sound like these bands, so I just thought this was an opportunity for us to make the kind of records that we wanted and make some money at the same time." - Buzz Osborne

MELVINS FACTFILE:

Start up year: 1985

Disband year: N/A

Home town: Aberdeen, Washington, U.S.A.

Members: Buzz Osborne, Lori "Lorax" Black, Dale Crover, Matt Lukin, Joe Preston, Mark Deutrom, Kevin Rutmanis

What you should check out/why: Houdini is arguably the pinnacle of the venerable noise rockers' records.

Worth looking out for: Buzz "King Buzzo" Osborne's participation in art rock supergroup Fantômas.

342 Bikini Kill

At a time when boys were wearing cardigans and trying to be sensitive, Kathleen Hannah was leading Bikini Kill in a punk rock call to arms for all women who were sick of being told to sit down, shut up and look pretty, breaking ground on the Riot Grrrl movement in the process. Often criticized for being anti-male, the songs were less against men as they were pro women, with songs like "Rebel Girl" exalting female friendship. While Kathleen Hannah started using her singing voice more than her screaming voice in later projects Julie Ruin and Le Tigre, her message stayed the same throughout: Revolution girl style now!

343 Bush

Taking their name from the members' home town of Shepherd's Bush, London, modern rockers Bush hit American shores at the perfect time. Unveiled at the height of post-Nevermind grunge mania and releasing their debut album Sixteen Stone, in 1994, Bush dominated the U.S. alternative airways with hits like "Everything Zen", "Comedown" and "Glycerine". Seeking a heavier edge and hoping to silence detractors who thought the band contrived, Bush recorded their sophomore album with indie-rock veteran Steve Albini, a man famous for his work with Big Black, the Pixies and Nirvana. Razorblade Suitcase entered the U.S. charts at number one.

344 Deftones

Chino Moreno, Abe Cunningham, and Stephen Carpenter formed the Deftones in 1998 while still in high school and were joined sometime later by bassist Chi Cheng. Early on, the band shared the aggression, density, and angst of other metal-oriented bands, but with an emphasis on space and atmosphere rarely found in their contemporaries' records. Lead songwriter Moren soon added turntablist Frank Delgado and folded the hip-hop and shoegaze elements into the Deftones' sound, and these elements are particularly evident on their 2000 album White Pony. Currently at work on a sixth album, the band recently weathered the loss of bassist Cheng who was badly injured in a car accident in 2008.

345 The Besnard Lakes

Who knew that songs about spies and secret lives could be so haunting and beautiful? On their first album, Montreal's Besnard Lakes dealt in a fairly experimental sound, while on 2007's Are the Dark Horse, subtle orchestration, powerhouse drumming and layered guitars create the perfect accompaniment to Jace Lasek and Olga Goreas's tales of the loneliness and adventure that are part and parcel of being a spy. The band's harmonies only elevate the proceedings, with every layer adding to the energy. Mysterious and explosive, the Besnard Lakes' live show is just as intense as their recordings.

346 The Black Keys

The Black Keys guitar and drum duo of Dan Auerbach and Patrick Carney play a stripped-down form of soulful, blues-drenched rock and have earned comparisons to Jimi Hendrix and the White Stripes. Auerbach and Carney released three albums, The Big Come Up, Thickfreakness and Rubber Factory, featuring the rump-shaking single "10 A.M. Automatic", between 2002 and 2005, as well as an EP, The Moan. Their most recent release, 2008's Attack & Release, continues to develop the raw edge of earlier recordings with a fuller band sound and production by Danger Mouse.

347 The Headcoats

With a slew of bands to his credit, England's Billy Childish was leading the garage rock revival years before the White Stripes or the Hives had even learned to play the guitar. The longest-lasting of Childish's bands, which also include Thee Milkshakes, Thee Mighty Caesars and the Pop Rivets, the Headcoats' music is unsurprisingly loud and catchy, but Childish's lyrics frequently ran against the grain, exploring issues like child abuse and alienation. Assuming the role of impresario, he created the band's female counterpart Thee Headcoatees featuring Holly Golightly. Their version of the Beatles' "Run for Your Life" is not to be missed.

348 Rare Earth

Detroit R&B powerhouse Rare Earth signed with Motown Records in 1969 where they scored a hit with a cover of the Temptations' "Get Ready". The radio edit was significantly shorter than the lengthy album version that takes up a whole side of the album Get Ready. Logging in at 20 minutes, "Get Ready" achieves the rare feat of maintaining, if not building upon, the song's energy over an extended period. A year later the pure funk of "I Just Want to Celebrate" gave them another smash hit. In spite of a shifting line-up the band continued to record into the '80s.

349 Blue Cheer

When they formed in 1967, few bands were as heavy as San Francisco's Blue Cheer. Their slow, fuzzed-out version of rock helped create the blueprint for what is now known as heavy metal. A power trio with the emphasis on "power", Dickie Peterson, Leigh Stephens, and Paul Whaley took their overdriven amps into the top 40 with a cover of Eddie Cochran's "Summertime Blues" that sounds closer to a meeting of Black Sabbath and Jimi Hendrix than to the rock 'n' roll pioneer who wrote the song. Blue Cheer gave future metal-heads a glimpse of what was to come. (See picture opposite)

350 Boris

Tokyo, Japan's Boris is a band that refuses to be pigeonholed. Taking their name from a song on the album Bullhead by the Melvins, it is no surprise that the band is fond of sludgy riffs and glacially paced tempos. If one looks beyond the doom metal roots of Boris, there is a trio equally capable of minimalist drone, pastoral psychedelic rock or blistering garage freak-outs. Along the way Boris have collaborated with the likes of loud American heavyweights SunnO))), Japanese noise legend Merzbow and avant-garde artist Keiji Haino, creating a lengthy discography that is consistently varied.

351 Carcass

Carcass helped to push the boundaries of the metal sub-genre of grindcore musically, lyrically and aesthetically. The Liverpool natives' early releases like Reek of Putrefaction and Symphonies of Sickness set new standards with their ultra low-tuned guitars, blast-beats and medical jargon-infused lyrics. Cover art that showed collages of dead bodies only helped to attract fans and send the squeamish running for the hills. Over time their musical abilities grew substantially and they implemented more melody and classic rock sensibilities resulting in metal classics such as Necroticism: Descanting the Insalubrious and their major label debut Heartwork. (See picture opposite)

CARCASS FACTFILE:

Start up year: 1985

Disband year: N/A

Home town: Liverpool, England

Members: Bill Steer, Ken Owen, Michael Arnott, Jeff Walker

What you should check out/why: Necroticism: Descanting the Insalubrious because songs like "Symposium of Sickness" and "Incarnated Solvent Abuse" will make you listen to death metal in a whole new way.

352 Dark Angel

Before expanding metal fans' palates for technical brutality in bands like Death and Strapping Young Lad, drummer Gene Hoglan was the creative force behind Los Angeles thrash pioneers Dark Angel. Joining the band after the recording of their debut album We Have Arrived, Hoglan helped push the band's raw sound into more intricate realms. Though faced with several line-up changes Dark Angel managed to push their sound forward. Leave Scars showcased their ability to craft lengthy songs ripe with tempo-shifting complexity. The band would be put to rest after the release of their swansong, 1991's Time Does Not Heal.

353 No Age

With the excellent independent record Weirdo Rippers already to their credit, Dean Spunt and Randy Randall of Los Angeles' No Age released Nouns on Sub Pop in 2008. This simple guitar and drums duo's sound is rooted in a lo-fi punk aesthetic but songs like "Eraser", for which they made a sweet and scrappy video, and "Teen Creeps" while too noisy for radio play are nevertheless wonderfully poppy singles. No Age's punk roots show most in the band's relentless touring schedule, which finds them on tour a good chunk of the year. (See picture opposite)

354 Davie Allan & The Arrows

Though Davie Allan recorded and released dozens of albums with various incarnations of the Arrows, his brisk, fuzz-guitar take on surf rock is most associated with the B-movie soundtracks he appeared on throughout the '60s as producer Roger Corman had tapped Allan to write and perform for his American International Pictures. Allan began to experiment with distortion on "Apache '65", a moderately successful single from the Arrows' first LP. Allan debuted his trademark fuzz sound with the soundtrack to the 1966 Peter Fonda film The Wild Angels and his personal sound is particularly evident on "Blues' Theme", which was Allan's most successful single. In the early '70s Allan went underground and reemerged in the early '90s with the critically acclaimed album Loud, Loose, and Savage.

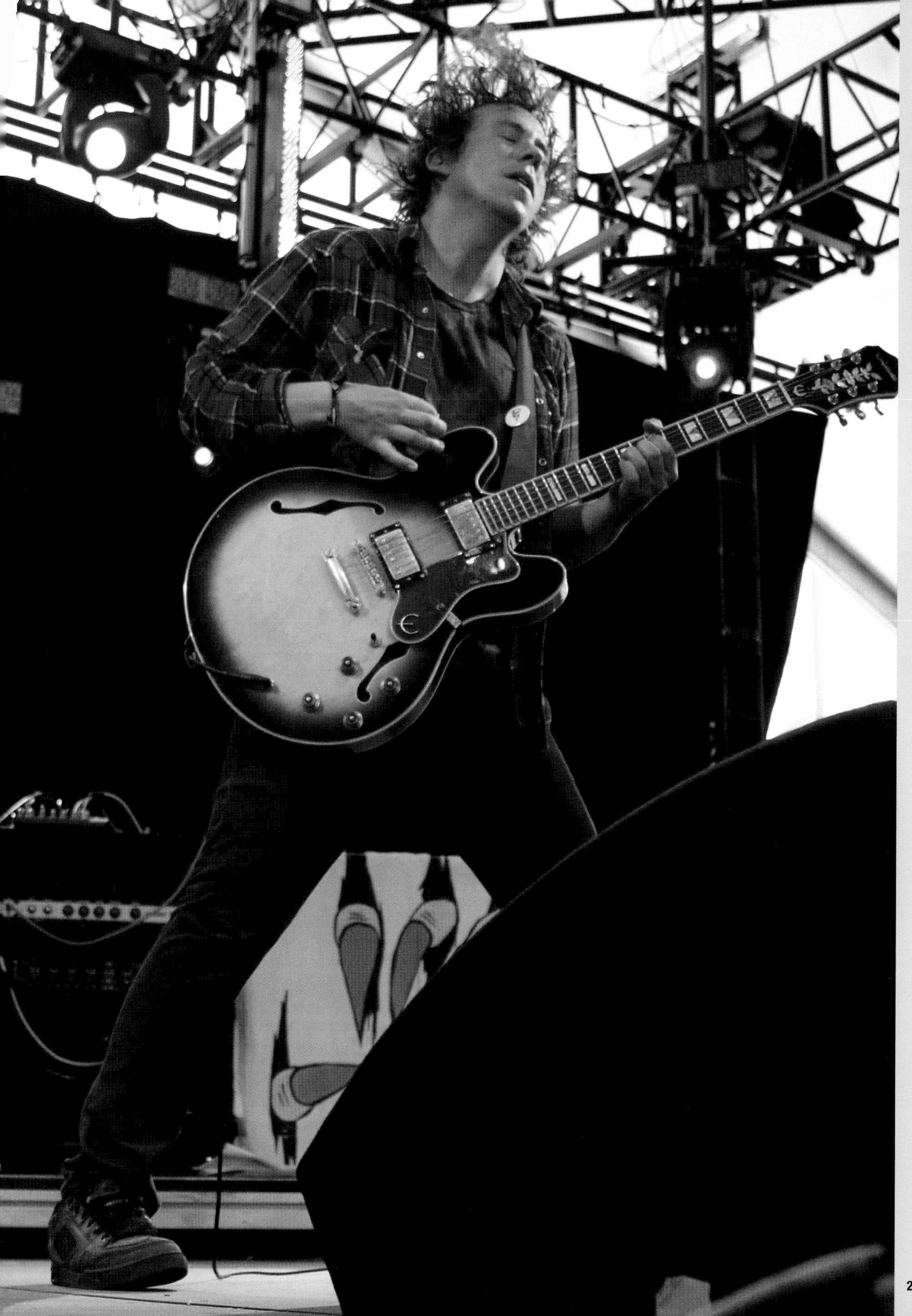

355 Dead Moon

Until 2006, Fred Cole on guitar and Toody Cole on bass, along with drummer Andrew Loomis, comprised Dead Moon. Based in Oregon, this trio spent almost twenty years playing raucous and spooky rock 'n' roll. Fred's voice rarely shouts or screams but it is still in the forefront and his tone almost always expresses a sense of urgency or sadness not unlike that of 13th Floor Elevators' Roky Erickson. Haunting is an apt descriptor, which makes the band's name especially fitting. While most of Dead Moons' albums had been released independently, Sub Pop Records released a Dead Moon retrospective collection called Echoes of the Past in 2006.

356 The Black Angels

Influenced by the psychedelic rock of the '60s, Austin, Texas quintet the Black Angels make dark and sexy music often based around a drone that creates an almost hypnotic effect that is not disturbed when singer Alex Maas's voice enters the reverie as his voice is just another layer added to the proceedings. First gaining attention with their 2006 debut Passover, two years later their Directions to See a Ghost further raised their profile. The Black Angels are currently working on their third album with producer Dave Sardy, who has previously worked with The Rolling Stones, Primal Scream and many others.

357 Jesu

With Jesu singer/songwriter Justin Broadrick's band lineage including such extreme bands as Napalm Death, Techno Animal and Godflesh, it may be a bit surprising that Jesu's music has more in common with the dreamy, atmospheric bands that got stuck under the shoegazer umbrella in the '90s than it does with any of his former bands. Broadrick has been quoted as saying he was thinking about bands like Teenage Fanclub when he started Jesu and those influences can be heard in Broadrick's vocal melodies and in songs like "Star" from the Silver EP, which is downright poppy, even if it is seven minutes long.

358 The Deadly Snakes

From 1996 to 2001, the Deadly Snakes ruled Toronto's rock 'n' roll scene. Although there were a couple of line-up shifts in that time, the band's two songwriters, Andre St. Clair and Max Danger (a.k.a. Andre Ethier and Max McCabe-Lokos) remained steadfast, leading the band on a journey from intensely exciting garage rock like Love Undone through to the thematically and musically ambitious Ode to Joy and Porcella. In 2001 Greg Cartwright of the Oblivians joined the band for I'm Not Your Soldier Anymore. On recordings the Deadly Snakes are excellent, but live they were without comparison and always left their audiences hoarse, sweaty and yearning for more.

359 Earth

Since 1990, Olympia, Washington's Earth has primarily been the work of the only constant member Dylan Carlson. Perhaps the most outsider band on the Sub Pop label in the early '90s, Earth's explorations of the lower frequencies earned Carlson a cult following that included occasional collaborator Kurt Cobain and robe-wearing Earth-worshippers Sunn O))). The music of Earth has evolved from the bass feedback-laden Sabbath-on-the-wrong-speed sound of Earth 2 to the melodic meditations on dusty Americana of Hex: or Printing in the Infernal Method. 2008's The Bees Made Honey in the Lion's Skull finds a more fleshed out Earth sound, in part due to collaboration with jazz guitarist Bill Frisell.

360 The Makers

Spokane, Washington's the Makers spent their first three years and five records as one of the world's finest garage rock revival outfits. Known for their energetic, sometimes verging on violent, live shows, singer Michael Maker's sneering and squawking vocals, and Tim Maker's fuzzy guitar sound, the Makers were ahead of the mid'90s garage rock explosion that made stars of the White Stripes and the Hives. Just as the freak beat sound was gaining mainstream popularity, the Makers switched gears and went glam rock with 1998's Psychopathia Sexualis, continuing down that road with their follow-up. They released Everybody Rise in 2005.

361 Eric's Trip

One of Canada's most beloved indie-rock bands, Moncton, New Brunswick's Eric's Trip epitomized the lo-fi sound, creating noisy masterpieces with Rick White (guitar) and Julie Doiron (bass) trading vocals that were integral to the band's sound, even if it wasn't always possible to hear what they were saying.
In 1993 they released Love Tara, a record that combined sweetly noisy pop songs like "Stove" with heartbreaking ballads such as "Behind the Garage". Subsequent albums Forever Again, Purple Blue and Long Days Ride 'Til Tomorrow made the band so popular that occasional reunions are still greeted with enthusiasm. (See picture opposite)

"We can't see clear, but what we see is a alright. We make up what we can't hear and then we sing all night."

ERIC'S TRIP FACTFILE:

Start up year: 1990

Disband year: 1996 (with occasional reunions)

Home town: Moncton, Canada

Members: Rick White, Julie Doiron, Mark Gaudet, Chris Thompson

What you should check out/why: The Sloan/Eric's Trip split-7" in which the two bands cover each other is the key to Canadian rock in the '90s.

362 The Fall

Though they emerged from Manchester in the late '70s, the Fall shares an affinity for Martin Hannett's production but little else connects it to the local scene. The Fall is known for clunky and sometimes atonal guitars, being one of the first bands given the post-punk tag. With 1980's Grotesque they enjoyed a semi-hit with the propulsive "Totally Wired". Founder Mark E. Smith's misanthropic sense of humor is evident in lyrics that he delivers in a sing-speak manner. Smith has recorded and toured with various versions of the Fall since 1977, maintaining a cynical outlook despite a brief lapse into more accessible pop in the '80s due to the influence of his then-wife Brix.

363 Amon Duul II

Forming in a Munich commune in 1967 under the name Amon Duul, a collective of artistic and politically minded Germans employed an open-door membership policy for their freeform psychedelic jams. Some of the more ambitious members of the collective broke off into a new group. Deciding they already had a decent name, they christened the band Amon Duul II to avoid confusion. Throughout the '70s Amon Duul II incorporated elements of progressive rock, experimental and improvisational techniques in their music, which was often delivered with a sense of whimsy that defied the seriousness of the work. The '80s saw the formation of a new faction named Amon Duul in the UK or Amon Duul III elsewhere.

364 Generation X

Before Billy Idol was known for sneering about a "White Wedding" he was the singer for Generation X, a band that came out of London's original punk scene and also included Tony James, who went on to one-hit wonder infamy with Sigue Sigue Sputnik. Generation X had a hit with "Ready Steady Go", an ode to the music TV show that introduced many bands to the kids of England, while subsequent single "Kiss Me Deadly" moved away from their earlier punky sound with this softer slower song. Idol's solo hit "Dancing With Myself" first saw the light of day with Gen X too.

365 Gin Blossoms

The Gin Blossoms travel similar musical terrain as the Jayhawks, combining power-pop melodies and guitars with a hint of country. Although they've been relegated to the second tier of alternative pop music they continue to be played in coffee shops and supermarkets. In 1992 they released New Miserable Experience and had a hit with "Hey Jealousy", a song that has some gorgeous jangle in its guitars and a catchy chorus. Sadly, songwriter Doug Hopkins didn't live to see just how popular his song would become. The band continued without him, having their biggest hit with "Til I Hear it From You" from the Epic Records soundtrack.

366 Nashville Pussy

Husband and wife Blaine Cartwright and Ruyter Suys formed Nashville Pussy in 1998 with drummer Jeremy Thompson and bassist and fire-eater Corey Parks, who remained with the band for its first two full-length releases, Let Them Eat Pussy and High As Hell. The band's sound is characterized by rockabilly swagger, shredding metal guitars, Cartwright's sneering vocals, and lyrical obsessions with sex, drugs, and machismo. Since High As Hell Nashville Pussy has seen two more bassists, Katielyn Campbell and Karen Cuda, who appeared on 2002's Say Something Nasty and 2005's Get Some.

367 The Jayhawks

With strong songwriter and glorious harmonies, the Jayhawks are one of the few bands who grew stronger with each subsequent album, becoming masters of the jangle-rock genre. From 1985 to 1997 the Jayhawks' were led by co-writers Mark Olson and Gary Louris and released Hollywood Town Hall, Smile and others. Although people feared Olson's departure would put an end to the band, 2003's Rainy Day Music is perhaps a more introspective affair than previous efforts but is still full of Louris's songwriting magic, especially on "Tailspin" and "Save It For A Rainy Day". Unable to stay apart for long, Louris and Olson started touring together and announced their reunion as the Jayhawks in 2009.

368 Uncle Tupelo

Influenced equally by Gram Parsons and the Minutemen, Uncle Tupelo is credited with bringing the alternative country genre to prominence. Fusing the relaxed blues structures and despondent lyrics of roots music with a brash post-punk edge, Jay Farrar, Jeff Tweedy and Mike Heidorn formed the band in 1984 and found the record label Rockville in 1988. Their first LP No Depression became an alt/country hallmark, featuring Tweedy and Farrar's take on the struggles of small-town life. The band released two more albums before Heidorn left. Tensions between Tweedy and Farrar led Uncle Tupelo to break-up after touring in support of their final album Anodyne. Both Tweedy and Farrar would go on to success with their own post-breakup bands Wilco and Sun Volt.

369 Gwar

If you are a believer in the absurd, Gwar is a band of monstrous alien warriors who reside in Antarctica and is hell-bent on the destruction of humanity. If you are prone to over-think things however, Gwar is a high concept art-work formed by a group of students from Virginia. By dressing in elaborate oversized costumes that celebrate the obscene and the macabre and by filling their stage show with phalluses, scatological humor and more than a few buckets of blood, Gwar has proven to be a consistent draw for concert-goers who want the "show" put back in "rock show".

370 High on Fire

Guitarist/vocalist Matt Pike emerged from the demise of his previous band the stoner metal outfit Sleep in 1998 to found High on Fire with Des Kensel and George Rice. Though decidedly dense and sludgy, High on Fire's sound is faster and given to muscular guitar solos. High on Fire released their debut The Art of Self-Defense in 2000 and followed it with Surrounded By Thieves two years later. Shortly thereafter Rice left and was replaced by Joe Preston, who appeared on Blessed Black Wings. Preston was replaced by current bassist Jeff Matz who appears on their most recent studio album Death Is This Communion. (See picture opposite)

TAMA

371 Stereolab

Together for almost twenty years, England's Stereolab has maintained a steadfast audience drawn to their intriguing sound. Drawing on numerous influences, not least of which is the drone-based sounds of Germany's Neu!, Stereolab made a name for themselves courtesy of singer Laetitia Sadier's voice mingling with Tim Gane's melodies. Blending jazz, bossa nova and ambient noises, Stereolab had their biggest hits with 1994's Moog-laden Mars Audiac Quintet and 1996's Emperor Tomato Ketchup, wherein Sadier and now-deceased keyboard player Mary Hansen's vocal interplay was at its peak. In 2008 Stereolab released Chemical Chords, and in the same year Sadier released Monstre Cosmic under the band name Monade. (See picture opposite)

STEREOLAB FACTFILE:

Start up year: 1991

Disband year: N/A

Home town: London, England

Members: Laetitia Sadier, Tim Gane, Mary Hansen, Andy Ramsay, Duncan Brown, Katharine Gifford, Morgane Lhote, Sean O'Hagan

What you should check out/why: Crumb Duck, the Stereolab/Nurse with Wound EP because it's what musical collaboration should be.

Worth looking out for: The Fluorescences EP

372 Isis

Formed by Hydra Head Records head-honcho Aaron Turner, the music of Isis holds a kinship with metal vagabonds Neurosis and Godflesh as well as post-rock mainstays like Do Make Say Think and Tortoise. Isis' music is built around epic songs heavily rooted in quiet/loud dynamics and lengthy instrumental passages and vocals that range from a menacing growl to a melodic whisper. Tours with Converge, Dillinger Escape Plan and Tool helped introduce new fans to Isis's challenging and rewarding music. Isis has collaborated with Scotland's Aereogramme, as well as members of Tool and Godflesh.

373 Slint

Slint only recorded two albums and one EP in its short lifespan but those releases, particularly 1991's Spiderland, are cited by critics and other artists as key to the development of post-rock. Brian McMahan, David Pajo, Brit Walford, and Ethan Buckler recorded their debut Tweez with Steve Albini in 1987, showcasing McMahan's spoken-word vocals and the non-linear song structures that would come to characterize math-rock. By comparison, Spiderland is more accessible, though each of its six tracks stretches past five minutes and exploits a broad dynamic range and guitars that shift suddenly from soft to loud and dissonant, juxtaposed with untreated vocals. Slint broke up in 1992 but reunited for performances in 2005 and 2007. (See picture opposite)

374 Southern Culture on the Skids

Though their name and the off-beat humor in their music suggests that Southern Culture on the Skids is a joke on the culture and conventions of the American South, the band, like their contemporaries the B-52s, balances sincere devotion to surf rock with campy homage. The band began with a straight-forward punk approach but founder and guitarist Rick Miller began exploring country and rockabilly and prompting a line-up shift. Miller, along with bassist Mary Huff and drummer Dave Hartman, honed their gonzo approach to country-rock over a number of years and released their first full-length Too Much Pork For Just One Fork in 1991. 1995's Dirt Track Date served as the band's major label debut and a summation of their career to that point.

375 The Go-Betweens

Some people are meant to work together, as were for example Australia's Grant McLennan and Robert Forster as the Go-Betweens. Although the original duration of the band was from 1978 to 1989 the pair played on each others' solo records and reformed the Go-Betweens in 2002 with The Friends of Rachel Worth and continued making records until McLennan's death in 2006. While every Go-Betweens fan has a favorite song and album, 1983's Before Hollywood and 1988's 16 Lovers Lane are two pinnacles, with the intense "Cattle and Cane" coming from the former and the beautifully bittersweet "Dive For Your Memory" from the latter.

376 Tav Falco's Panther Burns

Born with the distinctly non-rock 'n' roll name Gustavo Antonio Falco, the future singer and leader of Panther Burns did a little shortening (originally to Gus) and came up with the decidedly catchier Tav for a stage name. Starting his recording career in Memphis, Falco has gone through numerous band members over the years, variously relocating to New York City, Mississippi and Europe. Although Falco has never had any commercial success, for thirty years he has been making scrappy, frenzied rockabilly that influenced the psychobilly scene. Falco has also appeared in a number of movies, including Highway 61 and Great Balls of Fire.

377 The Apples in Stereo

One of the three original Elephant 6 projects along with Neutral Milk Hotel and the Olivia Tremor Control, the Apples in Stereo's ambitions sometimes outreached their abilities in the early days, but they still produced wonderful songs that recall the Kinks and the Beach Boys. The present line-up is John Hill, Eric Allen, Bill Doss, John Dufilho, John Ferguson and lead singer and songwriter Robert Schneider, who founded the band in Denver, Colorado in 1994. In an unlikely mainstream crossover, the song "Energy" from the Apples in Stereo's 2007 release New Magnetic Wonder has recently appeared in two commercials, one for a car and performed by American Idol contestants, the other for soda pop.

378 The Fleshtones

Kicking around since 1976, New York City's Fleshtones show no sign of slowing down, having released both Take a Good Look and the Christmas album Stocking Stuffer in 2008. With their sound firmly rooted in the freakbeat sound of the '60s, the Fleshtones sound is cemented by a Farfisa organ and Peter Zaremba's distinctive voice. One can detect his Queens accent even when he sings. Since the '90s the Fleshtones have been made up of Zaremba, Keith Streng onguitar, Bill Milhizer on drums and Ken Fox on bass. This line-up signed with Yep Roc in 2003 with Beachhead. (See picture om p304)

379 Sublime

Variously categorized as punk, ska, reggae, hip-hop, and any combination thereof, Sublime preferred to mix and match conventions in order to produce a laid-back sound free from the angst of alternative rock. Eric Wilson and Bud Gaugh began playing together in the mid'80s, and were joined shortly by guitarist/vocalist Bradley Nowell. Sublime was known for its live show before releasing 40 Oz. To Freedom. The popularity of the single "Date Rape" led to a spot on the Warped Tour. Sublime's self-titled third album was their most successful, spawning the singles "Doin' Time," "Santeria," and "What I Got". Nowell died of a heroin overdose shortly before the album's release, and Sublime broke up in 1996, though their popularity continues unabated.

380 The Plimsouls

Even a lengthy appearance as themselves in the '80s cult classic Valley Girl wasn't enough to turn Californian power-poppers the Plimsouls into superstars. However, that movie did introduce songs like "A Million Miles Away" and "Oldest Story in the World" to a new audience. Those songs also showed up on second record Everywhere at Once, which was more laid-back and jangling than their debut The Plimsouls, which included "Zero Hour", a song that has a chunkier guitar sound than they would have in the future. While singer Peter Case has a solid solo career, the Plimsouls are known to reunite from time to time.

381 Turbonegro

Like a funhouse mirror's refection of punk, metal and glam rock, the music and image of Norway's Turbonegro is warped distorted and fun. Crossing the boundaries of good taste on albums like Ass Cobra, Scandinavian Leather and Apocalypse Dudes, Turbonegro know how to bring the party. Vocalist Hanke Von Helvete, guitarists Euroboy and Rune Rebellion, keyboardist Pal Pot Pamperious and drummer Chris Summers inject their punk rock with a heavy dose of trash and an abundance of swagger. Boasting song titles that would get any self-respecting parental group's attention, Turbonegro showed that having your head in the gutter has rarely been as much fun. (See picture opposite)

TURBONEGRO FACTFILE:

Start up year: 1989

Disband year: 1998 (though reunited in 2002)

Home town: Oslo, Norway

Members: Hanke Von Helvete, Euroboy, Rune Rebellion, Pal Pot Pamperious, Chris Summers

What you should check out/why: Apocalypse Dudes because it's crass, lewd and pure rock 'n' roll.

Worth looking out for: Turbonegro: The Movie

382 Badfinger

Arguably the most tragic band in rock's back pages, Badfinger should have been on top of the '70s, riding the wave of hits like "Come and Get It" and "No Matter What", as well as writing "Without You", which was a smash for Harry Nilsson. The only band signed with the Beatles' Apple label to see international success, Badfinger was, sadly, at the mercy of Apple's disorganization and their own poor management. This meant that despite making some fine pop-rock they never saw any money. In a terrible series of events both of the band's songwriters, Pete Ham and Tom Evans, hanged themselves.

383 The Boo Radleys

For a few years in the mid-'90s, the Boo Radleys, named after a character in Harper Lee's To Kill a Mockingbird, were at the top of their game, releasing a triumvirate of excellent albums: Giant Steps, Lazarus and Wake Up. Starting out making pop that was hidden by layers of noise, by 1993 when Lazarus was made they were starting to shy away from that sound, so while single "Lazarus" still had lots of layered guitars, follow-up "Wish I Was Skinny" was clean pop-rock. The Boo Radleys' use of horns made them stand apart, bringing a brightness to their music that was absent from that of most of their contemporaries.

384 King Khan & The Shrines

Formerly a member of the Montreal garage rockers called the Spaceshits, Erick Khan took the stage name King Khan as a solo artist in Berlin. While recording with Spaceshits' guitarist Mark Sultan as The King Khan & BBQ Show, Khan assembled a band of jazz and R&B musicians and recorded the album Spread Your Love Like Peanut Butter in 2000. Two full-length albums followed before Vice Records signed the Shrines in 2008 and issued a career catch-all titled The Supreme Genius of King Khan & the Shrines. The band recalls the intensity and soul of Ike and Tina Turner focused through the fuzz of the Jon Spencer Blues Explosion in both their recordings and their flamboyant, high concept performances.

385 Alexisonfire

Ontario's Alexisonfire merges the chugging guitars and screaming vocals of hardcore punk with the melodic voice and more complex structures of early '90s emo, with the contrasting vocal styles often overlapping in the chorus. George Petit, Dallas Green, Wade MacNeil, Chris Steele and Jesse Ingelevics formed the band in 2001 and recorded their self-titled debut for indie label Distort in 2002. Despite the ensuing positive critical attention, word-of-mouth popularity and major label courtship, Alexisonfire stuck with Distort and released follow-up album Watch Out in 2004. Subsequent releases Crisis and Old Crows/Young Cardinal have found the band blending the once disparate melodic and aggressive elements of their signature sound.

386 The Lovin' Spoonful

New York's Lovin' Spoonful were ostensibly part of the folk-rock explosion in the '60s, though theirs was the sunnier and poppier side of that music. Fueled by singer/songwriter John Sebastian's pleasant voice and his incorporation of autoharp and harmonica into the standard guitar/bass/drums instrumentation, the Lovin' Spoonful was a hit-making machine. "You Didn't Have to Be So Nice", "Daydream", "Do You Believe in Magic" and the harder edged "Summer in the City" were just a few of their many charting singles. After leaving the band in 1968 Sebastian went on to moderate solo success.

387 Mclusky

Known for their brash and funny lyrics as well as a ragged and feisty musical sensibility, Mclusky was comprised of Andy Falkous on guitar, Jonathan Chapple on bass and Matthew Harding on drums. Not afraid of giving their albums long titles, the Welsh trio introduced themselves with 2000's My Pain and Sadness is More Sad and Painful Than Yours, but it was their second record, the economically titled Mclusky Do Dallas, that gave them their biggest success, getting rave reviews for songs like "Alan is a Cowboy Killer" and "To Hell With Good Intentions". After one last album Mclusky sadly called it a day.

THE MODERN LOVERS FACTFILE:

Start up year: 1970

Disband year: 1974 (The Modern Lovers was released in 1976)

Home town: Boston, Massachusetts, U.S.A.

Members: Jonathan Richman, Jerry Harrison, Ernie Brooks, David Robinson

What you should check out/why: The original Modern Lovers' only album because it might make you believe in the wonder of rock 'n' roll.

Worth looking out for: Galaxie 500's version of Jonathan Richman's "Don't Let Our Youth Go to Waste".

GOLDEN EARRING FACTFILE:

Start up year: 1964

Disband year: N/A

Home town: The Hague, Netherlands

Members: George Kooymans, Barry Hay, Eelco Gelling, Cesar Zuiderwijk, Rinus Gerritsen, and many more

What you should check out/why: Moontan has "Radar Love", an under-rated '70s hit.

Worth looking out for: The garage rock songs they recorded in the '60s, like "Daddy, Buy Me a Girl".

388 Mitch Ryder & The Detroit Wheels

Originally called Billy Lee & the Rivieras, guitarists James McCarthy and Joseph Cubert, bassist Earl Elliot, drummer Johnny Badanjek, and vocalist William Levise, Jr. attracted the attention of producer Bob Crewe, who renamed Levise "Mitch Ryder" and the band the Detroit Wheels. Best known for the top ten hits "Devil In a Blue Dress", "Jenny Take a Ride," and "Sock It To Me, Baby!", Mitch Ryder & the Detroit Wheels made a name in R&B circles due to their intense driving rhythms and Ryder's raspy soul call. Their success was cut short when Crewe persuaded Ryder to leave the group and go solo in 1967. (See picture opposite)

389 The Modern Lovers

Although Jonathan Richman would go on to call his backing band the Modern Lovers for years to come, the original band made one perfect album in 1976 before Richman decided that he didn't want to make loud music anymore. Sounding as vibrant and vital now as it did when it first came out, The Modern Lovers lays Richman's loves and hates out in the open. In "Old World" he finds pleasure in 1950s architecture while on "I'm Straight" he doesn't understand why the girl would choose a guy who is "always stoned" over teetotaler Richman. The Lovers also made "Roadrunner", which is the ultimate ode to rock 'n' roll.

390 Golden Earring

In 1974 Golden Earring seemed to come out of nowhere with the super catchy "Radar Love". The truth of the matter is that George Kooymans, Barry Hay and their band had been having hits in their native Netherlands for a decade prior to the rest of the world catching on to their hard rocking ways with Moontan. Subsequent albums didn't stick in quite the same way however and they fell from sight again. In 1982 Golden Earring revisited the international charts one more time with the moody "Twilight Zone", though they are still best remembered for "Radar Love".

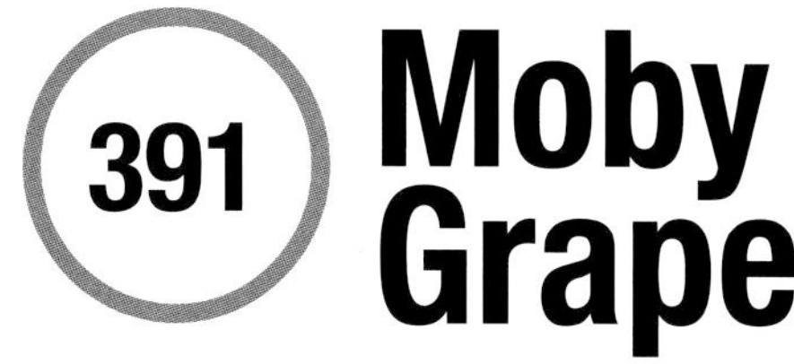

391 Moby Grape

For a moment in the mid '60s, Moby Grape was a contender as the best band from the San Francisco scene. With a similar blend of country, folk and boogie as fellow Bay Area band the Grateful Dead, Moby Grape's debut, while sounding of the time, does not sound dated. With all five band members contributing songs, it still sounds cohesive. From the boogie rock of "Hey Grandma" to the laid back "8:05" and the surprisingly sweet "Naked If I Want To", there's not a bum note to be found. Unfortunately, conflicts between members meant only one more album before the departure of Skip Spence and the absence was tangible. (See picture opposite)

MOBY GRAPE FACTFILE:

Start up year: 1966

Disband year: 1968

Home town: San Francisco, California, U.S.A.

Members: Skip Spence, Jerry Miller, Don Stevenson, Peter Lewis, Bob Mosley

What you should check out/why: Debut album, Moby Grape, is psychedelic without being silly; for a brief moment they ruled the San Francisco scene.

Worth looking out for: Skip Spence's solo masterpiece, Oar

392 Radio Birdman

Before the term punk became part of the vernacular, Australia's Radio Birdman were making loud and fast rock 'n' roll not unlike what the Stooges and MC5 were doing in Detroit. Fronted by singer Rob Younger and guitar player Deniz Tek, Radio Birdman's first album, Radios Appear, stands with the strongest of the '77 punk scene, with "New Race", "What Gives" and "Murder City Nights" being highlights. Splitting up in 1978 prior to the release of their second album, the legend of the band grew and eventually sparked a reunion that resulted in 2006's Zeno Beach, an album that retains the band's grit and intensity even three decades later.

393 The Nation of Ulysses

In the midst of Washington, DC's ever-so-serious punk scene that was guided by Ian McKaye's record label Dichord came the revolutionary Nation of Ulysses. Led by indie heartthrob Ian Svenonius, Nation of Ulysses incited near-riots with performances that were based as much on Svenonius's sermon-like banter as they were on the band's fiery music. Over the two albums 13-Point Program to Destroy America and Plays Pretty for Baby, Nation of Ulysses proved that punk didn't have to be dour and politics don't have to exist at the expense of good times. Since the band's demise Svenonius has gone on to lead numerous bands, including the Make-Up and Weird War.

394 Oneida

Primarily recording for the prestigious Jagjaguwar label, Brooklyn's Oneida started out as a quartet, but have been a trio since 2002's Each One Teach One, and bring extra people along when needed. Inspired by myriad styles, including psychedelic rock, krautrock, metal and soul, no two Oneida albums sound the same, with the band growing and expanding upon their sound every year. 2006's Happy New Year is a stunning album, starting off with the sombre "Distress" and the pastoral title track. But by "Up With People" the album is pure energy, with singer Bobby Matador exalting "You gotta get up to get free". Oneida released the triple-album Rated O in 2009.

395 Primal Scream

While still drumming with the Jesus & Mary Chain, Bobby Gillespie formed Primal Scream as a side-project, exploring a lighter pop sound than the brooding noise rock perfected by his other band. Kicked out of JAMC for his allegiance to his own band, Gillespie recorded two psychedelic pop albums, Sonic Power Groove and Primal Scream, before hitting the jackpot with 1991's Screamadelica, which fused rock guitar with acid house beats and samples. Since then, Primal Scream has moved back and forth between rock and experimental dance music, creating a catalogue of always interesting and often excellent albums.

396 Sleep

For a band with relatively little recorded output, Sleep managed to make major waves amongst metal and hard rock fans. Playing doom metal very much indebted to Black Sabbath, St. Vitus and marijuana, Sleep broke through with their second album Holy Mountain, which was a dense cloud of pummeling riffs. The follow up to Holy Mountain took over two years to finish and consisted of a single 60-minute stoner epic called Jerusalem. The band's new label London Records took exception to the bands refusal to break the song up into individual tracks and the album was shelved. At that point Sleep decided to call it a day.

397 The Spencer Davis Group

Birmingham, England's Spencer Davis Group was one of the hottest R&B-based rock bands of the British Invasion. While Davis was the bandleader and guitar player the Group was best known for Stevie Winwood's organ playing and vocals. Winwood's voice sounded like a man much more mature than someone still in his teens. Catching people's attention with the insistent "Keep on Running", the Spencer Davis Group really took off with the soulful singles "I'm A Man" and "Gimme Some Lovin". Right at the moment the Group was ready to take off Winwood left to join Traffic.

398 Jeff Buckley

With only one full-length album, one EP, and a smattering of singles released before he drowned at the age of 30, Jeff Buckley has amassed an enormous following. Building his chops in coffee houses and often playing solo as heard on the Live at Sin-E EP, Buckley assembled a band that allowed him to intersperse gentle acoustic numbers like his cover of Leonard Cohen's "Hallelujah" with Led Zeppelin-style rockers like "Dream Brother" when it came time to make his album Grace. An album of songs he was working on prior to his death was released as Sketches (For My Sweetheart the Drunk) in 1998.

399 Spoon

Formed in Austin, Texas in 1994 by singer/guitarist Britt Daniel and drummer Jim Eno, Spoon fused post-punk influences with blues, R&B and rockabilly to produce hybrid high-energy yet laid-back rock characterized chiefly by Daniel's raspy vocals. Spoon released albums on Matador and Elektra Records before signing with Merge in 2000 and releasing Girls Can Tell. While that record raised Spoon's profile, they broke into the mainstream with 2002's Kill the Moonlight and in particularly the single "The Way We Get By", which seems to be film and television's quirky soundtrack go-to song. Greater critical and popular attention followed and Spoon's sixth full-length album Ga Ga Ga Ga Ga debuted at #10 on the Billboard 200.

400 The Stranglers

For most of the Stranglers' hit-making period, they were equally loved by record buyers and reviled by activists who didn't buy that the band's blatant misogyny on songs like "Peaches" and "Bring on the Nubiles" was just a joke. Regardless of the band's intentions, the Stranglers continued to have hits, primarily in the U.K., for almost two decades. Led by singer Hugh Cornwell, the Stranglers are best known for songs like "No More Heroes", "Skin Deep" and perhaps most fitting of all, "Nice 'N' Sleazy". Cornwell left the band in 1990 though the band still continues without him.

401 Sunn O)))

Stephen O'Malley (ex- Khanate) and Greg Anderson (ex-Goatsnake) make trance-inducing, droning, bass-heavy music inspired by Seattle's Earth. On record, the listener can control the volume. In a live setting Sunn O))) is so loud and so heavy that audience members have described it as feeling like their insides were trying to escape their bodies. Japanese avant-garde noisemaker Merzbow mixed two songs on Sunn O)))'s 2002 release Flight of the Behemoth, adding a new element of noise to Sunn O)))'s sound. 2009's Monoliths and Dimensions is the coalescing of the many forms of experimental music they've worked with to date. (See picture opposite)

SUN O))) FACTFILE:

Start up year: 1998

Disband year: N/A

Home town: Seattle, USA

Members: Stephen O'Malley, Greg Anderson

What you should check out/why: Their version of CandleGoat from Blackone and the lyrics from Freezing Moon, arguably one of their best covers.

Worth looking out for: Footage of their minitour marking the 10th anniversary of The Grimmrobe Demos

402 The Thermals

Over four albums, Portland, Oregon's Thermals have etched their place in indie rock's history making soaring, inspiring and perhaps even cathartic music. Bassist Kathy Foster and singer/ guitar player Hutch Harris make up the Thermals' core and various people have played on the drums since the band's inception in 2002. By the time they released More Parts Per Million in 2003 they already had fans based on their intense and rambunctious gigs. Third album The Body, The Blood, The Machine from 2006 skewers hypocrisy in religion and the government. In 2009 they released Now We Can See on Kill Rock Stars.

403 Trans Am

Nathan Means, Phil Manley and Sebastian Thomson didn't begin recording as Trans Am until 1996 although the band existed as a hobby while its members were still in college. Their self-titled debut on Thrill Jockey Records saw the trio using guitars, drums and electronics to experiment with classic rock riffs and the minimalist electronic compositions that dominated their subsequent albums which eventually incorporated Means' vocals. Although their skill as straightforward musicians and songwriters is obvious Trans Am balance sincerity and irony in their work and poke fun at genres to which they have made significant contributions.

404 Mastodon

Georgia's Mastodon is at the forefront of contemporary heavy metal and melds thrash, sludge, and progressive rock with lyrical themes often based on film and literature. Their breakthrough release, 2002's epic Leviathan, was based loosely on Herman Melville's Moby Dick and found the band at the top of many critics' favorite lists. Tours with metal giants like Slayer, Slipknot, and Tool have helped introduce the band to fans worldwide. In 2009 Mastodon released Crack in the Skye, an ambitious offering with lyrics based around astral projection, Tsarist Russia, and the theories of Stephen Hawking. Mastodon was selected as the opener for the European leg of Metallica's 2009 World Magnetic Tour. (See picture opposite)

405 Bedhead

Figureheads of the slowcore genre Bedhead 's body of work reveals a band content to let guitar-driven melodies and hushed vocals stretch, with harmonies resolving over several measures, rather than several beats. Brothers Matt and Bubba Kadane formed Bedhead with drummer Trini Martinez, guitarist Tench Coxe and bassist Kris Wheat in 1991. In 1993 the band signed with Trance Syndicate Records, who released WhatFunLifeWas, Bedheaded, and Transaction de Novo. Transaction de Novo featured some louder, more aggressive arrangements that would later appear in the music of the Kadane brothers' post-Bedhead band New Year.

406 X-Ray Spex

Stunning listeners with the spoken introduction to first single "Oh Bondage! Up Yours!", X-Ray Spex singer Poly Styrene made clear her feminist intentions from the outset and made a song as punchy, brave and listenable as that of her punk brethren. The Spex followed up their unaffected and defiant single with Germ Free Adolescents, an album that saw the departure of original saxophonist Lora Logic but retained the immediacy for which they were known. This album and a few unreleased tracks that made their way onto 2006's Let's Submerge collection make up the band's entire recorded output.

407 Descendents

Though they first recorded in 1978, the Descendents only released six albums and a handful of EPs, the most recent of which, Cool to Be You, came out in 2004. Bill Stevenson, Frank Navetta and Tony Lombardo released one single before returning in 1980 with vocalist Milo Aukerman and taking on a more hardcore punk sound. Debut album Milo Goes to College demonstrates the short, loud blasts of comic anger that would come to define the Descendents' sound. By the time they released Enjoy! in 1986 they were also aiming for more mature songs. With lengthy breaks between records, the band's line-up rarely remained constant and founder Navetta passed away in 2008.

408 Nick Lowe

In the late '70s and early '80s Stiff Records was the epicenter of cool, launching the careers of, among others, Ian Dury, the Damned, Madness, Elvis Costello, and Nick Lowe. Lowe already had some notoriety around the U.K. for his previous band Brinsley Schwartz and went on to worldwide success as a solo artist with "Heart of the City", "So It Goes" and "Cruel to Be Kind". While he's best known for early albums like Jesus of Cool and Labour of Lust, he continues to put out good, if more mellow and country-tinged, music today.

409 Rocket From the Crypt

Rocket From the Crypt tweaked the conventions of punk, filling out the gritty guitar sound with horns, strings and background vocals, and easing the breakneck tempo into more of a backbeat-heavy stomp. The original line-up, which included guitarist/vocalist John "Speedo" Reis, guitarist Andy Stamets, bassist Pete Reichert, drummer Sean, and vocalist Elaina, recorded their debut album, Paint as a Fragrance, in 1991 before adding new drummer Adam "Atom" Willard and saxophonist Paul "Apollo 9" O'Beirne for a follow-up album. Rocket From the Crypt signed with Interscope in 1992 and released Scream, Dracula, Scream! in 1995 to popular and critical acclaim. Reis then wanted to focus on other projects so Rocket From the Crypt played their final show on Halloween in 2005.

410 Pere Ubu

Pere Ubu's influence is inversely proportional to its popularity. While the band, fronted by singer/multi-instrumentalist David Thomas, has long eschewed conventional success, their idiosyncratic interpretation of avant-garde rock, jazz, and musique concrete has had an impact on bands from the Talking Heads to TV on the Radio. Thomas formed the initial line-up from the remnants of his previous band Rocket From the Tombs in 1975 and soon released the two singles "30 Seconds Over Tokyo" and "Final Solution" that showcase Thomas' middle-pitched, calling vocals and the band's emphasis on rhythm and texture over melody. The band released three albums, The Modern Dance, Dub Housing, and New Picnic Time, before disbanding in 1979. Pere Ubu emerged in a different configuration in 1987 with a more pop-oriented sound.

411 Down By Law

The only consistent member in the band's 19 year history, guitarist/vocalist Dave Smalley formed Down By Law in 1990 and soon after released a self-titled debut album on Epitaph. Taking influence from Black Flag and X, Down By Law apply a social and political perspective to their propulsive punk sound, characterized chiefly by Smalley's shouting vocals. Unlike his peers in the punk revival who celebrated a young, decidedly male world-view, Smalley's songwriting was mature and focused, but no less energetic. Down By Law signed with Go Kart Records for 1999's Fly the Flag. Though the band has been quiet since 2003's Windwardtidesandwaywardsails, Down By Law is said to be writing and recording a follow-up.

DOWN BY LAW FACTFILE:

Start up year: 1991

Disband year: N/A

Home town: Los Angeles, U.S.A.

Members: Dave Smalley, Chris Bagarozzi, Kevin Coss, Jack Butts, Ed Urlik, Dave Nazworthy, Sam Williams, John DiMambro, Hunter Oswald, more

What you should check out/why: PunkRockDays: The Best of DBL is a fine introduction to DBL's brand of punk rock.

412 Dio

Inside the petite frame of Ronnie James Dio is one of the most powerful voices in the history of rock 'n' roll. After performing in Ronnie and the Red Caps, Elf, Richie Blackmore's Rainbow, and as the replacement for Ozzy Osbourne in heavy metal titans Black Sabbath, it was finally time for Dio to take the reins of a new self-titled group. Building off the mystical, dungeons and dragons imagery he had established in his previous groups, Dio found great success with albums Holy Diver, Last In Line and Dream Evil. Dio reunited recently with his Black Sabbath cohorts under the name Heaven and Hell and released The Devil You Know in 2009.

413 Jerry Lee Lewis

Putting any of today's rock 'n' roll rebels to shame, Jerry Lee Lewis is the original bad boy of rock. Who else could earn the nickname The Killer? While the piano isn't really considered a rock 'n' roll instrument these days, Lewis, like Little Richard, proved that you did not need a guitar to get the kids on their feet. Songs like "Shake, Rattle & Roll" and "Great Balls of Fire" flew to the top of the charts. However, right at Lewis's peak, he married his underage cousin Myra and was awash in a sea of controversy. In the ensuing years he has had continued success in the country market and as a brilliant performer.

414 Ash

Never attaining the popularity Stateside that they achieved in the U.K., Northern Ireland's Ash first grabbed attention in the early'90s with their guileless songs that can be considered pop-punk although they have little in common with other bands of that genre and retain a closer musical relationship with spirited pop-rock groups like Supergrass. Break-through singles "Kung Fu" and "Girl From Mars" established them prior to the release of their first album 1977. Surviving ever-changing popular tastes, Ash had a British Number One hit with Free All Angels which featured the lovely "Shining Light". At this time Ash plan to only release singles, believing audiences are no longer interested in albums. (See picture on p326)

415 At the Drive-In

After tireless touring and a couple of albums gained El Paso, Texas's At the Drive-In a solid following of devotees, it was a breathtaking live performance on MTV that gave the band a late career hit with "One Armed Scissor" from Relationship of Command. For over six years Omar Rodriguez-Lopez, Paul Hinojos, Jim Ward, Cedric Bixler-Zavala and Tony Hajjar made intelligent and aggressive music that challenged audiences to think for themselves. Internal dissent and musical differences caused the band to split while at the peak of their commercial success.

416 Dead Horse

Though not widely known outside of their home state of Texas, Houston's Dead Horse crafted some of the most eclectic and imaginative thrash metal of the 1990s. Dead Horse had the uncanny ability to walk the line between pained emotional turmoil and reckless, playful abandon. One has to look no further than their warped take on the B-52s' classic "Rock Lobster" to see that their roots run deeper than the metal scene with which they were connected. After a few self-funded releases the band found major distribution for Peaceful Death and Pretty Flowers, which is a rewarding listen for all headbangers who like surprises.

417 ...And You Will Know Us By the Trail of Dead

The band that would become ...And You Will Know Us by the Trail of Dead began as a noise rock duo comprised of childhood friends Conrad Keely and Jason Reece, who recorded together in Austin, Texas. After forging a noise-rock framework, Trail of Dead found significant critical acclaim and a broader audience with 2001's Source Tags & Codes. The album featured the abrasive dissonance and complex song structures of their previous albums, but also tighter songwriting structures that only served to make them sound more urgent. The band released its sixth full-length The Century of Self in 2009.

418 Modest Mouse

For over ten years Modest Mouse was among the most popular American indie rock bands around, releasing albums on Calvin Johnson's K Records and generally building a reputation around Isaac Brock's oblique songwriting and yelpy vocals. A steadily growing secret, Modest Mouse maintained a cool cachet among music snobs. All that changed in 2004 with the release of Good News for People Who Love Bad News, the band's second major label release and the album containing "Float On", a clunky yet catchy song that hit the charts and became as ubiquitous in boutiques as it was on dance floors.

419 Sunny Day Real Estate

Sunny Day Real Estate is often credited for helping to create the equally celebrated and maligned punk rock sub-genre of emo. While many up and coming emo bands borrowed greatly from Sunny Day's musical bag of tricks, one should not hold them responsible for the crimes of the others. The intricate drum and bass interplay, melodic guitar lines, and vulnerable hushed-to-scream vocals of front man Jeremy Enigk on their 1994 debut Diary were a breath of fresh air in a sea of frat rock and grunge wannabes. They have disbanded and reformed a few times now, including a 2009 reunion tour.

420 The Dead Boys

Before he headed the goth-friendly Lords of the New Church, Stiv Bators was the voice of the Dead Boys, one of the raunchiest punk bands to ever call Cleveland, Ohio home. Finding an audience at legendary New York club CBGB, the Dead Boys live shows often resulted in violence, often at the behest of Bators' confrontational demeanor. Although the Dead Boys did not have any commercial popularity they penned two of the era's most significant songs, "Sonic Reducer" and "Ain't it Fun". Officially disbanding in 1979, the Dead Boys reunited periodically throughout the '80s. In 1990 Bators died of complications after being hit by a car. (See picture opposite)

MODEST MOUSE FACTFILE:

Start up year: 1993

Disband year: N/A

Home town: Issaquah, Washington, U.S.A.

Members: Isaac Brock, Eric Judy, Jeremiah Green,

What you should check out/why: Good News for People Who Love Bad News includes the catchy "Float On."

SUNNY DAY FACTFILE:

Start up year: 1994

Disband year: N/A

Home town: Seattle, U.S.A.

Members: Jeremy Enigk, Dan Hoerner, Nate Mendel, William Goldsmith, Jeff Palmer, Joe Skyward

What you should check out/why: The reissues of Diary and LP2 include bonus tracks.

421 7 Seconds

While singer Kevin Seconds is beloved by a handful of the population for the solo albums that showcase his acoustic pop songs, most music fans know him for his work with tenacious hardcore band 7 Seconds. Before punks started recording ironic cover versions of pop hits, 7 Seconds edged into the public's conscious with a cover of Nena's "99 Red Balloons". Their version toughened up the song and took away the synthesizers, but it wasn't hard to hear that Seconds embraced the song's anti-war message. Together for almost 30 years, 7 Seconds released Take It Back, Take It On, Take It Over in 2005.

7 SECONDS FACTFILE:

Start up year: 1979

Disband year: N/A

Home town: San Francisco via Reno, Nevada, U.S.A.

Members: Kevin Seconds, Troy Mowat, Steve Youth, Bix Bigler, Bob Adams

What you should check out/why: Walk Together, Rock Together features a fast and furious cover of Nena's anti-war song, "99 Red Balloons."

Worth looking out for: Kevin Second's gentle solo albums. The song "Stoudamire" is a gem.

422 The Mars Volta

When At The Drive-In broke up amidst a storm of mud-slinging and musical differences, three members formed Sparta. The other two, Cedric Bixler-Zavala and Omar Rodgriguez-Lopez, formed The Mars Volta, thus giving them an outlet to explore whatever jazzy, progressive, experimental and psychedelic avenue they chose. As with their former band, a lot of attention was given to the band's exuberant performances, which has resulted in two live records in addition to their studio work. Premiering with the acclaimed De-Loused in the Comatorium they set the standard for what was to come. Anyone looking for straight-ahead punk rock was looking in the wrong place. They released Octahedron in 2009.

423 The Raincoats

Beloved by Kurt Cobain, Robert Wyatt, Sonic Youth and countless other musicians, filmmakers and artists, the Raincoats proved that technical prowess was not essential for making meaningful music. Undergoing numerous reconfigurations, the classic Raincoats line-up is Vicki Aspinall, Gina Birch, Ana DaSilva and Palmolive (previously of The Slits), with saxophone provided by Lora Logic of the X-Ray Spex. Over the course of three studio albums including their self-titled debut that includes a scrappy take on the Kinks' "Lola" and one live release, the Raincoats forged their place in experimental rock history. They reunited in 2006 for Looking in the Shadows and occasionally play special events.

424 Arch Enemy

After parting ways with influential English grindcore band Carcass, guitarist Mike Amott assembled Arch Enemy in his homeland of Sweden. After a few years with former Carnage singer Johan Liiva handling the vocal duties, Arch Enemy found a star in Angela Gossow, who had given a tape to the band's rhythm guitarist Christopher Amott, who is also Mike's brother. Though a female vocalist in a death metal band is an unfortunate rarity, Gossow possesses a powerful growl that can stand up to any of her more testosterone-fueled peers. The current line-up is rounded out by bass player Sharlee D'Angelo and drummer Daniel Erlandsson. (See picture opposite)

425 The Slits

Anybody who considers "I Heard It Through the Grapevine" to be the sole property of Motown has never heard the Slits punky reggae version. Alternately trilling and speaking, singer Ari Up and crew roughen up the Marvin Gaye classic and make it their own. First album Cut also features "Typical Girls", a song that lists a variety of tasks and behaviors women are expected to follow, then asks the astute question; "Who invented the typical girl?" After breaking up in 1981 Up and bassist Tessa Pollitt recruited some new members in 2006 and released an E.P. titled Revenge of the Killer Slits, with the intention of more to follow.

426 Dillinger Escape Plan

Mathematically complex time signatures, rapid-fire riff jumping, and dizzying displays of musical dexterity are the foundation for the hardcore assault that is New Jersey's Dillinger Escape Plan. Known for their jazz-based chops as much as they are for their highly energized and violent live shows, Dillinger Escape Plan gained notoriety in the punk and metal worlds. Their album Calculating Infinity made a fan of former Faith No More singer Mike Patton who then invited them to open for his band Mr. Bungle. That relationship resulted in a collaboration with Patton as vocalist on the release Irony Is A Dead Scene.

427 Bachman-Turner Overdrive

Following his departure from the Guess Who, Randy Bachman took his guitar and hooked up with his brother Robbie and Chad Allan and Fred Turner to form Bachman-Turner Overdrive. While his former band mixed their rock with pop and even a little soul, B.T.O. plays straight-ahead, blues-based rock. Although their first album failed to spark, 1973's Bachman-Turner Overdrive II reversed the band's fortunes and scored hits with "Let It Ride" and, most notably, "Takin' Care of Business", which is perhaps the ultimate working man's anthem. Randy Bachman quit the band in 1977, though he eventually sued his former band-mates for rights to the band's name.

428 Kings of Leon

Nashville, Tennessee's Kings of Leon spent the '00s slowly and stealthily becoming one of the world's most popular bands. When 2003's Youth and Young Manhood came out, the band gained attention for bringing a hint of Southern boogie to their garage rock underpinnings. Subsequent albums Aha Shake Heartbreak in 2005 and Because of the Times in 2007 strengthened the fan base of brothers Caleb, Nathan and Jared Followhill and cousin Matthew Followhill. But it was 2008's Only by the Night and the single "Sex on Fire" that made stadium headliners of the Kings of Leon by showing a bigger and more ambitious sound than ever before.

429 The Klaxons

Given the label "nu-rave" by the press, the Klaxons may have some dance-music inspirations and it would not be remiss to dance to some of their songs, but for the most part they are a band working from a fairly traditional pop-rock standpoint. Formed in 2005, the Klaxons are Jamie Reynolds, James Righton, Simon Taylor-Davis and Steffan Halperin. They take most of their song titles and lyrical themes from science fiction, outer-space, lost worlds and literature. Two of their biggest dance hits are "Atlantis to Interzone" and "Gravity's Rainbow". They released their lone album Myths of the Near Future in 2007.

430 The Troggs

With three chords and a swagger Reg Presley led the Troggs stomping up the charts with their version of Chip Taylor's "Wild Thing", a song that Jimi Hendrix would lend an air of sensuality during his performance at the Monterey Pop Festival. While "Wild Thing" is the best known of their canon, the Troggs had two softer though equally compelling successes with the sweet shuffle of "With A Girl Like You" and the equally endearing "Love is All Around". Although they stuck around for quite a while and continued to release records they were never able to recapture the magic of those early singles.

431 Darkthrone

While many of their Norwegian black metal pioneering peers have evolved into more progressive, musically complex projects or ended up in prison, the highly influential Darkthrone has managed to avoid both scenarios. If anything, the music of Darkthrone seems to be getting rawer and more primitive with each release. Celebrating their love of Mötörhead and all things crusty, the duo of Fenriz and Nocturno Culto has found longevity in relative obscurity. Their classics Under a Funeral Moon and Transylvanian Hunger are a must for anyone interested in black metal. (See picture opposite)

DARKTHRONE FACTFILE:

Start up year: 1988

Disband year: N/A

Home town: Oslo, Norway

Members: Fenriz, Nocturno Culto

What you should check out/why: If you're in need of some true black, why not give Ravishing Grimness a listen?

Worth looking out for: Their NWOBHM album, out July 2009

432 Avenged Sevenfold

Combining pop-punk melodies and emotion with metal's grit and loud guitars, California's Avenged Sevenfold found themselves sitting on a goldmine when the high school friends decided to form a band. Having already kicked around for six years when they released their major label breakthrough City of Evil, Avenged Sevenfold climbed the charts, notably helped along by the success of single "Bat Country". Having hits on both sides of the Atlantic with "Critical Acclaim", "Dear God" and "A Little Piece of Heaven", Avenged Sevenfold may be maturing, but they're taking their fans with them.

AVENGED SEVENFOLD FACTFILE:

Start up year: 1999

Disband year: N/A

Home town: Huntington Beach, California, U.S.A.

Members: Synyster Gates, The Reverend, Zacky Vengeance, M. Shadows, Johnny Christ

What you should check out/why: Sounding the Seventh Trumpet is where it all began.

433 Nickleback

Like many successful post-grunge bands, Nickelback relies on heavy guitar riffs and stomping rhythms and they add singer Chad Kroeger's raspy, clenched-jaw vocals to the mix, though all those characteristics are softened for ballads, which are another staple of the genre. The band found success in their native Canada with second album The State, and crossed over to the U.S. with 2001's Silver Side Up, which featured the single "How You Remind Me." Nickelback continues to find international success and their later singles, "Hero" from the Spiderman soundtrack and "Photograph", continue to benefit from the legacy of early'90s alternative. (See picture opposite)

NICKLEBACK FACTFILE:

Start up year: 1996

Disband year: N/A

Home town: Vancouver, British Columbia, Canada

Members: Chad Kroeger

What you should check out/why: Silver Side Up features "How You Remind Me."

434 Unwound

Coming from Olympia, Washington's independent music scene of the 1990s, Unwound had more in common musically with noise and punk rockers than with scrappy lo-fi combos like Beat Happening. Regardless of genre, Unwound made fierce, caustic, and cathartic music. Originally formed with Justin Trosper on voice and guitar, Vern Rumsey on bass and Brandt Sandeno on drums, the band released some well-received singles and was ready to drop their first album when Sandeno left the band. His replacement Sara Lund attacked her drums with ferocity. Following the release of 2001's Leaves Turn Inside You the band announced it was breaking up.

435 Supersuckers

There's something about Tucson, Arizona that incites members of its population to join or form full-throttle rock 'n' roll bands. Such was the case for Eddie Spaghetti aka Edward Daly, who formed the Supersuckers in 1988 and started hammering out raunchy punk-spiked rockabilly. La Mano Cornuda from 1994 is the Supersuckers' second album and still ranks among the band's best work fifteen years and almost as many releases later. Countless tours, starting up their own label (Mid-Fi) and continuing to record ensure the Supersuckers have little time on their hands. Get it Together, a relatively mature effort, was released in 2008.

UNWOUND FACTFILE:

Start up year: 1991

Disband year: 2001

Home town: Olympia, Washington, U.S.A.

Members: Justin Trosper, Vern Rumsey, Brandt Sandeno, Sara Lund

What you should check out/why: Repetition is loud, disciplined and gut-shaking hardcore punk rock.

SUPERSUCKERS FACTFILE:

Start up year: 1988

Disband year: N/A

Home town: Tucson, Arizona

Members: Eddie Spaghetti, Ron Heathman, Dan "Thunder Bolton, Dan Seigal, Eric Martin, more.

What you should check out/why: Must've Been High for Willie Nelson's guest appearance.

436 Godspeed You Black Emperor

For all the bands that think success can be determined by the frequency with which a band's face graces the cover of a magazine or by the number of column inches an interview runs, there is Godspeed You! Black Emperor. Shrouded in mystery, this nine-piece band from Montreal made haunting, graceful, powerful instrumental music that explored the extremes of dynamics and never insulted its listeners' intelligence. Shunning media attention and only putting faces to the music during performances Godspeed was always reclusive. Athough the band has never officially broken up, at least not publicly, their last album release was
35138. was Yanqui U.X.O. in 2002.

437 Fu Manchu

These days, there is a plethora of bands mining Black Sabbath's cavern of heavy riffs, slow tempos and thunderous rhythm sections, but there was a time when that sound wasn't so popular. Credit for the resurgence in that heavy sound can go, at least in part, to California's Fu Manchu. In 1990 Fu Manchu started releasing singles and building their name so that by the time they released 1994's No One Rides for Free, they already had fans salivating to hear a whole album's worth of material. Never angling for mainstream success, Fu Manchu continue to make heavy music exactly the way they want to play it, ironically calling their 2007 album We Must Obey.

GYBE FACTFILE:

Start up year: 1994

Disband year: 2002?

Home town: Montreal, Quebec, Canada

Members: Efrim Menuck, Mauro Pezzente, Dave Bryant, Aidan Girt, Sophie Trudeau, Thierry Amar, Bruce Cawdron, Norsola Johnson, more

What you should check out/why: Lift Your Skinny Fists Like Antennas to Heaven requires, and deserves, time and attention to be enjoyed.

Worth looking out for: Other albums released on Constellation Records, home of GYBE!

FU MANCHU FACTFILE:

Start up year: 1990

Disband year: N/A

Home town: Orange County, California, U.S.A.

Members: Scott Hill, Brad Davis, Bob Balch, Brant Bjork, more

What you should check out/why: Try The Action is Go for Fu Manchu's cover of SSD's "Nothing Done."

438 Megadeth

Dave Mustaine is one of metal's most unique personalities. As a founding member of Metallica he helped define the California thrash sound, but he was kicked out of the band when stardom was just out of reach. Immediately forming Megadeth, he built on the style he helped to create in his old band by increasing the speed and filling the lyrics with his cynical wit and nihilistic worldview. With his partner bassist Dave Ellefson and a rotating cast of drummers and lead guitarists, Megadeth released landmark albums like Peace Sells…But Who's Buying? and Rust in Peace. (See picture above)

439 Neurosis

Originally formed in Oakland, California in 1985 as a hardcore band, Neurosis has grown to explore doom metal, folk, ambient and experimental styles. With an expansive catalog exploring so much terrain that Neurosis is a musical movement unto itself, the band favors long dirge-like songs that employ minimalist concepts at maximum volume. Sometimes referred to as post-metal, Neurosis exterts an influence on many genre-defying acts, including Isis, Nadja and Pelican. The band also operates its own record label, Neurot Recordings, and has released albums by like minded artists including Oxbow, Om, and their own side-project Tribes of Neurot. (See picture above)

440 Slipknot

In the music business, where being noticed is half the battle, it does not hurt to be a nine-piece band in Halloween masks and matching orange jumpsuits. Des Moines, Iowa's Slipknot, whose members took the numbers zero-to-eight as their stage names, became one of the biggest bands to come from the metal movement. Fusing blistering guitars, pounding drums, industrial samples, and the agonized screams of lead vocalist #8 Corey Taylor, Slipknot found their way into the angst-filled hearts of young people around the world and terrified parents in the process. That is the way rock 'n' roll was meant to be. (See picture opposite)

SLIPKNOT FACTFILE:

Start up year: 1995

Disband year: N/A

Home town: Des Moines, Iowa, U.S.A.

Members: Corey Taylor, Josh Brainard, Paul Grey, Craig Jones, Joey Jordison, Sid Wilson, Chris Fehn, Shawn Crahan, Mick Thompson, Jim Root

What you should check out/why: The 10-year reissue of Slipknot because it comes with a live DVD and bonus songs.

"You can only stare at a clown mask so long. After a few minutes it's no big deal anymore. So people start paying attention to the music instead of what the clown is doing, or what he is wearing, or how cool his spikey hair is."
-Paul Gray

NIRVANA
VESTIBULE - THE INDECISIVE
CIRCLE I - LIMBO
CIRCLE II - THE LUSTFUL
CIRCLE III - THE GLUTTONOUS

441 Ladyhawk

Ladyhawk makes grandly melancholy guitar rock that rushes from whisper to wail with distorted guitars accompanying guitarist/ singer Duffy Driediger's earnest vocals and emotive lyrics, though the band's variety of angst is often expressed as sarcasm. "The Dugout" and "My Old Jacknife" from their self-titled debut epitomize the band's expansive guitars, off-kilter melodies, and heart-on-sleeve lyrics. Often cited as disciples of Neil Young and Crazy Horse, Ladyhawk revels in that same mid-tempo, riff-laden churn, but tend to fill in the spaces with background vocals and yet-stronger guitars. Their follow-up Shots finds the band experimenting with a heavier atmosphere contrasted with graceful backing harmonies. (See picture opposite)

LADYHAWK FACTFILE:

Start up year: 2006

Disband year: N/A

Home town: Vancouver, British Columbia, Canada

Members: Duffy Driediger, Darcy Hancock, Ryan Peters, Sean Hawryluk

What you should check out/why: "The Dugout" and "My Old Jacknife" can both be found on Ladyhawk, stand-outs on an all-around solid debut.

442 Hanoi Rocks

Rock 'n' roll history has made Finland's Hanoi Rocks best known for the car accident that killed drummer Nicholas "Razzle" Dingley, who was the passenger in a car driven by Motley Crue's Vince Neil. Prior to that unforeseen tragedy Michael Monroe, who was born Matti Fagerholm, had been in the process of making his band famous. A glammed-up cover of Creedence Clearwater Revival's "Up Around the Band" from the album Two Steps from the Move hit the British charts and Hanoi Rocks had their eyes set on America. Although the band broke up in 1985 Munroe and guitar player Andy McCoy reunited Hanoi Rocks in 2002.

443 Black Label Society

Guitar God Zakk Wylde became Ozzy Osbourne's lead guitarist and right hand man at the ripe old age of nineteen, thus joining the rich tradition of Ozzy guitarists Randy Rhodes and Tonni Iommi. In his free time Wylde fronts his own band, Black Label Society, where he handles the guitar, vocal, and songwriting duties. Not surprisingly, Black Sabbath is an obvious influence, but Black Label Society also shares a kinship with Alice in Chains and southern rockers like the Allman Brothers and Lynyrd Skynryd. In 2009 they released their eighth studio album, Pride and Glory.

444 BellRays

When California's BellRays first started making their fiery soul-rock in the '90s, no one had heard of Amy Winehouse and it had been a long time since a woman with vocals as smoky and vulnerable as Lisa Kekaula's had been heard on the radio or had a top ten hit. Releasing their sixth album, Hard, Sweet and Sticky, in 2008, the BellRays still have not found widespread commercial favor, but that has not stopped fans and critics from falling in love with them time and time again. The Red, White and Black from 2003 is a great place to start as this is where the bands' confluence of soul, garage rock and jazz hits its stride.

445 Constantines

Hailing from Toronto by way of smaller Canadian towns, Constantines make rock 'n' roll that owes a little to Bruce Springsteen, a little to Fugazi and a smidge to The Band, which is to say they play narrative, occasionally country-flavored art rock with a some shouty punk moments but don't shy away from a rousing chorus. With four albums to Constantines' credit, their critical peak so far has been 2003's Shine a Light, featuring "Nighttime/Anytime (It's Alright)", a single for the band and a highlight of their intense live shows. As the band's singers Bry Webb and Steve Lambke have both moved to Montreal now, Constantines is not quite as busy as previously but they've still played a ton of shows in support of 2008's Kensington Heights.

446 Boss Hog

Not exactly a prolific band, Boss Hog has released three albums in its 11-year existence. Based around the married duo of Jon Spencer and Cristina Martinez, Boss Hog's music is not far removed from Spencer's other band, the Blues Explosion, combining sleazy rock 'n' soul with punk adrenaline and an experimental vibe. On their major label debut Boss Hog (1995), Martinez and Spencer duet on a cover of Ike and Tina Turner's "I Idolize You" and it does not take much imagination to hear the truth in their vocals. Although they have not released an album since 2001's Whiteout, Boss Hog play the occasional show.

CONSTANTINES FACTFILE:

Start up year: 1999

Disband year: N/A

Home town: Guelph, Ontario, Canada

Members: Bryan Webb, Steve Lambke, Will Kidman, Doug McGregor, Dallas Wehrle

What you should check out/why: Shine a Light features "Nighttime/Anytime (It's Alright)", one of the best rock songs of the 00s.

Worth looking out for: Constantines duet with Feist on the "Islands in the Stream" 7".

BOSS HOG FACTFILE:

Start up year: 1995

Disband year: 2001 was their last album, though they occasional perform live

Home town: New York, New York, U.S.A.

Members: Cristina Martinez, Jon Spencer, Hollis Queens, Charlie Ondras, Pete Shore, more

What you should check out/why: Boss Hog for the down 'n' dirty cover of Ike and Tina Turner's "I Idolize You."

447 Vampire Weekend

One of the biggest names of 2008 was New York City's preppy crew, Vampire Weekend. Defying their near-goth name, the guys in Vampire Weekend make up-tempo Afro beat-inspired rock that doesn't sound entirely unlike what Haircut 100 was trying to do in the '80s. They dress similarly, too. Song lyrics about grammar and college life abound on Vampire Weekend, which may leave some listeners in the dark while keeping young fans enraptured and finding a niche with audience with grammar teachers everywhere, particularly with the song "Oxford Comma".

448 Tad

Tad weighs in on the heavier end of the grunge scale, easily outclassing even Mudhoney in its plodding, metal-derived guitar riffs and pummeling drums. It is no surprise then that the band never found the mainstream success of their Seattle peers whose youthful rebellion was more palatable than Tad Doyle's darkly comic lyrics, throaty vocals and Tad's sludgy guitar assault. Tad released two albums with Sub Pop, God's Balls and 8-Way Santa, the latter produced by Butch Vig, but neither attracted much attention outside of controversy over cover art. Inhaler, Tad's first for a major label, features a somewhat lighter sound and earned positive critical attention.

VAMPIRE WEEKEND FACTFILE:

Start up year: 2008

Disband year: N/A

Home town: New York, U.S.A.

Members: Ezra Koenig, Chris Baio, Rostam Batmanglij, Chris Tomson

What you should check out/why: Their self-titled debut is their only record to date.

TAD FACTFILE:

Home town: Seattle, Washington, U.S.A.

Members: Tad Doyle, Kurt Danielson, Gary Thostensen, Steve Wied, Josh Sinder, Mike Mongrain

What you should check out/why: 1993's Inhaler is a grunge-era standard.

Worth looking out for: The original cover of 1991's 8-Way Santa.

449 Bloc Party

Though not as overtly funky as their dance-punk forefathers Gang of Four, British quartet Bloc Party retain the earlier band's tension and unsettling marriage of guitar and synth. Singer Kele Okereke provides polished, dynamic vocals that tie the sound together. Among the energetic, staccato dance numbers that populate Bloc Party albums, particularly their debut, Silent Alarm, are soaring ballads that draw from Radiohead's Kid A in their use of beats and atmosphere. These moments dominate their second album, A Week in the City, which has a warm, emotionally honest feel that continues on the more blatantly political, Intimacy.

450 Skid Row

When your singer's name is Sebastian Bach, how can you lose? In the case of Skid Row the salad days didn't last long but they left an indelible print on the hard rock landscape. In 1989, just a couple of years before Nirvana would change the sound of radio for a while anyway, Skid Row's self-titled debut gave them the two giant hits "18 and Life" and power ballad "I Remember You". While Bach only stuck it out with the band for two more records, including Slave to the Grind which debuted at #1 in the U.S., Skid Row soldiers on today. Bach is better known for his acting these days, and has enjoyed a recurring role on the television show The Gilmour Girls.

BLOC PARTY FACTFILE:

Start up year: 2004

Disband year: N/A

Home town: London, England

Members: Kele Okereke, Matt Tong, Gordon Moakes, Russell Lissack

What you should check out/why: Silent Alarm ushered in a dance-rock trend, but Okereke's lyrics set it apart from those that came in their wake.

SKID ROW FACTFILE:

Start up year: 1986

Disband year: N/A (although without singer Sebastian Bach)

Home town: Toms River, New Jersey, U.S.A.

Members: Sebastian Bach, Rachel Bolan, Scott Hill, Dave Sabo, Rob Affuso, Phil Varone, Johnny Solinger

What you should check out/why: Skid Row includes "18 and Life" and "I Remember You", two hair metal classics.

451 The Walkmen

In the midst of the garage rock revival, Brooklyn's Walkmen opted to slow their tempos, incorporate piano and organ and drench everything in a pensive but peaceful atmosphere to create a rock sound that still fit alongside contemporaries the Strokes and Interpol. The band's debut album Everyone Who Pretended to Like Me is Gone was met with critical acclaim and a wide mainstream audience when the song "We've Been Had" appeared in a car commercial. Subsequent albums, including their 2006 full-length cover of Harry Nilsson and John Lennon's Pussy Cats, have found the band the band experimenting with a fuller sound that often involves horns and exploring blues and folk colors. (See picture opposite)

THE WALKMEN FACTFILE:

Start up year: 2000

Disband year: N/A

Home town: New York, New York, U.S.A.

Members: Hamilton Leithauser, Paul Maroon, Peter Bauer, Walter Martin, Matt Barrick

What you should check out/why: Bows & Arrows is a wonderfully atmospheric album and features, "The Rat".

Worth looking out for: Records by Jonathan Fire*Eater, whose ashes begat a number of Walkmen.

452 J. Geils Band

After years of under the radar popularity as a bar band steeped in early rock 'n' roll, doo-wop and blues, it took a fairly radical change in sound for Boston's J. Geils to have their biggest hits. A hint of success came with 1980's Love Stinks album and the single of the same name. But it took them injecting a lot more pop into the J. Geils sound with songs like "Centerfold" and "Freeze Frame" from the album Freeze Frame before they became one of the most played bands of 1981. Unfortunately, they could not keep it together and broke up soon after.

453 Social Distortion

After 30 years and numerous changes to the band's make up, only Mike Ness remains to carry the name of Social Distortion into the next decade. With his recognizable vocals that sound a bit like the Clash's Joe Strummer as filtered through a Californian twang, Ness is the X-factor that led the song "Bad Luck" to get some radio play and expand Social D's faithful audience. Ness's admiration of Johnny Cash led to his band's slash-and-burn covers of "Folsom Prison Blues" and "Ring of Fire". (See picture opposite)

454 The Flamin' Groovies

Finding at least in the U.K. a brief flash of commercial success with the album Shake Some Action eight years after the band's inception, the Flamin' Groovies never took off with mainstream audiences, although they remain integral to the fabric of rock 'n' roll. Formed in 1968, the Flamin' Groovies released one album, Supersnazz, for Epic Records before being dropped by the label. Making music that was decidedly unfashionable for the times, when everyone else was letting their hair grow and wearing sandals, the Groovies sported four-button suits and made music that still sounds great today.

455 The Mummies

Wrapped up like, well, mummies, California's ultimate garage band the Mummies took the '60s party rock sound to a place even more straightforward, primitive and tough than where it had originated. Loud, snarling, confrontational and fast, Larry Winther, Maz Kattuah, Trent Ruane, and Russell Quan kept the Mummies together for four years from 1989 to 1992. One of the band's finest moments was the song "You Must Fight to Live on the Planet of the Apes", an original that obviously pays homage to the science-fiction classic. After years of being out of print the Mummies' classic Never Been Caught is now available on CD.

456 The Mamas and the Papas

John and Michelle Phillips, Denny Doherty and Cass Elliot came from jazz and folk backgrounds to form the signature vocal group of the '60s, bringing with them some of the harmonies and structures of their previous work to craft rich, layered pop that spawned ten successful singles in only three years. The Mamas and the Papas 1966 debut album If You Can Believe Your Eyes and Ears featured "Monday, Monday" and "California Dreaming," two of their biggest hits that both demonstrate light melodies, closely harmonized voicing, and wistful, idealistic lyrics. The group broke up in 1966 but briefly reunited in 1971.

457 Richard Hell and the Voidoids

After bailing from a still-nascent Television, Richard Hell, who was born Richard Meyer, hooked up with Johnny Thunders in the Heartbreakers, but it wasn't long before the charismatic and poetic Hell decided to head up his own band. Thus the Voidoids were formed. Hell didn't have much initiative so he only released two albums with the band, not including 2002's Time that compiled bits and pieces of the past with a couple of new songs thrown in for fun. But 1977's Blank Generation and 1982's Destiny Street show as much growth in two albums as many bands do in two decades and they remain essential listening for anyone interested in New York punk rock.

458 Dire Straits

In the midst of the '70s divide between punk's aggression and arena rock's bluster came Dire Straits. "Sultans of Swing", a no-frills blues-based song about a bunch of guys who love to play music, set up the band's mandate and gave them their first hit. That was in 1978 and while their next three albums were critically lauded it seemed that the hits had dried up. Then they released Brothers in Arms in 1985 and became one of the biggest bands in the world based on "Money for Nothing", "So Far Away" and "Walk of Life". The songs still had Mark Knopfler's dry vocal delivery and bluesy guitar leads, but they also featured more synths and sounded good on the radio.

459 The Boomtown Rats

On the strength of early songs "Lookin' After No. 1" and "Mary of the Fourth Form", Ireland's Boomtown Rats were considered a punk band from the outset. While the band has punk's energy, singer Bob Geldof's narrative lyrics are closer to those of Thin Lizzy's Phil Lynott or Bruce Springsteen, a similarity underscored by the saxophone breaks on "Rat Trap". Already popular in 1979, they blew up with "I Don't Like Mondays" and headed straight to Number One on the U.K. charts. Too controversial for U.S. radio because the lyrics are based on reports of a school shooting, the song did not attain the same heights there but remains one of the most powerful songs of the time.

460 Hot Snakes

For four albums John "Speedo" Reis and Rick Froberg, who are both ex-Drive Like Jehu members, along with Jason Kourkounis and Gar Wood, were Hot Snakes, a scrappy, pure rock 'n' roll band that lasted from 1999 to 2005. Releasing most of their albums through Reis' own label Swami, Hot Snakes was truly an independent band. First album Automatic Midnight introduced the loud, guitar-soaked fun that made Hot Snakes such an engaging live band. On a bittersweet note, Hot Snakes have the honor of being the final band to record for BBC DJ John Peel's Peel Sessions.

461 Suicide

Suicide, also known as the duo of Alan Vega and Martin Rev, made incredibly terrifying, harrowing and depressing music considering just two people were involved. Although mainstream success eluded the synthesizer and drum machine-reliant pair, today they are best known for the song "Frankie Teardrop". Taken from their first album, "Frankie" tells the story of a guy struggling to make it and then decides he can't take it anymore, sort of like a character from one of Bruce Springsteen's songs of lost hope. Not for everyone, Suicide is beloved by nihilists everywhere. (See picture opposite)

"I always said I was never gonna be an entertainer, Suicide was never supposed to be entertainment." – Alan Vega

SUICIDE FACTFILE:

Start up year: 1971

Disband year: N/A

Home town: New York, New York, U.S.A.

Members: Alan Vega, Martin Rev

What you should check out/why:

Worth looking out for: Nick Hornby's essay about why he never needs to hear "Frankie Teardrop" again.

462 Los Lobos

By now an institution of American pop music, Los Lobos have performed and recorded together without a line-up shift and with only a single brief hiatus for 35 years, drawing on rock 'n' roll, Spanish and Mexican folk music, soul, and other genres to craft a refined, expressive pop sound. Their early EPs and LPs, particularly 1984's How Will the Wolf Survive, were celebrated by critics for their clarity and brisk, Tex-Mex tinged rock feel, but the band found its biggest audience with the soundtrack for the film La Bamba, which found them covering tragic rock 'n' roller Richie Valens' songs.

463 Corrosion of Conformity

Starting out in 1983 in Raleigh, North Carolina, Corrosion of Conformity was part of the first wave of hardcore, helping define the genre with the breakneck speed and near-incomprehensible lyrics that form first album Eye for an Eye. Undergoing lineup and label changes throughout their early existence, they found crossover success when they started incorporating sludgy '70s rock riffs and Ministry-style vocal distortion into their sound, hitting their peak of popularity with 1991's Blind. Together for over twenty-five years, Corrosion of Conformity released Arms of God in 2005.

464 The Undertones

Derry, Northern Ireland's entry into the punk rock melee was the Undertones, who shared the Buzzcock's blend of melody, energy and songs that painted vivid lyrical images. Singer Feargal Sharkey's adenoidal quaver was perfect for songs about adolescent lust and anxiety. Given the seal of approval by influential and sorely missed BBC DJ John Peel, who once named the Undertones' first single "Teenage Kicks" as his favorite song, helped the struggling band gain some well-deserved attention. The band's first two albums, The Undertones and Hypnotised, are both excellent and gave them hits with "Jimmy, Jimmy" and "My Perfect Cousin". (See picture opposite)

LOS LOBOS FACTFILE:

Start up year: 1973

Disband year: N/A

Home town: Los Angeles, U.S.A.

Members: Cesar Rosas, David Hidalgo, Steve Berlin, Conrad Lozano, Louie Pérez

What you should check out/why: The Town and the City shows that some bands get better with age.

Worth looking out for: The band's appearance in the Richie Valens biopic, La Bamba

COROSSION OF CONFORMITY FACTFILE:

Start up year: 1983

Disband year: N/A

Home town: Raleigh, North Carolina

Members: Pepper Keenan, Reed Mullin, Woody Weatherman, Eric Eycke, Simon Bob, Karl Agell, Phil Swisher, Mike Dean

What you should check out/why: Blind shows Corrosion of Conformity heading toward metal, but still retaining punk lyrics and song structure.

Worth looking out for:

465 The Bobby Fuller Four

In a tragically short career Bobby Fuller demonstrated unique songwriting gifts as well as an affinity for the tight rockabilly and early rock 'n' roll sounds that were just beginning to pass out of fashion when he entered the spotlight. In fact, Fuller's career mimed that of his fellow Texan and greatest influence, Buddy Holly, who's light, driving rhythms, bright guitar, and quavering vocal twang he emulated. Fuller's biggest hit "I Fought the Law", was penned by Sonny Curtis of the Crickets and he also hit with a cover of Holly's "Love's Made a Fool of You". And, like Holly, Fuller died young, at age 23.

466 Sebadoh

Sebadoh began as a creative outlet for Dinosaur Jr. bassist Lou Barlow, whose songwriting contributions to that band were sidelined by J. Mascis. When Mascis decided to replace Barlow, Sebadoh became Barlow's full-time concern. Barlow began writing and recording a mix of quiet, acoustic songs featuring his low, mournful vocals, and lo-fi noise jams with Eric Gaffney and Jason Lowenstein. Sebadoh's fourth album Bubble and Scrape demonstrates the band's split personality, alternating between songs like gently strummed, heart-breaking "Soul and Fire" and the thrashing of "No Way Out". Other Sebadoh favorites include 1994's Bakesale and its follow-up Harmacy. (See picture opposite)

467 Slowdive

Though often mentioned in the same breath as Ride, Chapterhouse, and other noted shoegazers, Slowdive has little to do with that "movement" outside of a shared affinity with My Bloody Valentine and the Cocteau Twins. In three albums released over a five-year span, Neil Halstead, Rachel Goswell, Nick Chaplin, Christian Savill and Simon Scott dabbled in pop, dub, ambient, techno, and country, and washed it all in distortion. Slowdive's 1993 album Souvlaki, widely regarded as the band's best record, is also its most diverse, ranging from the whirling guitars of "Allison" to the synth-heavy "Missing You." It also contains a cover of Lee Hazelwood and Nancy Sinatra's "Some Velvet Morning" that arguably ups the psychedelic ante.

468 Charlatans

While Manchester's Charlatans' first hit, "The Only One I Know", with its Hammond organ hook and shuffling rhythm, was a product of the same scene , known as "baggy", that begat the Stone Roses and Happy Mondays, the Charlatans lived to outgrow the label and outlast most of their colleagues. Led by the Jagger-like Tim Burgess, the Charlatans have had more commercial success (1993's Up to Our Hips, 1997's Tellin' Stories) in the U.K. than the U.S., though tours in both countries are met with excitement from fans. In 2008 the Charlatans released their tenth album You Cross My Path.

SLOWDIVE FACTFILE:

Start up year: 1989

Disband year: 1995

Home town: Reading, England

Members: Neil Halstead, Rachel Goswell, Nick Chaplin, Christian Savill, Simon Scott

What you should check out/why: Souvlaki for the dreamy, trippy "Allison."

CHARLATANS FACTFILE:

Start up year: 1989

Disband year: N/A

Home town: Manchester, England

Members: Tim Burgess, Tony Rogers, John Baker, Mark Collins, Jon Brookes, Rob Collins

What you should check out/why: Up to Our Hips is a mid-'90s look at the music of the past, featuring "Can't Get Out of Bed."

469 Clap Your Hands Say Yeah

One of the earliest bands that owes its popularity to blog chatter and other forms of grassroots online promotion, Clap Your Hands Say Yeah self-released both of their full-length albums, Clap Your Hands Say Yeah and Some Loud Thunder, and seem content to enjoy their independence. The band makes up-tempo, danceable guitar-pop characterized by singer Alec Ounsworth's David Byrne-derived nasal, yelping vocals. In fact, the rhythmic drive, lightly chugging guitars and bass rumble of "Let the Cool Goddess Rust Away" from the band's first record suggests the nervous energy of the Talking Heads, while the second features the band beginning to experiment with noise and unusual song structures. (See picture opposite)

CLAP YOUR HANDS SAY YEAH FACTFILE:

Start up year: 2004

Disband year: N/A

Home town: Brooklyn, U.S.A.

Members: Alec Ounsworth, Lee and Tyler Sargent, Sean Greenhaigh, Robbie Guertin

What you should check out/why: The self-titled debut is a good introduction to this band's all-over-the-map indie rock.

470 Deerhunter

One of the most enigmatic singers of the '00s, Deerhunter's Bradford Cox, who also makes music under the name Atlas Sound, has already confounded fans by putting out three disparate albums. Their debut Deerhunter, was a dissonant take on new wave which they followed with the dance beats of Cryptograms. Microcastle from 2008 includes some of Cox's most ear-catching songs, including the moving "Agoraphobia" and the excellent title song, which jumps from being a meandering exercise in space to having a driving rhythm and distorted guitars.

DEERHUNTER FACTFILE:

Start up year: 2001

Disband year: N/A

Home town: Atlanta, U.S.A.

Members: Bradford Cox, Moses Archuleta, Josh Fauvre, Colin Mee, Lockett Pundt

What you should check out/why: Microcastle for the glorious one-two punch of "Cover Me (Slowly)" and "Agoraphobia".

Worth looking out for: Records by Bradford Cox's other band, The Atlas Sound

Marshall
Marshall

471 Bardo Pond

With only a passing interest in making music that adhered to popular conventions, brothers Michael and John Gibbons founded Philadelphia's Bardo Pond in 1989. For twenty years Bardo Pond has explored spacey, experimental, psychedelic music that has at various times dabbled in free jazz conventions and musique concrete. Throughout the '90s Bardo Pond made some of their best records for the Matador label, including 1996's Amanita, which found singer/flutist Isobel Sollenberger's voice becoming one with the instruments on these languid, mesmerizing, and often disorienting songs. (See picture opposite)

BARDO POND FACTFILE:

Start up year: 1991

Disband year: N/A

Home town: Philadelphia, Pennsylvania, U.S.A.

Members: Michael and John Gibbons, Isobel Sollenberger, Joe Culver, Clint Takeda

What you should check out/why: Try Aminita for lots of drones, fuzz and feedback.

472 Raveonettes

Sharin Foo and Sune Rose Wagner of the Raveonettes take characteristics of their namesakes, notably the close harmonies and doo-wop dynamics of the Ronettes and the rock drive of Buddy Holly's "Rave On", and wash them in distortion and feedback. The Danish duo came to international attention with their first album Whip It On, which introduced their postmodern take on '50s rock 'n' roll in gritty, up-tempo songs like "Attack of the Ghost Riders". Although the Raveonettes' second and third albums found Foo and Wagner recording with a full band, their fourth full-length Lust Lust Lust is a return to their origins. (See picture opposite)

473 The Decemberists

Putting literacy and history back into popular music seems to be the unofficial mandate of Decemberists' singer Colin Meloy. As a solo artist he has released a number of limited edition albums in tribute to his favorite performers including esoteric folk icon Shirley Collins. With his band, the Portland, Oregon Decemberists, Meloy has released five albums, including 2009's rock opera The Hazards of Love which also finds the band beefing up their expansive pop sound with more reverb and, if such a thing can be said for such a bookish lot, more muscle.

RAVEONETTES FACTFILE:

Start up year: 2001

Disband year: N/A

Home town: Copenhagen, Denmark

Members: Sharin Foo, Sune Rose Wagner

What you should check out/why: Lust Lust Lust for the excellent "Aly, Walk With Me."

THE DECEMBERISTS FACTFILE:

Start up year: 2000

Disband year: N/A

Home town: Portland, Oregon, U.S.A.

Members: Colin Meloy, Jenny Conlee, Nate Query, Chris Funk, John Moen, Ezra Holbrook, Jesse Emerson

What you should check out/why: Picaresque is this literate, lyric-heavy band at its finest.

Worth looking out for: Singer Colin Meloy's tribute to English folk singer Shirley Collins, Colin Meloy Sings Shirley Collins.

474 Wolves in the Throne Room

Sometimes, even in the darkest places, light remains. So it is with Olympia, Washington black metal mavens Wolves in the Throne Room. While their music throbs and pulses under masses of bass and low-end guitar, Wolves in the Throne Room radiates a sound that isn't rooted in evil or even in ambivalence. Even when the lyrics are impossible to decode, the message is clear. The band members' commitment to the earth and environment is a focal point of their lives and music. Wolves in the Throne Room may be one of the most inspiring bands of our time.

475 ? and the Mysterians

Punk progenitors ? and the Mysterians formed in Michigan in the early '60s and made an indelible impression on modern music with the single "96 Tears". Characterized by a catchy central organ riff, minimal chord changes, and singer Question Mark's unsentimental, attitude-heavy vocals, "96 Tears" became a national hit in 1966. Critic Dave Marsh used the label "punk" to describe the band's sound in 1971, and their minimal rock sound influenced the Ramones and other first-wave punk bands. The band's lineup changed several times over its career, but the original Mysterians reunited with ? for a few performances in the early 2000s. (See picture opposite)

476 Saint Vitus

Back in the days when punk and metal was first starting to admit they could be friends, Black Flag's Greg Ginn released doom metal band Saint Vitus's self-titled premiere on his influential SST label. With support from all sides, the Californian band who worshipped at the altar of Black Sabbath should have been a success. And, in the sense that they've gone on to influence bands that have sprung up since their mid '90s demise, they were successful. While they found more success with the mid '80s introduction of Scott "Wino" Weinrich as their singer, they still remained obscure and eventually disbanded in 1996.

477 Brian Jonestown Massacre

It is likely that more people have seen the documentary Dig! that chronicles the dramatic machinations of Brian Jonestown Massacre singer Anton Newcombe than have ever heard the band's records. That is unfortunate, because when San Francisco's BJM hit the mark, as they did on songs like "Going to Hell" and "Anemone", they were one of the finest psychedelic rock bands around. While albums like Take It From the Man! and Strung Out in Heaven often have an easy-going vibe, the band's live shows often disintegrate into name-calling, bottle-throwing and violence.

SAINT VITUS FACTFILE:

Start up year: 1979

Disband year: 1996 (reunions have followed)

Home town: Los Angeles, U.S.A.

Members: Scott "Wino" Weinrich, Mark Adams, Dave Chandler, Armando Acosta, more.

What you should check out/why: Live gives fans of the band – of which there is a far greater number now than there was during the band's existence – a chance to hear what Saint Vitus sounded like live.

BRIAN JONESTOWN MASSACRE FACTFILE:

Start up year: 1990

Disband year: N/A

Home town: San Francisco, California, U.S.A.

Members: Anton Newcombe, Joel Gion, Matt Hollywood, Dean Taylor, more

What you should check out/why: Strung Out in Heaven for the trippy jangle of "Going to Hell."

478 The Coral

Attempting to discern the Coral's key influences is akin to flipping through a used record bin labeled "The '60s". Ennio Morricone, Dick Dale, the Beatles and Syd Barrett are only a handful of potential touchstones. Formed in the mid'90s in Hoylake, England by six high school friends, Coral weaves the sounds of their forbearers into clear, pop- rock distinguished by a quavering surf guitar, organs, horns, and vocalist James Skelly's croon. Their self-titled 2002 debut album earned a Mercury Prize nomination. The Invisible Invasion, Coral's fourth full-length, features less ornate arrangements, and layers a moody atmosphere over the proceedings. (See picture opposite)

479 The Clean

Two of the most significant figures in Dunedin, New Zealand's underappreciated yet influential music scene are brothers Hamish and David Kilgour. Signing with the Flying Nun label in the early'80s, the Clean released the simple and addictive single "Tally Ho!", which was the song made the charts in the band's homeland and got music fans around the world excited to hear more from this young band. Releasing albums and EPs since their inception, the Clean were at the forefront of indie rock's Do It Yourself spirit and recorded most of their music with a four-track. The Clean released their eighth album Mister Pop in 2009. (See picture opposite)

480 Joan of Arc

Perhaps because Tim Kinsella's previous band Cap'n Jazz played a significant role in emo's development in the early '90s, Joan of Arc is considered emo as well. And while that classification speaks to the band's facility with melodic rock and Kinsella's yowling vocals, it ignores the band's versatility and flirtation with krautrock in its use of electronics, loops and dense sound collages. Joan of Arc's first three studio albums chart a trajectory from the gentle guitars and synths of A Portable Models Of… to the spacious sound concept of The Gap, though later albums would find the band returning to more recognizable song structures

481 King Crimson

In 1969, Robert Fripp, Ian McDonald, Greg Lake, Michael Giles and Peter Sinfield effectively invented the genre known as prog-rock when they released In the Court of the Crimson King. Packaged in one of the most haunting album sleeves ever created, Crimson King brings jazz, folk, Mellotron, musical virtuosity and fantastical lyrics to the table in one ambitious album that divides music fans into those who consider it one of the finest musical creations of the 20th century, and those who think it is self-aggrandizing gobbledygook. Fripp and the gang continued exploring their vast musical palettes. The band broke up in 1974, though different versions of the band appeared for years to come. (See picture opposite)

KING CRIMSON FACTFILE:

Start up year: 1969

Disband year: 1974

Home town: England, with English and American band members

Members: Robert Fripp, Ian McDonald, Greg Lake, Michael Giles, Peter Sinfeld, Bill Bruford, Adrian Belew, Tony Levin, more

What you should check out/why: In the Court of the Crimson King is the apex of progressive rock.

482 Free

Prior to leading Bad Company into the hearts and minds of classic rock fans everywhere, Paul Rodgers pretty much defined the era of fist-pumping stadium rock with Free. With band members culled from the cream of England's blues scene, there was no shortage of talent among the ranks of Free, although there were as many internal clashes and substance abuse issues among Free as there typically were with bands whose careers spanned decades, even though Free spent only five years together. Nonetheless, the guys from Free had one of the most enduring hits of the era with "All Right Now".

FREE FACTFILE:

Start up year: 1968

Disband year: 1973

Home town: London, England

Members: Paul Rodgers, Andy Fraser, Paul Kossoff, Simon Kirke

What you should check out/why: Tons of Sobs is a British blues-rock classic.

483 Living Colour

Considering that rock 'n' roll's founders are African-American, it seems strange that it would be such a big deal when Corey Glover, Vernon Reid, Muzz Skillings and Will Calhoun formed hard rocking Living Colour and released Vivid in 1988. Their touring with the Rolling Stones on the Steel Wheels tour gave audiences a chance to check out Reid's guitar skills and Glover's skills as a singer and front man. In the meanwhile, "Cult of Personality" and "Glamour Boys" were getting tons of radio play. The follow-up, Time's Up sold well, too, although it didn't have as memorable songs as the debut. Everything is Possible: The Very Best of Living Colour was released in 2006. (See picture opposite)

LIVING COLOUR FACTFILE:

Start up year: 1984

Disband year: 1995 (but have since reunited)

Home town: New York, U.S.A.

Members: Corey Glover, Vernon Reid, Muzz Skillings, Will Calhoun

What you should check out/why: Debut album, Vivid, for the acerbic "Funny Vibe".

Worth looking out for: Singer Corey Glover's appearance in the movie Platoon.

484 Whiskeytown

Like Uncle Tupelo and the Jayhawks, Whiskeytown mined the conventions of country music, particularly the country-rock of Gram Parsons, and mixed in some of the Replacements' rock 'n' roll energy. Ryan Adams formed the band in Raleigh, North Carolina, with Caitlin Cary, Eric Gilmore, Steve Grothman, and Phil Wandscher, but, with the exception of Adams and Cary, Whiskeytown's line-up changed frequently. Faithless Street, the band's first album, introduced its characteristic down-tempo country swing and Adams' raspy vocals. Its success attracted the attention of Geffen Records, who signed Whiskeytown and released its follow-up album Strangers Almanac. The band recorded a third album, Pneumonia, which was shelved until 2001. By then Whiskeytown was no more and Adams' solo career was underway.

485 The Blasters

If the Blasters' brand of late'70s punk-influenced rockabilly R&B sounds more authentic than many other revivalists, it may be due to Phil and Dave Alvin's early association with blues legends T-Bone Walker, Lee Allen and others. The brothers capitalized on that tutelage and began performing rock that shot the blues swagger of their guitars, drummer Bill Bateman's thick backbeats, and Phil Alvin's soulful vocals through a scrim of raw punk energy. They found a sympathetic audience in Los Angeles and frequently appeared with like-minded, though more obviously punk, bands like X and Black Flag, though their diversity and broad appeal led to appearances on tour with bands as diverse as Queen and the Cramps.

WHISKEYTOWN FACTFILE:

Start up year: 1994

Disband year: 2001

Home town: Raleigh, North Carolina, U.S.A.

Members: Ryan Adams, Caitlin Cary, Eric Gilmore, Steve Grothman, Phil Wandscher

What you should check out/why: Try Rural Free Delivery for Whiskeytown's alt.country take on Black Flag's "Nervous Breakdown".

Worth looking out for: Singer Ryan Adams' Heartbreaker; anything by Caitlin Cary.

THE BLASTERS FACTFILE:

Start up year: 1979

Disband year: N/A (without Dave Alvin)

Home town: Los Angeles, California, U.S.A.

Members: Phil and Dave Alvin, Bill Bateman, John Bazz, Gene Taylor, Steve Berlin, Lee Allen, more

What you should check out/why: First record American Music is rock 'n' roll bliss, especially the title track and "Marie, Marie".

486 The Saints

In 1976, The Saints were one of Brisbane, Australia's finest punk bands, making people sit up and listen with first single "(I'm) Stranded", a bouncy, melodic bit of rock 'n' roll that also served as the title song for the Saints' first album. Formed by singer Chris Bailey and guitar player Ed Kuepper, the Saints released two stunning albums in their homeland before Kuepper left the group and Bailey, whose vocals had always been more pop than sneer, took the band in a more mature direction. While the Saints never found worldwide mainstream acceptance, they are beloved in Australia and with classic punk fans everywhere.

487 The Action

While their contemporaries the Who and the Yardbirds developed a hard-edged rock sound based on that of the blues musicians they admired, the Action turned to soul, particularly Motown and Curtis Mayfield, as the impetus for a softer, expressive variation of British beat. Their cover of Gerry Goffin/Carole King's "Just Once in My Life," a song popularized by the Righteous Brothers, demonstrates their subtle touch. Whereas the Righteous Brothers belt the melody, cushioned by strings, the Action's Reg King croons plaintively, backed by gentle guitars and tambourine. Although the band released several singles from 1965 to 1967 none of them charted. The Reaction label reissued the Action's Rolled Gold in 2002.

THE SAINTS FACTFILE:

Start up year: 1976

Disband year: N/A

Home town: Brisbane, Australia

Members: Chris Bailey, Ed Kuepper

What you should check out/why: Debut record, (I'm) Stranded because it's one of the best punk albums of the '70s.

THE ACTION FACTFILE:

Start up year: 1965

Disband year: 1967

Home town: London, England

Members: Reggie King, Pete Watson, Martin Stone, Roger Powell, Ian Whiteman, Alan King, Mike Evans

What you should check out/why: The collection Rolled Gold because the song "Something to Say" is the cream of the Mod crop for a start.

RAZZLE DAZZLE

488 Therapy?

For a while in the early '90s it was near-impossible to pick up a music magazine without the faces of Belfast, Ireland's Therapy? jumping out from the pages. Singer/guitarist Andy Cairns, drummer Fyfe Ewing and bassist Michael McKeegan had a huge hit with "Screamager" from their first album Troublegum. This song was as angst-ridden as anything that got stuck with the grunge tag, but Therapy? had a stronger facility for melody than many of those bands. Two decades later they continue to make catchy hard rock, including Crooked Timber from 2009. (See picture opposite)

489 Venom

When a non-fan is asked to describe what a heavy metal band looks like, chances are they'll come up with something that looks like the members of venom. Often bare-chested and bedecked in leather and bondage gear, with long flowing hair, Newcastle's Venom dabbled with Satanic imagery, playfully called their third album To Hell With Satan, and played music that was a little darker and heavier than that of their peers. It was a sound that connected with fans and helped the band to survive for over twenty five years. In 2008 they released Hell, keeping fans happy for another year.

490 The Electric Flag

Rock 'n' roll is full of sub-genres and labels, but the Electric Flag is one of the few bands that truly defy description. While singer Nick Gravenites doesn't do much to distinguish himself, guitar player Mike Bloomfield, previously of Paul Butterfield Blues, and drummer Buddy Miles are two of the most striking on their respective instruments. As for the music, over the course of making four official albums including the soundtrack to The Trip, the Electric Flag dipped into jazz, soul, rock 'n' roll, funk and blues. Sometimes the sound was laid back and blissful and at other times it was a cosmic dance party freak-out. Either way, there's pretty much no arguing with the groove that permeates most of second album A Long Time Comin'.

491

The Waitresses

Best known for "I Know What Boys Like" and the holiday chestnut "Christmas Rapping", Akron, Ohio's Waitresses released two excellent albums and an EP before things fell apart. Most interestingly, the songs were written by Chris Butler from a distinctly female, and often feminist, point of view. Singer Patty Donahue, with her ultra-deadpan delivery was the ideal mouthpiece for wry yet empowering songs like "No Guilt", wherein Donahue lists all the useful things she's done since breaking up with a beau, culminating with the observation "I'm sorry I can't be helpless / It wasn't the end of the world". (See picture opposite)

THE WAITRESSES FACTFILE:

Start up year: 1980

Disband year: 1983

Home town: Akron, Ohio, U.S.A.

Members: Patty Donahue, Chris Butler, Billy Ficca, Dave Hofstra, Mars Williams, Dan Klayman, Tracy Wormworth, Ariel Warner, Ralph Carney

What you should check out/why: Wasn't Tomorrow Wonderful? has "I Know What Boys Like" and the world's best break-up song, "No Guilt".

Worth looking out for: The Waitresses' appearance on the pilot episode of Square Pegs.

492 Pansy Division

It seems obvious that punk rock should embrace and be embraced by the queer community, although to this day few bands have done it as successfully as San Francisco's Pansy Division. While Pansy Division is no longer a full-time job for singer/songwriter Jon Ginoli and bassist Chris Freeman, who played with numerous drummers, they've been incorporating gay themes and lyrics, often in parodies of popular songs like "Smells Like Queer Spirit", into catchy pop-punk melodies since 1991. While opening for Green Day on the Dookie tour Pansy Division widened their audience while remaining unabashed about politics, love and sex.

493 Cracker

David Lowery formed Cracker in 1990 after his previous band, indie rock favorites Camper Van Beethoven, broke up. They had an early hit with "Teen Angst (What the World Needs Now)" but found greater success with their follow-up album, Kerosene Hat. That album's single, "Low", is evidence of Lowery's decision to focus Camper Van Beethoven's rock lurch and wit into blues-based alternative rock, turning up the volume and distorting the guitars. Cracker has never repeated Kerosene Hat's success, but subsequent albums have been well-received critically and the band tours extensively, with Lowery splitting time between it and a reunited Camper Van Beethoven.

PANSY DIVISION FACTFILE:

Start up year: 1991

Disband year: N/A

Home town: San Francisco, California, U.S.A.

Members: Jon Ginoli, Chris Freeman, various drummers

What you should check out/why: Pile Up for "Smells Like Queer Spirit", a gay-positive re-written take on Nirvana's hit.

Worth looking out for: Singer Jon Ginoli's book, Deflowered.

CRACKER FACTFILE:

Start up year: 1990

Disband year: N/A

Home town: Richmond, Virginia, U.S.A.

Members: David Lowery, Davey Faragher, Johnny Hickman, Phil Jones, Michael Urbano, Frank Funaro, Kenny Margolis, more

What you should check out/why: The Garage D'Or collection has a fine cover of The Flamin' Groovies' "Shake Some Action."

Worth looking out for: Teenage Fanclub's cover of Lowery's other band Camper Van Beethoven's "Take the Skinheads Bowling".

494 Killing Joke

What defines Killing Joke is not their sound, which varies from a disco-flecked post-punk squall to a more experimental thudding rock. It lies more in the cynicism and outrage that founders Jaz Coleman and Kevin "Geordie" Walker express with those varied sounds. Not merely a political band, Killing Joke is content to criticize society as unjust and hypocritical, often employing disturbing imagery that complements Coleman's harsh vocals and the clashing dissonance of guitars and synth. In spite of or maybe because of Coleman's worldviews, Killing Joke still had some alternative rock hits, with singles "Eighties" and the near pop of "Love Like Blood". (See picture below)

Grand Funk Railroad

The trio of Mark Farner, Mel Schacher and Don Brewer formed in 1968 and found an audience for their bluesy hard rock the following year at the Atlanta Pop Festival. Persistent touring and a laid-back, sing-a-long sound helped the band gather a sizable following in the '70s. Their singles "We're An American Band" and "Some Kind of Wonderful" and their cover of "The Loco-motion" have become staples of classic rock radio. Grand Funk Railroad also looked to soul, particularly Motown, as an influence, which can clearly be heard in Farner's vocals. Grand Funk disbanded in 1977 but reunited briefly in 1996.

496

Little Feat

Little Feat songwriter Lowell George was one of the brightest lights in the Laurel Canyon scene that spawned the Eagles, Jackson Browne, the Byrds, and many others. But while George watched his peers become increasingly successful, some among the biggest names of the era, George remained respected but relatively obscure. Adept in rock and blues and having also a foundation in the jazz-and-art explosion that was Frank Zappa's Mothers of Invention, George seemed less interested in having hits than he did in just making music he enjoyed. Lowell George passed away in 1979 but a version of Little Feat remains on the tour circuit.

497 Exodus

Prior to joining Metallica guitar player Kirk Hammett was a founding member of thrash metal progenitors Exodus. Formed in 1981 by Hammett, Paul Baloff, Gary Holt, Geoff Andrews and Tom Hunting, Exodus built up a significant following by combining the speed and energy of punk with the heaviness and technical skill of Iron Maiden. Plagued by problems within the band and at a label level, Exodus never saw the commercial success of other bands that followed in their footsteps. When their debut Bonded by Blood was released a full year after recording in 1984 their moment had already passed.

498 Bob Log III

Tucson, Arizona one-man band Bob Log III is a one-man rock 'n' roll revival, playing slide guitar and drums while singing into a modified telephone handset that is soldered to a motorcycle helmet. His records, School Bus, Trike, Log Bomb and 2009's My Shit Is Perfect, mine similar musical and lyrical territory. His sound, culled from Delta blues, AC/DC, and rockabilly weirdo Hasil Adkins, is frenzied and ramshackle. His lyrics can generally be categorized as being about liquor, women, rock 'n' roll or a combination of the three. The records are fun but it is Bob Log's live show where all the elements coalesce perfectly.

EXODUS FACTFILE:

Start up year: 1981

Disband year: N/A (minus Kirk Hammett)

Home town: San Francisco, U.S.A.

Members: Kirk Hammett, Paul Baloff, Gary Holt, Geoff Andrews, Tom Hunting, Steve Souza, John Tempesta, Rob McKillop, Rick Hunolt, more

What you should check out/why: Bonded By Blood may seem a little tame now, but in 1985, it set the standard for thrash metal. It still sounds great.

BOB LOG III FACTFILE:

Start up year: 1998

Disband year: N/A

Home town: Tucson, Arizona, U.S.A.

Members: Bob Log III

What you should check out/why: Log Bomb for the hit "Boob Scotch".

Worth looking out for: Music by Bob Log's old band, Doo Rag.

499 Dashboard Confessional

Chris Carrabba began Dashboard Confessional as a solo project while still with Further Seems Forever and released his first album, Swiss Army Romance, shortly before his other band entered the studio for the first time. Carrabba left the band soon after and found mainstream success as a solo act with 2001's The Places You Have Come to Fear the Most, which featured the songwriter's unsparingly personal lyrics and saw his acoustic guitar occasionally supplemented by a full band. Subsequent releases, including an MTV Unplugged appearance, a song on the Spider-Man 2 soundtrack, and 2003's A Mark, A Mission, A Brand, A Scar, further raised Dashboard's profile and helped introduce emo to mainstream audiences. (See picture opposite)

500 Atomic Rooster

Ex Crazy World of Arthur Brown members convened in 1969 to create the prog-rock band Atomic Rooster. Regular line-up changes have meant that keyboard player, Vincent Crane, has been the only constant member of the band since its conception. They went on hiatus in 1975 after Farlowe, Mandale and Parcell left the band, but reformed in 1980 following a reconciliation between Crane and Cann.

DASHBOARD CONFESSIONAL FACTFILE:

Start up year: 1999

Disband year: N/A

Home town: Boca Raton, Florida, U.S.A.

Members: Chris Carrabba

What you should check out/why: The Places You Have Come to Fear Most for showing that it's ok for boys to cry.

"My hopes are so high, that your kiss might kill me.
So won't you kill me, so I die happy.
My heart is yours to fill or burst, to break or bury,
Or wear as jewelery, whichever you prefer."

ACKNOWLEDGEMENTS

The publishers would like to thank the following picture libraries for their kind permission to use their images:

Getty (Redferns Collection): 3, 11, 12, 13, 15, 16, 18, 20, 23, 26, 28, 30, 31, 34, 36, 38, 39, 41, 42, 44, 46, 49, 51, 52, 55, 56, 59, 60, 65, 66, 68, 71, 72, 74, 76, 80, 82, 84, 86, 87, 89, 90, 92, 94, 96, 98, 100, 104, 106, 108, 110, 112, 114, 116, 118, 122, 124, 127, 128, 130, 136, 140, 142, 144, 146, 148, 150, 151, 152, 154, 156, 158, 161, 164, 166, 168, 171, 174, 176, 178, 182, 186, 190, 192, 196, 198, 202, 207, 208, 213, 214, 216, 220, 223, 226, 230, 232, 235, 238, 240, 242, 245, 246, 248, 250, 254, 256, 258, 261, 265, 266, 270, 272, 277, 278, 280, 284, 290, 290, 293, 301, 302, 305, 308, 312, 323, 326, 331, 334, 338, 340, 344, 345, 346, 349, 354, 357, 360, 363, 364, 366, 368, 371, 372, 374, 376, 378, 382, 384, 387, 388, 390.

Istockphoto: 120, 296, 317, 326, 332.

Swami Records: 188..

Merge Records: 375.

Southern Lord: 320.

Duned in Music: p190

Every effort has been made to contact the copyright holders for images reproduced in this book.

Any omissions are entirely unintentional, and the details should be addressed to Quantum Publishing.

GLOSSARY

Acid Rock: rock music with a repetitive beat and lyrics hat suggest psychedelic experiences

Alternative: guitar-based rock with male or female vocalists which grew in the 1970's and later enjoyed commercial success

Black metal: an extreme sub-genre of heavy metal with fast tempos, shrieked vocals, highly distorted guitars played with tremolo-picking, double-kick drumming and unconventional song structure

Blues: a style of music that evolved from southern African-American secular songs and usually has a slow tempo and flatted thirds and sevenths

Death Metal: an extreme sub-genre of heavy metal, with fast tempos, heavily distorted guitars, growling vocals, blast beat drumming and complex song structures and tempo changes

EBM: Electronic Body Music is a genre that combines elements of industrial and electronic dance music

Funk: a type of popular music combining elements of jazz, blues and soul with syncopated rhythm and a heavy, repetitive bass line

Glam Rock: a style developed in the UK, marked by flamboyant costumes, subversion of typical gender roles and references to sci-fi and old movies

Goth Metal: a genre of music that combines the aggression of heavy metal with the melancholy of goth rock lyrics

Grunge: a type of rock featuring distorted guitars, whining vocals and flannel-shirted front men, made popular by Seattle bands Nirvana and Alice in Chains

Heavy Metal: a form of metal featuring brittle, flash guitar work, high-pitched male vocals and an attraction to the darker side of human experience

Indie Rock: a sub-genre of rock music that is usually used to describe music that has been produced and distributed independently, as well as the style of music associated with earlier music in this category

Industrial: an experimental music style that often includes electronic music that draws on transgressive of provocative themes

New Age: modern music featuring quiet improvisation on the piano, guitar and synth to produce a dreamy, relaxing sound

New Wave: emotionally detached rock music with a synth sound and repetitive beat

Nu Metal: a sub-genre of heavy metal that combines grunge, alternative, funk metal and hip hip with various other influences such as industrial, groove and thrash

Progressive Rock: sometimes called 'Art Rock', prog rock pushes the conventions of chorus-verse-chorus formations and often use concept albums to tie pieces together

Punk: a raw form of rock music that is fast, hard-edged and often political/anarchist lyrically

Rock: probably the most popular form of 20th century music, combining African-American rhythms, urban blues, folk and country music of the rural south, which developed since the 1950's into hundreds of sub-genres

Rockabilly: one of the earliest forms of rock music, which emerged in the early 1950s – the name is a fusion of the words 'rock' and 'hillbilly,' which show the major influences

Ska: a brisk form of Jamaican-born rock derived from reggae and rock-energy which now forms a lighter faction of the punk movement

Thrash Metal: a sub-genre of heavy metal with a fast tempo, aggressive percussion and low-register guitar tiffs

INDEX